The Antioch Factor

The Hidden Message in the Book of Acts

Ross Paterson

with

Christine Paterson

Sovereign World

Sovereign World Ltd
PO Box 777
Tonbridge
Kent TN11 0ZS
England

All Scripture quotations are taken from the New King James Version, copyright © 1983 by Thomas Nelson, Inc.

Extracts from *On This Day*, by Robert J. Morgan, used by permission of Thomas Nelson, Inc.

ISBN 1 85240 284 9

The publishers aim to produce books which will help to extend and build up the Kingdom of God. We do not necessarily agree with every view expressed by the author, or with every interpretation of Scripture expressed. We expect each reader to make his/her judgement in the light of their own understanding of God's Word and in an attitude of Christian love and fellowship.

This Sovereign World book is distributed in North America by Renew Books, a ministry of Gospel Light, Ventura, California, USA. For a free catalog of resources from Renew Books/Gospel Light, please contact your Christian supplier or call 1-800-4-GOSPEL.

Typeset by CRB Associates, Reepham, Norfolk.
Printed in England by Clays Ltd, St Ives plc.

Contents

Dedication

To Christine, my wife, best friend and co-author,
and Deborah, Hannah, Sharon, Joanna and Esther,
our five 'golden flowers'.

Author's Preface

There are many who have helped with the task of preparing this book. First and foremost, my wife Christine. She is responsible this time for one whole chapter in this book, as well as numerous edits and insights. She takes much credit for the work. I believe her chapter is of great significance for the Church of Jesus Christ.

Christine Hobson also, as usual, did a great deal of work, editing every chapter as it was written and rewritten. I said the following words about her in my last book, and I cannot improve on them: 'She did an enormous amount of work in her usual humble and effective way. She has been a great gift to me and to the ministry.'

Craig Dahlberg also worked with us again. Thanks are due too to Lita, Ben, Bill, James, Ian and others for their encouragement, patience and help. Millie did some typing for the book and helped to keep emails at bay by typing those as well. Thanks, Millie. Allen came in with some crucial material; so did Corinne and Paul. Rod and Barry were also very helpful to Christine for her chapter. Thanks to you all.

And that is not to exclude many others in our Antioch Missions/CCSM and DPM teams. Brothers and sisters, you are special. Consider yourself mentioned, please. God has given us great colleagues in the task of world mission in Singapore and elsewhere, and we are grateful to every one of you. Singapore has a special place in world mission, and it is my fervent prayer that her Church would indeed become an 'Antioch'.

Alec probably does not realise how much he has contributed to make this book possible. He truly is a unique brother to whom we owe more than we could ever repay. Thanks Alec!

Thanks to my five daughters for your patience and to my parents, as well as Christine's Mum. You have all played your part, and I am thankful for that.

Finally, thanks are richly due to those who, in past and present generations, dared to obey God and go to the nations of the world with the Gospel of Jesus Christ. Some died, some suffered and lost much, some laboured and saw little. Others were privileged to see great things in their own lifetime. But the Lord knows it all and their labour was not in vain in Him. We are grateful to them for their courage to be Antioch Factor people – for daring to read the Bible's 'hidden' message and to be different.

'On the basis of what God has revealed through His Son and what is recorded for us in Scripture, I affirm that missionary obedience is the only sufficient response to life's imperatives. There is no other way of aligning ourselves with God's purposes or adequately confronting the world's problems. Mission is basic to God's relationship with humankind.'

'... This saving mission of God is so big it can never be shunted to the sidelines and dismissed as of secondary concern. Where both local and global mission do not head the churches' agendas, then they have dismally failed in reading God's agenda. To ignore mission is to show oneself unaware of the central movement in the whole of history. To minimise it is to belittle God; to trivialise mission is to insult Him.' [1]

Introduction

This book has been at least twenty years in the making. I began serving as a missionary in Asia in 1969. I have been involved in missions since then – for over thirty years. During all this time the message of the Antioch Factor has been forming and developing, as I have moved between East and West, sharing it in many places. I believe finally the time has come to put it down in book form.

For all my familiarity with the subject matter, it has not been an easy book to write. But God encouraged me greatly in the process a few weeks ago, when I had almost completed the first draft, and the title had been long since chosen. At that time, my colleagues showed me material by Don Richardson from his book *Eternity In Their Hearts*. I was amazed to find that one of the key chapters of his book was called: 'The Hidden Message Of "Acts"' – almost exactly the same words as, after prayer, I had chosen for my subtitle! Richardson is a senior statesman in the world of mission. We had both reached the same conclusion, almost in the same words, without collaboration. If I had been looking for encouragement for the substance of this book, I do not think I could have asked for anything clearer than that!

Richardson remarks:

> 'Hundreds of millions of Christians think that Luke's Acts of the Apostles records the 12 apostles' obedience to the Great Commission. Actually it records their reluctance to obey it.' [2]

That on the negative side is the essence of this book. Strong stuff! How could he possibly presume to say that? Read this book, and you will find out!

But there is a positive side to the Antioch Factor. God desires us to make a difference – if we will let Him take us from the ranks of those to whom the Antioch Factor is 'hidden' and propel us into the ranks of the ordinary people who have seen the 'mystery' and are running with it.

Let God through these pages birth in you the confidence that you and I can, as churches and as individuals, bring His blessing to the unreached masses of our world today – those who do not yet know that the Son of God died for their sins and rose again for them.

Many today are searching for significance. Perhaps you will find yours in the Antioch Factor!

Ross Paterson
Singapore, July 2000

Chapter 1

'Sit Down, Young Man'

'Sit down, young man! When God pleases to convert the heathen, He'll do it without consulting you or me.' Doctor John C. Ryland, a senior Baptist minister in the 1780s in England, glared at the young man before him, William Carey. Doctor Ryland was annoyed at the presumption of this unlettered Christian. What was the cause of the offence? Carey had suggested that the Great Commission, the mandate of Jesus Christ to go to the ends of the earth so that every man and woman might have a chance to hear the Gospel, was binding not just in the Acts of the Apostles, but also upon every succeeding generation of Christians – including their own. That idea suffered rejection from many preachers, including apparently Doctor Ryland, who was firm in his acceptance of the common Protestant belief of the time that the Great Commission had been given only to the original apostles, and was not relevant to the Eighteenth Century Church.

Ryland called Carey a 'miserable enthusiast'. His comments were particularly disheartening because he had been the man who had baptised Carey.

On the face of it, there was good reason for pouring cold water on the young man's ideas. Carey was not, as one writer observes, a likely prospect to become the 'Father of Modern Missions.'[3]

'William Carey was born in August 1761 in a forgotten village (Paulerspury in Northamptonshire) in the dullest period of the dullest of all centuries. His family was poor, and he was poorly educated. A skin affliction made him sensitive to outdoor work, so he apprenticed to a nearby shoemaker. When he didn't do well at cobbling, he opened a school to supplement his income. That didn't go well either. He married, but his marriage proved unhappy. A terrible disease took the life of his baby daughter and left Carey bald for life. He was called to pastor a small church, but he had trouble being ordained because of his boring sermons.'[4]

That hardly looks like the curriculum vitae of a man targeted for greatness. But he was. In the midst of his battles even to find gainful occupation, let alone his destiny in life, an event had occurred that radically changed Carey's life – and to some extent the views and values of the Protestant Church in generations to come. He read a book that transformed his views and values. Carey had borrowed a copy of the record of Captain Cook's Voyages. The famous sailor's journals gripped him, and he started thinking of overseas evangelism. On the wall of his cobbler's shop he hung a home-made map of the world, and jotted down facts and figures concerning some of the people groups in various countries on the map. And he began to feel that something should be done to reach the world for Christ, or at least the people represented on the map. It was that simple. God had spoken to Carey about the needs of the lost in other lands. And Carey wished to respond. After all, was that not what the Bible told him to do?

Ryland's rebuke, far from causing Carey to 'sit down', resulted in his writing a book, published on May 12th, 1792. The book had a long title: *An Enquiry into the Obligations of Christians, to use means for the Conversion of the Heathens in which the Religious State of the Different Nations of the World, the Success of Former Undertakings, and the Practicability of Further Undertakings, are Considered*. The modern reader might struggle with the title – it is hardly an eye-catcher or a compulsive purchase candidate on Amazon.com. Yet, despite its unwieldy title, 'this 87-page book became a classic in Christian history that deserves a place alongside Luther's Ninety-five Theses in its influence on subsequent Church history.'[5]

Carey did more than write a book, however effective that might have been. As with all who wish to make a genuine contribution to world evangelisation, he put his life on the line for his missionary convictions. He formed a missionary society. Carey himself was the first candidate, and launched himself forth to serve the Lord in India, beginning a ministry of enormous significance. In so doing, he began the modern era of missions. He became the model for the book, not just its author.

But in our day, as then, Careys are few and far between. We therefore must consider carefully the real possibility of Ryland's thought being alive and well in our midst. In other words, if in Carey's time the prevalent Protestant culture was that world missions were not important, and indeed that it was presumptuous, unspiritual and in contradiction to the will of God to engage in reaching a dying world, could we not be doing exactly the same thing today? We may think that our basic attitudes are not the same; yet they may still result in the same level of ignorance or even opposition.

Few of us might speak in quite the same way as Doctor Ryland. We may pay more lip service – but not necessarily more real service – to reaching the billions of people who have not yet heard that Jesus saves. Ultimately, the question is not whether I agree with Carey or Doctor Ryland. The real issue is whether my church is involved in training and assisting and sending out the Careys of our generation, and of what it will cost me and my Christian community to model that agreement. It cost Carey a very great deal. But it also enabled him to be a man of life and blessing to many, many people.

This book, indeed the very process that I am calling 'The Antioch Factor', is based on the proposition that the forces of Ryland are much more alive today than we might think. We should not assume for one moment that Ryland was less zealous, or less committed to the Word of God, or less desirous of obeying the Lord in his generation than we are. We should not even assume that he was not in many ways a successful man of God. There is no evidence to suggest that. But the evidence that we do have clearly shows us that, despite his zeal for the Lord, he did not know what the Lord wanted him to do in one vital area of Christian service, that of world evangelisation. Not only was he himself ignorant, but he also discouraged strongly those who did want to obey God in the matter of reaching the nations for Jesus. That is the awesome implication of Ryland's words to Carey. It is not that Christians like him do not want to obey the Lord. They are genuine in what they think, and committed to their core beliefs. And yet they still are missing God's main agenda in their generation.

The Antioch Factor addresses that question. Indeed, it will argue that Ryland's thinking even existed, in a different form, in the book of Acts. The lessons from the book of Acts that will be studied in these pages therefore offer a vital warning to us today. It is that we should not assume that our growing churches, or our 'successful' worship meetings, or our powerful sermons, or our miracles, or our websites, video tapes, radio and TV programmes, or our 'influence in society', will necessarily lead to obedience to all of the will of God for our lives. We must look again at our Christian values today, and if necessary admit that we are missing something, even as Ryland was. The next chapter will outline in more biblical detail what that means from the book of Acts. The chapters after that argue that blessing, powerful blessing, can actually cause us to miss the central will of God for which that blessing was given, rather than to find it. If it happened in the early Church, we must face the possibility that it could also be happening in our churches today.

For now, it is enough to face the reality that it is possible, as individual Christians and also in our churches, to be doing well in many areas, and yet still to miss what is perhaps the most urgent matter on the agenda of God in our generation, the task of reaching men and women everywhere with the knowledge of salvation in Jesus Christ.

We have already seen that Doctor Ryland and his Protestant contemporaries firmly believed that the Great Commission had been given only to the original apostles, not to the Eighteenth Century Church. We presumably see that as preposterous. But it was not preposterous to them. It was their understanding of the Scriptures. They believed the Bible was the revealed Word and therefore a directive from God to mankind, just as we do. If good men and women were able to think and behave like that in their day, then, in different ways with different means, it may very well be that we today are doing the same thing. Might future generations – if the

Lord tarries and there are any – consider us equally misguided? Or worse?

Morris of Clipstone, who was present at that meeting of ministers held in 1786 at Northampton, remembered the events of the Ryland-Carey encounter this way:

> 'Doctor Ryland invited the younger brethren to propose a subject for discussion at the ministers' meeting. There was no reply, till at last Carey suggested, doubtless with an ill-restrained excitement, "whether the command given to the Apostles, to teach all nations, was not obligatory on all succeeding ministers to the end of the world, seeing that the accompanying promise was of equal extent." ... The aged chairman shouted out the rebuke – "You are a miserable enthusiast for asking such a question. Certainly nothing can be done before another Pentecost, when an effusion of miraculous gifts, including the gift of tongues, will give effect to the commission of Christ as at first." Carey had never before mentioned the subject openly, and he was for the moment greatly mortified.'

'Certainly nothing can be done before another Pentecost, when an effusion of miraculous gifts, including the gift of tongues, will give effect to the commission of Christ as at first.' We cannot tell if the good Doctor expected that to happen or not. But how are we to respond to that remark two hundred or more years later? Another Pentecost? Is that still what we are waiting for, after the frequent visitations by the Spirit of God in the last one hundred years – Azusa Street, the Welsh Revival, Korea, Toronto, Pensacola, to name but a few? We now have a set of denominations built around and named after Pentecost, as well as the charismatic move amongst traditional churches and much, much more. How much more of Heaven's throne gift do we need, before we will begin to go? It is true that we need more moves of God – we need revival urgently, desperately. Yet surely at the same time we are, by now, on the other side of 'another Pentecost'! We have seen 'an effusion of miraculous gifts, including the gift of tongues'. But what then has changed with respect to 'the commission of Christ as at first'? Our modern version of the argument has come to be that until we have reached some as yet undefined quantum of spiritual experience, something more than we have already seen, we will not venture forth.

Yet the reality is that while we wait, our world does not. All around us it goes from bad to worse, on a scale impossible for Carey and his generation to imagine, as populations explode and the numbers of those who have never heard increase daily. Carey did not wait for whatever the good Doctor Ryland was waiting for. Carey went out, and Carey made a difference. Will we do the same?

God delights to use the most unlikely vessels. Carey, as we have seen, was an unsuccessful shoemaker, a failed school-master, a struggling pastor. But part of his real significance to our generation is that God used one whom others would have passed over without a second glance. The history of obedience to the Great Commission is full of such examples. Behind this reality is a truth that God will use any who will submit to and obey His purposes for mission in their generation. As I write, throughout the nations of the world, there are those whose courage and obedience is known only to God and to a very few fellow believers. They are not seen in the pulpits of our great churches, in the magazines of our denominations. Indeed, when they return home from years away in foreign lands, they may only be granted three minutes in their home church pulpits to share about a life's work.

But these 'little people', those who may not be honoured or lionised elsewhere, are the heroes and heroines of our modern Christian era. This book will show how the greatest church of its day in the New Testament, the church at Antioch, was planted by a group of unknown believers. We do not know the name of a single individual whose life and ministry and witness birthed that great church. Yet this book will show that it was the Antioch church, not the star-studded Jerusalem church, that impacted the unreached world of its day, bringing life and joy to multitudes. It is not stretching the point too far to say that 'little people changed the world'. That 'anonymous' process is being repeated today, amongst the hidden and unreached people groups of our generation.

The sad truth is that many believers today are becalmed in their local churches in frustration because there is no space for them, and because they are not taught or encouraged to venture out into the nations of the world. 'Sit down' they are told – until they have completed some five-year church training programme, or worked their way through the ranks of local church activity. But there is a place of destiny for them, if we may but see what the Antioch Factor seeks to bring to them and to us. It says that unknown Christians, ordinary people who walk with an extraordinary God of grace and power, really can make a difference in other as yet unreached lives.

In central China a few years ago a young girl languished in emptiness and rejection. A severe fire had hit her family home, causing her life-long injuries. Perhaps her parents, under China's one child per family policy, decided to get rid of her in order to have another child, wanting the one child permitted to them by the government to be a fully healthy one. Perhaps they were not able to care for her with those severe injuries. Whatever the reason, this damaged child was placed in a state children's home, uncared for emotionally and, to some extent, physically. An Australian grandmother, Barbara, visiting the children's home to work there on one of our teams, [6] bonded with her. As a result, the rejected child found the Lord – and also experienced genuine love expressed through this Australian grandmother and others. How moving it was to hear Barbara describe how little Lydia, as Barbara brushed her hair one day, turned to her and said: 'You are my mother.'

This grandmother and others like her are not the superstars of our local churches. Indeed they may find it hard to find their place of service or to feel useful in a local church. But on the mission field they can find a place of significance and destiny that changes lives – theirs and others.

William Carey was an ordinary man who made an extraordinary difference. The English philanthropist William Wilberforce, a man of no mean achievement himself, described the mission to India founded by Carey, Joshua Marshman and William Ward (collectively known as the 'Serampore Trio') as 'one of the chief glories' of the British nation.

Carey's impact in the field of world mission in the UK and the US, and subsequently elsewhere, was immense. As others considered his life work, they were changed. Through his work, men and women found Christ. That in itself is enough – that the unreached should hear the good news, and some of them respond. But Carey also translated the Bible into Bengali, Oriya, Marathi, Hindi, Assamese, and Sanskrit. Parts of it he translated into 29 other languages and dialects. The Word of God became intelligible for millions through his work.

It goes without saying that he also made a huge impact in the field of literacy and education in India. He edited, with Marshman, a grammar in Bhotia and prepared six other grammars in different languages. In addition to dictionaries in Bengali, Sanskrit, and Marathi, Carey and Marshman prepared a translation of three volumes of the Hindu epic poem *Ramayana*.

He brought social and practical benefit too. Having established a press at Serampore, Carey edited and published two works of the horticulturist William Roxburgh, *Hortus Bengalensis* (1814) and *Flora Indica* (1832), and helped distribute prose texts for use in schools. He led in the formation of the Agricultural Society of India in 1820. His social work extended beyond education to urge the government to outlaw such practices as infanticide and *suttee* (in which Hindu widows burnt themselves to death on their husbands' funeral pyres). He also encouraged Indians to go out as missionaries to other people groups.

His obedience to the Great Commission, his willingness to ignore the instructions of Doctor Ryland, changed the temporal and eternal destinies of a multitude of lives. One contemporary, Robert Hall, defined Carey's impact in this way:

> 'That extraordinary man who, from the lowest obscurity and poverty, without assistance, rose by dint of unrelenting industry to the highest honours of literature, became one of the first of Orientalists, the first of Missionaries, and the instrument of diffusing more religious knowledge among his contemporaries than has fallen to the lot of any individual since the Reformation; a man who unites with the most profound and varied attainments the fervour of an evangelist, the piety of a saint, and the simplicity of a child.'

And yet, for all that he achieved, Carey remained an ordinary man. Like the Antioch founders mentioned above, he was no superstar. Another writer records:

> 'It (a dilapidated collection of Carey's letters) contains one passage of value, however. Carey once said to his nephew, whose design (to write a biography) he seems to have suspected, "Eustace, if after my removal any one should think it worth his while to write my life, I will give you a criterion by which you may judge of its correctness. If he give me credit for being a plodder he will describe me justly. Anything beyond this will be too much. I can plod. I can persevere in any definite pursuit. To this I owe everything." ' [7]

A plodder, no more or less! No one special, no one remarkably gifted. What a remarkable personal secret: 'I can persevere in any definite pursuit'!

How then was it possible for this ordinary man to achieve so much? The secret lies in understanding and obeying the will of God, as revealed in the Scriptures. Carey was simply a man who, in his day, understood that the Word of God commands us to go, and went, even though that meant swimming against the tide of Christian opinion. He took the words of Jesus in Matthew 28 to heart, words which have transformed his and many other lives.

> 'And Jesus came and spoke to them, saying, "All authority has been given to Me in heaven and on earth. Go therefore and make disciples of all the nations, baptizing them in the name of the Father and of the Son and of the Holy Spirit, teaching them to observe all things that I have commanded you; and lo, I am with you always, even to the end of the age.' Amen.'
> (Matthew 28:18–20)

Recently I sat with some of my colleagues who labour for the Lord with us in a remote part of China, negotiating with Chinese Communist officials for permission to work on practical projects amongst an unreached and deprived people group in China. Obviously I could not in such a context make any reference to my Christian faith or missionary convictions. And yet at the same time it would be logical for them to wonder why on earth this mixed bunch of Western and Asian men and women should be wanting to go off into the mountains of China to help a largely ignored people group. I gave a reason, stripped as it was of Christian content. I was born, I said, in a privileged land in a privileged family, and was given a good education, which enabled me to enter Cambridge University, and emerge later with a Masters degree. The folk that we wanted to help, I said, were at the very opposite end of the scale of privilege. We had been amongst them a few days before, in the midst of drought and poverty. If, I told the officials, my life was to have significance, it would be found in making a difference in the lives of such people, sharing something of what we have with them.

Their response was interesting. You, I was told, are *wei-da* (a great man). I politely rejected that. I was then given a brief lecture on the thoughts of Chairman Mao. Greatness, it was explained, lies not in high or outstanding ability. It lies simply in the willingness to use what we have for others. The greater the 'other-people' dimension, the greater our personal 'greatness'.

I am not a great fan of Chairman Mao. Yet, cut and pasted and changed, that statement by a Chinese official is not entirely unbiblical, and is in one sense the message of this book. Greatness is obedience to what Jesus said, to the commission to go to the ends of the earth. It means setting out to make some difference somewhere to someone, in the Name of Christ. The recruitment takes place from the ranks of Plodders Anonymous. Yet such people can really make a significant difference.

The only reason why history knows of Doctor Ryland is because of his error. It was Carey, not Ryland, whose radical obedience changed many lives in India and at the same time influenced Christian thinking and priorities in the years to follow. How many destinies depended on his ignoring the Doctor's discouragement! Today you and I face that same choice. Who can say what might be the repercussions of the choices we need to make in our lives? It is my prayer that you and I will be changed – Carey-like. My desire for you and for me is that we should not be so busy with a million legitimate local church events and priorities, absorbing everything into local visions, that we are do not obey this significant element of the will of God in our generation, which is to reach the nations for Him.

One of my closest colleagues in world mission wrote this to me recently:

'I watched a secular documentary last weekend about five young Aussies (Australians) who cycled for about 3200 kilometres over a period of two months throughout the remote regions of Outer Mongolia. It was a very honest account of their struggles, pains, heartaches, conflicts, etc ... What impacted me the most was the comments of the young people at the end of their journey, in response to a question from the interviewer: "Why did you do the trip?" ... The last young lad really challenged me. He said that when he was a young boy, in a dream, he stood at the end of his life before five judges who were there to pass judgement on his life. After a long silence, one of the judges threw down the gavel and said, "Guilty of a wasted life." He said that this dream had impacted him greatly, and he did not want to get to the end of his life and hear the verdict pronounced, "Guilty of a wasted life."

I considered the fact that, although these folk were not Christians, yet they were thinking this deeply about life. As Christians, we have two lives that we will have to give account for ... our natural life and our new spiritual life in Christ Jesus ... Are the children of the world more switched on than the children of light? Do we come to Christ and fall asleep and wait for the rapture? Do we forget that one day each one of us will stand before a Judge, not just in a dream, but in reality, and we will be required to give an account of all the deeds that we have done in the body, of the talents that He has given to us? Even if we have despised the one talent that He has given us and thought it of no worth so that we have hidden it, we will have to give account, whether we like it or not. But how sweet will be the sounds of "Well done, My good and faithful servant..."'

If you have the time at the close of this opening chapter, would you consider before the Lord those questions in the paragraph above? They are important, even life-changing, in their implications. Oh that God would visit us in our generation with that 'map on the wall' revelation with which He visited Carey. May God help us to shrug off our Ryland traditions and embrace Carey's ambition to make a difference for Jesus in our world, coupled with the faith that God will use us, however inadequate we might feel! Carey's core personal statement says it all. Why not now embrace it for yourself, in the context of reaching our generation everywhere for Jesus:

'Attempt great things for God, expect great things from God.'

It worked for him. It will work for us. God has not changed.

Chapter 2

What *is* the Antioch Factor?

*'If indeed you have heard of the dispensation of the grace of God which was given to me for you, how that by revelation He made known to me the **mystery** . . . that the Gentiles should be fellow heirs, of the same body, and partakers of His promise in Christ through the Gospel . . . To me, who am less than the least of all the saints, this grace was given, that I should preach among the Gentiles the unsearchable riches of Christ . . . '*

(Ephesians 3:2, 3, 6, 8)

The title of this book implies that there are events in the book of Acts that are more than just history. There is a message for today, even if it seems still hidden from many believers. If that message is not yet understood, that is because we have not seen it yet, not because God desired it to be concealed from us. If we do not in our day want to face continued reruns of the battle that Carey faced with Doctor Ryland, we will have to learn that 'hidden' lesson. The place to do that is in the pages of the Bible. This chapter aims to give a basic summary from the book of Acts of what is meant by the Antioch Factor. The 'Carey experience' needs to be rooted in the teaching of the Bible.

The Ephesians passage at the top of this chapter puts this challenge very clearly. Paul used the word 'mystery' and then defined what that mystery is – *'that the Gentiles should be fellow heirs, of the same body, and partakers of His promise in Christ through the Gospel'*! A mystery in the New Testament language is something that has been revealed by God, but yet has not been understood by most believers. Therefore this 'open secret'

of which Paul talks is that the Gentiles must hear the Gospel.
Indeed in numerous passages of the New Testament Paul
makes it clear that this open door to the Gentiles was at the
heart of his own calling from God. However he also makes it
clear that the mystery was hidden from others and was not by
any means widely accepted in the Church of his time. Paul
shows us that in God's heart there is and always has been an
agenda running, which is that Jew and Gentile alike (that
means all mankind) should be *'partakers of His promise in
Christ.'* This 'mystery' is also totally central to Jesus' parting
words to His disciples (see Matthew 28:18–20; Mark 16:15–18
and Acts 1:8). The problem in the early Church, however, was
that God's heart was not fully shared by His people – the
disciples were very happy to share the Gospel with their own
people in Jerusalem, but reluctant to cross any geographic or
ethnic boundaries beyond that. The 'mystery', in other words,
remained veiled to most of them. My purpose in this book is to
show what God did to address this problem and how we might
expect Him to act in our day too, if we fail to embrace the
'mystery' Paul is describing in his letter to the Ephesians – that
God's heart is as much for those who so far are *'strangers and
foreigners'* as it is for those of us who are already *'saints and
members of the household of God'* (see Ephesians 2, especially
verses 19–22).

Don Richardson's words, already quoted in the Introduction, bear repeating, as they give a most provocative
expression of this truth:

> 'Hundreds of millions of Christians think that Luke's Acts
> of the Apostles records the 12 apostles' obedience to the
> Great Commission. Actually it records their reluctance to
> obey it.'[8]

How God overcomes His people's reluctance, then and now
– that is our investigation in this book and the very essence of
the Antioch Factor.

In its rawest form the Antioch Factor presents us with a
warning and a **promise**, both of which are woven within the
narrative in the book of Acts. There we can see how, although
the church in Jerusalem was a great and successful church and

much can be learned from it, yet also it missed it fullest destiny. Clearly it was God's original church of choice, yet by Acts 11 it had ceased to be the front line church of its generation, and was not central to the main plot of the book of Acts after that. It was replaced in the central purposes of God by the vibrant church in Antioch, which did not even exist in the first ten chapters of Acts, when the church at Jerusalem was at its height.

This process has a real application to us as Christians today. The marginalisation of Jerusalem's role was not random or accidental. It was for a specific reason. That reason is equally applicable to us today. Its logic states that the ultimate purpose of the Church of Jesus Christ is to reach out to a dying world with the good news of salvation. Jerusalem did that with real excellence and success locally, in ways that are a real model to us today. But it did not desire to do it in all the world. Instead, it desired only to care for Jerusalem and for the Jews. Indeed, as a friend (herself a Messianic Jew) commented to my wife recently, 'If the Gospel had remained exclusively with the apostles in Jerusalem, followers of Yeshua (Jesus) would have remained forever within Judaism!'[9] That is how high the stakes were. No wonder God had to raise up another man (Paul) and another church (Antioch) to take Jerusalem's place! The book of Acts assumes as one of its central themes that the church belongs to Jesus, not to us. We have to do what He wants, or He may have to bypass us to get the job done and go to other churches that will obey Him.

On the other hand, through the Antioch church, God presents us with a promise that balances this serious warning. God may raise up individuals and even entire communities to be significant in their generation. This offers the possibility for ordinary folk, 'Carey' folk, to make a definitive impact in the world. Under God, that which does not even exist can be raised up to change lives and even communities, to make a real difference. Thus the Antioch church is both an example for us and also presents us with an invitation to engage in a new destiny under God, by doing what He wants us to do.

It is of course easy to disagree with so basic an analysis of the book of Acts and especially of the Jerusalem church. Summaries are dangerous, because they give conclusions, but not the full evidence or reasons for those conclusions. The evidence regarding this 'hidden message' of the book of Acts follows in detail in later chapters. However, there is a simple exercise that illustrates this hidden lesson in a most remarkable way from the pages of Scripture. If we compare the references to the church in Jerusalem in the first half of Acts with the references in the second half of the book, we find a most astonishing contrast in the importance given by the writer to that church.

Most readers will be aware that the Church was born at Jerusalem. There the events that changed time and eternity took place. The Lord Jesus died there for our sins; there He rose from the dead; and from there He ascended into heaven. Jerusalem was the cockpit of history. It is also clear in the early chapters of Acts that there was remarkable growth in the church at Jerusalem. It did not just start well. It continued well – for quite some time.

> *'However, many of those who heard the word believed; and the number of the men came to be about five thousand.'*
>
> (Acts 4:4)

> *'And believers were increasingly added to the Lord, multitudes of both men and women.'*   (Acts 5:14)

Here we have five thousand men who believed, who are then joined by *'multitudes of both men and women.'* It is impressive and in that period of history represents unparalleled church growth.

Then comes a dramatic and significant change. Half way through Acts 11 we have the record of the birth of the church at Antioch (Acts 11:19ff). Suddenly, from that point, Jerusalem becomes secondary in importance. It is no longer the cockpit of the book of Acts, as it was before Acts 11:19. From this point on, Jerusalem's church is never mentioned again for its own sake. It is only mentioned when Paul or Barnabas (the Antioch church leaders) visit it. After Acts 11:19 the writer of Acts only looks at Jerusalem through the eyes of Paul and his missionary ministry from Antioch, from where he laboured to reach the Gentiles, the 'ends of the earth' people.

For the rest of the book of Acts, Jerusalem is never considered for its own sake alone. As far as we know, it still experienced much of the blessing of God. Clearly that was so in the first ten chapters. After that, it is more difficult to see what happened there, because the explicit references that abounded in the first ten chapters are discontinued. No doubt it still retained considerable status in church affairs. It certainly remained the headquarters, the source of orthodoxy:

> *'And as they went through the cities, they delivered to them the decrees to keep, which were determined by the apostles and elders at Jerusalem.'* (Acts 16:4)

Yet, though it still had status, Jerusalem did not remain on the cutting edge of God's activity on earth. Jerusalem from this point 'dropped off the map' in Acts as a major influence in the growth of the Church. This reality – that Acts begins with an exclusive focus on Jerusalem and then reduces its influence – is quite extraordinary. Either it is a very bad piece of writing, or there is a hidden message. There is: it is the message of the Antioch Factor!

Imagine a writer today beginning to write a book on the game of golf. He would start in Scotland. My own people invented the game. But in a relatively short space of time the writer would change his focus away from Scotland to England, to the United States and to other countries. Scotland would only be mentioned when the rest of the world came to play on its old and famous courses. It would not rate much of a mention apart from that. That is exactly what happened to Jerusalem. Jerusalem ceased to be central because it ceased to be on the front line of God's agenda of development, which was that of taking the Gospel to where it had not been heard before, to the lost in the unreached nations. Jerusalem is only mentioned, to continue the golf book analogy, when the main players come to town to play! If they are not there, the focus is gone.

That is perhaps difficult for us to embrace because Jerusalem was not a struggling church. It was and continued to be a very successful one. It saw great growth, as mentioned above. It also saw almost everything we could wish to see: wonderful teaching from men who had been with Jesus during His ministry on earth; sovereign acts of God in healing, raising the dead, dealing with sinners, and even rescuing His people from physical death (sometimes). It saw church life the like of which has not often been seen since, with deep sharing, mutual care and community. God's Presence was powerfully there. It was not a failed or failing church. It was highly successful in the best and purest sense of the word.

And yet – it missed God's agenda, and had to be replaced by Antioch, so that God could do what He wanted to do. At the beginning of the book of Acts we are given the key to that process:

> *'But you shall receive power when the Holy Spirit has come upon you; and you shall be witnesses to Me in Jerusalem, and in all Judea and Samaria, and to the end of the earth.'*
>
> (Acts 1:8)

The reason for the birth of the Jerusalem church, according to this scripture, was that it might not stop reproducing until it had reached 'the end of the earth' with its testimony to Jesus. That is why Jesus spoke Acts1:8 into it at the very moment of its birth. But Jerusalem did not obey Jesus in this matter. And so another church, the Antioch church, had to be raised up to do that work. That is the Antioch Factor.

There was no excuse for the early Church, any more than there is for us today. Jesus had made His plans clear throughout His ministry on earth:

> *'And this Gospel of the kingdom will be preached in all the world as a witness to all the nations, and then the end will come.'*   (Matthew 24:14)

Indeed, the nearer He got to His ascension, the more Jesus emphasised the need for the Church to be 'end of the earth' minded. It was a repeated theme in His teaching to the Church, both in Acts 1:8 and in all four Gospels:

> *'And Jesus came and spoke to them, saying, "All authority has been given to Me in heaven and on earth. Go therefore and*

> *make disciples of all the nations, baptizing them in the name*
> *of the Father and of the Son and of the Holy Spirit, teaching*
> *them to observe all things that I have commanded you; and lo,*
> *I am with you always, even to the end of the age." Amen.'*
>
> (Matthew 28:18–20)

'*Go . . .* ' But the church in Jerusalem did not go. They did not do what He commanded. And so their influence waned. Antioch was raised up to replace them.

This was not a capricious act of God. Reducing Jerusalem's influence and promoting Antioch was devastatingly logical, from God's point of view. Jerusalem had ceased to do what God wanted in this most vital area. That is why the church at Antioch was born and raised up in the way that it was, and it is also why the Antioch Factor is so important for us today. It is not random. It is necessary – and therefore may happen again today.

God wants the lost to be reached with the good news of Jesus, and He needs to find churches that will train and encourage their folk to go out to do just that. The work cannot be done without those who are willing to go out. One of our China team, a very special sister, wrote to me recently. She is working amongst an unreached people group in China, who number in the hundreds of thousands, but have no church, no pastors and probably no Christians amongst them. Her words beautifully illustrate why God must have Antioch people who are willing to go – then and now:

> 'Missionaries are needed on the front line, where the Gospel has not yet reached, because there is something in that name of "Emmanuel" ("God with us"). God through us comes to these unreached people. They will touch God, see God, hear God – through us. These people have not touched God in a specific way, only in God's general revelation of Himself through His creation. How will they hear? How can they hear unless someone goes to them? *"And how shall they preach unless they are sent? As it is written: 'How beautiful are the feet of those who preach the gospel of peace, who bring glad tidings of good things!'"* (Romans 10:15).

During my last trip to visit the X people,[10] I had the powerful sense that our presence meant that God was in their midst. They needed to touch God through human arms, human smiles, human interaction. We gave them that as we worked amongst them, as strangers who battled to make their lives better in practical ways. In a sense, as they saw us helping them in that battle, they could say: "This is what God is like..."'

This is not ecclesiastical theory. God is not proving some theological point in the Antioch Factor. It is much, much more than that – it is the difference between life and death for multitudes today. God needs His church amongst the ends of the earth people, that they might have a chance to know Him. My colleague went on to give this example of what she had articulated above:

'The team did not know that the heads of the households of the first two families that they helped were actually the village bullies. They were often drunk, often threatened others and routinely hit their children. At first, the villagers refused to work with the team as we helped these two families. "Why would no one help?" we wondered. Finally, through negotiations with the village chief, the team was able to let the people know that whoever would come to help, they in turn would be helped when it came time to building water tanks for their households. Seeing that they too needed help, they began to pick up the shovels, the sieve, the trowels and began to work alongside the team. The outcome of this part of the story is that the two men who had been the village bullies were so touched by the love of the team members, that, when it came to saying goodbye on the last day, they cried! These tough men cried! Why? Because they had been touched by the love of God, His care and concern shown through the team members. The miracle is that both men stayed through to the end helping the other eight families build their tanks as well. A measure of healing of relationships between the households in that village had taken place!'

The event above describes a small but significant report of some work by a team that is labouring amongst some of the poorest people in Asia, an unreached minority group who need to know that there is a God Who cares for them, and Who sent His Son to open to them the doorway to an eternity with Him. Such examples could be multiplied a million times over, often in much more significant ways. Yet in a small way this one expresses the heart of the Antioch Factor. God needs willing volunteers to go in our day – to go to remote places for Him to express His love to those who have urgent practical and spiritual needs. Therefore He will not guarantee ongoing significance to any group or individual Christian, if they refuse to make that a part of their agenda.

'Missionaries are needed on the front line.' This is the challenge of the Antioch Factor, in the book of Acts and now, two thousand years later. It is actually the main message of the book of Acts – a message for every Christian and for every church. Yet because we have begun to overlook that fact, I have described that challenge to world mission, the Antioch Factor, as the 'hidden message of the book of Acts'. It is there, plainly there. But we have begun to gloss over it. Somebody once said that the Church is the only club that was invented for the benefit of its non-members. There is a substantial biblical truth in that statement. However, the reality is that most of the Church lives as if that were not so. That is why the Antioch Factor is so vital.

A friend, who has herself been out to serve in China and elsewhere and whose writings have also challenged others to go, sent me this shocking and challenging parable. It speaks to me of some tendencies in the Jerusalem church and its modern equivalent:

> 'On a dangerous seacoast where shipwrecks often occur, there was once a crude little life-saving station. The building was just a hut, and there was only one boat. But the few devoted members kept a constant watch over the sea, and with no thought for themselves went out day and night tirelessly searching for the lost. Some of those who were saved, and various others in the surrounding area, wanted to become associated with the station and

give of their time and money and effort for the support of its work. New boats were bought and new crews trained. The little life-saving station grew.

Some of the members of the life-saving station were unhappy that the building was so crude and poorly equipped. They felt that a more comfortable place should be provided as the first refuge of those saved from the sea. They replaced the emergency cots with beds and put better furniture in the enlarged building.

Now the life-saving station became a popular gathering place for its members, and they decorated it as sort of a club. Fewer members were now interested in going to sea on life-saving missions, so they hired lifeboat crews to do this work. The life-saving motif still prevailed in this club's decoration, and there was a liturgical lifeboat in the room where the club initiations were held.

About this time a large ship was wrecked off the coast, and the hired crews brought in boatloads of cold, wet and half-drowned people. They were dirty and sick and some had black skin and some had yellow skin. The beautiful new club was in chaos. So the property committee immediately had a shower house built outside the club where victims of shipwrecks could be cleaned up before coming inside.

At the next meeting, there was a split in the club membership. Most of the members wanted to stop the club's life-saving activities as being unpleasant and a hindrance to the normal social life of the club. Some members insisted upon life-saving as their primary purpose and pointed out that they were still called a life-saving station. But they were finally voted down and told that if they wanted to save lives of all the various kinds of people who were shipwrecked in those waters, they could begin their own life-saving station down the coast. So they did just that.

As the years went by, the new station experienced the same changes that had occurred in the old. It evolved into a club, and yet another "spin-off" life-saving station was founded. History continued to repeat itself, and if you visit that sea coast today, you will find a number of exclusive clubs along that shore. Shipwrecks are frequent in those waters, but most of the people drown.'

When will we draw the line? When will we cry out to God to make us Antioch people, who care more for the fact that 'most of the people drown' than we do for our 'life-saving stations'? If this book helps one Christian or one church to see the hidden truth of the Antioch factor, then it will have achieved its purpose.

It is time to return to studying the Word of God in order to define what the Spirit of God is saying in our own and indeed in every generation. It is not enough to experience God. We have to find out His purpose and destiny in any visitation of His Spirit. The Bible, the Word of God, will define that for us. Jesus Himself stated it succinctly in the following manner:

> *'Jesus answered and said to them, "You are mistaken, not knowing the Scriptures nor the power of God."'*
>
> (Matthew 22:29)

The secret then is not just to know the Scriptures or merely to experience the power of God. We have to walk in the power of God to energise our obedience to the Scriptures, and to know well the Scriptures that they may tell us where to go and what to do with the power.

Smith Wigglesworth was a remarkable Pentecostal in the early part of the last century. Many decades ago he gave a prophecy that tied together the Word of God and the Spirit of God. His word concerned a great revival that he believed was coming. It is all the more compelling because he spoke of two distinct moves of God, which would occur before that revival occurred. These moves have now already largely come to pass as he foretold them. He declared that during the next few decades (he was speaking over half a century ago), there would be two distinct moves of the Holy Spirit across the Church. The first move would affect every church that is open to receive it and would be categorised by a restoration of the baptism and gifts of the Holy Spirit. The second move of the Holy Spirit would result in people leaving historic churches and planting new churches. His prophetic statement was that 'in the duration of each of these moves, the people who are involved will say, "This is the great revival." But the Lord says, "No, neither is this the great revival but both are steps towards it."' Then, he said, there would be a third stage:

> 'When the church phase is on the wane, there will be evidenced in the churches something that has not been seen before: The coming together of those with an emphasis on the Word and those with an emphasis on the Spirit. When the Word and the Spirit come together, there will be the biggest movement of the Holy Spirit that the nation, and indeed the world, has ever seen. It will mark the beginning of a revival that will eclipse anything that has been witnessed within these shores, even the Wesleyan and the Welsh revivals of former years. The outpouring of God's Spirit will flow over the United Kingdom to the mainland of Europe, and from there will begin a missionary move to the ends of the earth.' [11]

Leaving aside the emphasis on Britain, there is a crucial statement here regarding the role of the Word of God in any move of the Spirit of God. That statement is relevant in any nation upon earth. This is it: **without the coming together of the Word and the Spirit, we will not see the revival for which we hunger**. Furthermore and most significantly, the climax of these great events is to be a missionary move to the ends of the earth.

The central argument of the Antioch Factor is that when we are willing to study seriously the purpose of the activity of the Spirit of God as revealed in the Word of God, we will inevitably be made to look to the ends of the earth. That is what Antioch people do, because they are Word and Spirit people, not one or the other.

Conversely, if we refuse to do this and remain determined to be Jerusalem people, in the Acts sense, we will miss the fundamental purpose of any visitation of God. We may enjoy it and be blessed by it, but we will not find God's ultimate purpose in it. Any move of God, whether in the Bible's terms or in Wigglesworth's, is designed to impact the ends of the earth people, who have not yet heard.

Our agendas then must be defined from the Word of God, the Bible. That is what this book seeks to do, and will do in the chapters that follow, as we investigate the book of Acts more closely. It is the prayer of the writer that this crucial hidden secret of the book of Acts, this Antioch Factor, would remain hidden no longer, as God speaks to us from His Word!

Chapter 3

How Far Will We Go?

'Some wish to live within the sound of church or chapel bell,
I want to run a rescue shop within a yard of hell.'

(C.T. Studd) [12]

We concluded the previous chapter with the observation that we must define our agendas by the Word of God and learn the lessons He has placed there for our benefit. Even a cursory look at Church history (such as the example of Doctor Ryland in Chapter 1 and of the Jerusalem church in Chapter 2) will demonstrate that it is all too easy, unknowingly and for apparently good reasons, to miss the purposes of God in any generation. If we want to avoid that in ours, we must be diligent to apply what we learn from our study of God's Word.

The relevant passage of early Church narrative which we must now consider comes between Acts 1:8 and Acts 6:7 – it covers a period of between five and ten years. It is the first 'teaching block' in the hidden message in the book of Acts from God to His Church. The lesson is simply this, that **to be experiencing blessing is no test of obedience. Alignment with the revealed word of Scripture is the only valid test**.

The chapters that follow Acts 1:8 reveal a period of great excitement, power and growth in the Church. These events could be summed up in the following two statements:

- Everything that happened, happened for evangelism, and thus almost every event resulted in the salvation of souls.

- But all of this only happened within Jerusalem's boundaries.

First we need to look at the evidence for the first statement, that everything that happened, happened for evangelism, and thus almost every event resulted in the salvation of souls. We need here to consider briefly the variety of these events, and their identical result – church growth.

1. **Direct evangelism**: The first event, which was the birth moment of the Church of Jesus Christ on earth, was the blessing of Pentecost (Acts 2:1–4), the coming of the Holy Spirit in power. This was more than just a visitation alone. It had a specific result – the salvation of many souls (Acts 2:40–47):

   > *'And with many other words he* [Peter] *testified and exhorted them, saying, "Be saved from this perverse generation." Then those who gladly received his word were baptized; and that day about three thousand souls were added to them.'*   (Acts 2:40–41)

   The coming of the Holy Spirit was designed to bring evangelism to the lost, and that is just what happened. The timid Peter, who had three times denied Christ, now under the fullness of the Holy Spirit preached Jesus to those who had crucified Him, and saw three thousand men and women turn to Christ (Acts 2:41). Furthermore there came real life and love into the church in the period following that initial ingathering of new believers (Acts 2:42–47). It was a solid foundation.

2. **Healing**: Chapters 3 and 4 see a repetition of this trend, but in different ways. The healing of the lame man (Acts 3:1–11) again resulted in evangelism. Many turned to the Lord (Acts 4:4). Surely the Holy Spirit's message to us from that is that the miraculous should lead to witness and to salvation. It did here.

3. **Persecution**: Then we learn of the arrest of Peter and John (Acts 4:1ff). But even persecution and opposition, under the Hand of God, led in God's sovereignty, through answered prayer, to boldness and more evangelism. As an added bonus the early Church experienced great blessing in their community life (Acts 4:32–33).

> *'Now the multitude of those who believed were of one heart
> and one soul; neither did anyone say that any of the things
> he possessed was his own, but they had all things in
> common. And with great power the apostles gave witness to
> the resurrection of the Lord Jesus. And great grace was upon
> them all.'*   (Acts 4:32)

Later (Acts 5:17ff) there is a further arrest of Peter and
John. But the same is true again – aggressive evangelism
seemed to increase, not decrease, as a result of the
threatening and the danger.

> *'So they departed from the presence of the council, rejoicing
> that they were counted worthy to suffer shame for His Name.
> And daily in the temple, and in every house, they did not
> cease teaching and preaching Jesus as the Christ.'*
>
> (Acts 5:41)

4. **Church discipline**: Even church discipline under God led
    to evangelism (Acts 5:1–14). Ananias and Sapphira lied to
    God and to the church leadership about money – a very
    dangerous thing to do. Though the severity of the divine
    punishment brought fear on Christian and non-Christian
    alike, it also brought more to salvation – multitudes of
    both men and women (Acts 5:14).

5. **Internal church disputes**: In Acts Chapter 6 we learn that
    even disputes and divisions (along ethnic lines) in the
    church, when dealt with sensibly and under the guidance
    of God, resulted in the spread of the Gospel – in both
    quality and quantity:

    > *'Then the Word of God spread, and the number of the
    > disciples multiplied greatly* [quantity] *in Jerusalem, and a
    > great many of the priests were obedient to the faith* [qual-
    > ity].'*   (Acts 6:7)

Acts 1:8–6:7 is thus a most amazing section of Church
history. The Church grew in leaps and bounds. Everything –
whether it was blessing from the Holy Spirit, with miracles;
or persecution, opposition, dispute and discipline – seemed
to result in church growth, as God's servants sought His Face
and trusted and obeyed Him. The Bible does not lie. The 3,000
in Acts 2:41 is followed by the 5,000 men of 4:4, and the

multitudes of both men and women of 5:14 and the multitude of 6:7. A huge number was saved. Every activity, whether seemingly forward-moving in terms of blessing, or a seeming reversal in terms of opposition or dispute, resulted only in many more being saved.

A reasonable assumption from these early chapters of Acts would be that the Jerusalem congregation is the perfect model of church life. But that is not true. In a significant way, the hidden lesson is that quite the opposite is true. Jerusalem might have been having revival, but what about the 99.99% of people alive in the world at that time who did not live there in that city? By Acts 6:7, five or more years have passed from the Ascension of Jesus, five years of uninterrupted growth and success. But still no one was moving out of Jerusalem.

The real issue in these chapters is this: how big does the Jerusalem church have to grow before they are willing to go out to Judea or Samaria, far less the ends of the earth? How many thousands of believers does the church in Jerusalem need before it will reach out to Samaria?

What a lesson, what a warning there is here. We can read in these events of success, growth, the power and Presence of God – everything except obedience to the Great Commission so clearly stated in the second half of Acts 1:8. The Jerusalem church of Acts Chapters 1–6 was a Ryland church, not a Carey church.

There is a deep warning here to our modern successful churches. I realise that many reading this will not come from successful churches, and may indeed be struggling. But we are seeing as never before the elevation of the successful church. We flock to their meetings and their conferences, we emulate their techniques, study their books and videos. That is good, for they have much to teach us. But Acts 1–6 says something else – that it is possible to do all of that, and yet to be short of the purposes of God. What a sobering warning to us. God is not looking for success on any terms. He is looking for obedient success.

One great danger is that when we go from struggle to success, we lose our cutting edge, our desperation to obey the Lord and to find His will. We lose our dependence on His will and power. We become self-dependent. Are we, the modern

Church or a section of it, at ease in this wrong way? In our conferences, in our worship meetings, in our evangelical Bible conferences, is our focus just on our 'Jerusalem', that it may grow and prosper, whilst at the same time we neglect a world dying without Christ? If we are like that, then we need to read what happened next in the book of Acts after the Acts 1:8–6:7 events, for it was a terrifyingly sudden reversal of the fortunes of the church.

The issue which lies at the heart of this matter is found in the text of Acts 1:8, a verse very familiar to most Bible-aware Christians. What seems to be less familiar is that the verse contains two promises (not just one), both of equal authority and importance. Our embracing of both of these promises with equal weight is the key to our avoiding Doctor Ryland's error and thus being free to walk in Carey's path.

> 'But you shall receive power when the Holy Spirit has come upon you; and you shall be witnesses to Me in Jerusalem, and in all Judea and Samaria, and to the end of the earth.'
>
> (Acts 1:8)

There are then two statements here from the lips of the Lord Jesus. They are the more significant because He was about to leave His disciples and ascend into heaven, having conquered sin and death on the cross, and manifested that victory in His resurrection.

The first statement is a promise of power:

> 'But you shall receive power when the Holy Spirit has come upon you ...'

Recent generations, especially in some sectors of the Church, have majored on that first promise. Some have emphasised, with good reason, the promise of the power of the Holy Spirit, and have developed teaching and impartation around this theme. It is not necessary for me to outline to most readers the multitude of ministries, conferences, teaching and so on that have grown up in what is called the Pentecostal and the Charismatic sectors of the Church. Even in recent years, churches have sprung quickly to international fame because of a visitation of the Spirit of God, imparting the promised power of the Holy Spirit. It is not the purpose of this book to argue the rights and wrongs of individual movements. It is enough to state that countless lives, including the writer's, have been impacted and helped by a new encounter with Jesus through His Holy Spirit, often bringing gifts of power.

But Jesus gave a second promise in Acts 1:8.

> '...*and you shall be witnesses to Me in Jerusalem, and in all Judea and Samaria, and to the end of the earth.*'

The second promise is more significant than is at first obvious. It seems to be a general statement about evangelism and mission. That indeed it is. But it is more than that. It actually states that the validating test of any visitation and experience of the Spirit of God is whether or not we go out and testify for Jesus, and whether or not our parameters for doing that include the ends of the earth, the unreached. The ultimate test of genuine Holy Spirit activity in our lives is not to be defined in terms of gifts or of experience. It is in terms of specific obedience, the kind that leads us ever outward in surrender to the Great Commission.

Jesus states here that the innate desire of the Christian to stay within the warm confines of the local church is not of the Spirit of God. On the contrary, His desire is to lead us continually outward in four concentric circles. The first circle is our 'Jerusalem', our local community. The second is our 'Judea', which may be seen as our nation or our ethnic people group. The third is our 'Samaria', a similar but yet different people. For the British that might be France. For the American Christian, that might be Canada or even certain parts of South America. For the Singaporean, that might be Malaysia. The fourth circle is entirely different. It means what it says, 'the ends of the earth' – the peoples whose language and culture are totally alien to us, those who are remote and unreached.

Jesus then is saying here in Acts 1:8 that no experience of the Holy Spirit is real in the fullest sense of that word until part of our Christian community breaks out of its local territory and known culture and engages with the 'ends of the earth' people!

And it must do that not to make money in business, nor for political power, nor personal influence or any other selfish motive, but exclusively to make disciples by preaching the Gospel of Jesus.

Put in those terms, Acts 1:8 gives a whole new definition of the gifts and ministry of the Holy Spirit. The movement of the Holy Spirit in our lives is intended to be a means to an end, not an end in itself. The genuine end is defined as the Church reaching the distant peoples with her testimony to the Gospel. Some will go, some will stay, but those who stay should support those who do go. It is a whole Church endeavour. Anything less than that is short of the biblical end of the work of the Holy Spirit. We should not be satisfied with our experience of God until the hidden folk, the ends of the earth folk, know that the Saviour Jesus has died for them.

Thousands of Christians are thus using the means, the blessing of the Holy Spirit, for ends other than Acts 1:8 ends. For that we will give answer to God. We are stewards, not bosses, of His blessings. The means, the coming in power of the Holy Spirit, can be so exciting that we think the experience is all there is to it. It is not. It never is.

Some believers and churches might then need to reconsider the way forward for them in respect of the Holy Spirit. They may need to consider the example of Doctor Walter Lewis Wilson, rather than seek for yet another deeper experience of the Spirit. Wilson was a medical doctor and a Christian in the United States in 1913. But he agonised over his fruitless efforts at witnessing.

> 'One day in 1913 a French missionary visiting in the Wilson home asked the doctor, "Who is the Holy Spirit to you?" Wilson replied, "One of the Persons of the Godhead ... Teacher, Guide, Third Person of the Trinity." The friend challenged Wilson: "You haven't answered my question." To this Wilson replied sadly: "He is nothing to me. I have no contact with Him and could get along quite well without Him."
>
> The next year, on January 14th, 1914, Wilson heard a sermon by James M. Gray, Reformed Episcopal clergyman and later president of Moody Bible Institute.

Gray was speaking from Romans 12:1–2:

"I beseech you therefore, brethren, by the mercies of God, that you present your bodies a living sacrifice, holy, acceptable to God, which is your reasonable service. And do not be conformed to this world, but be transformed by the renewing of your mind, that you may prove what is that good and acceptable and perfect will of God." (Romans 12:1–2)

Gray leaned over the pulpit and said, "Have you noticed that this verse does not tell us to Whom we should give our bodies? It is not the Lord Jesus. He has His own body. It is not the Father. He remains on His throne. Another has come to earth without a body. God gives you the indescribable honour of presenting your bodies to the Holy Spirit, to be His dwelling place on earth."

Wilson returned home and fell on the carpet. There in the quiet of that late hour, he said, "My Lord, I have treated You like a servant. When I wanted You, I called for You. Now I give You this body from my head to my feet. I give You my hands, my limbs, my eyes and lips, my brain. You may send this body to Africa, or lay it on a bed with cancer. It is Your body from this moment on."

The next morning, two ladies came to Wilson's office selling advertising. He promptly led both to Christ, and that was the beginning of a life of evangelistic fruitfulness. Wilson later founded Central Bible Church in Kansas City, Flagstaff Indian Mission, Calvary Bible College, and he wrote the best-selling *Romance of a Doctor's Visits*. "With regard to my own experience with the Holy Spirit, the transformation in my life on January 14, 1914 was much greater than the change that took place when I was saved December 21, 1896.' '[13]

Some might find that last statement questionable, but the reality is undeniable. The power of the Holy Spirit deeply impacted the doctor, and found in him a surrendered vessel through whom He could work. The Wilson model makes this statement: any experience of the Spirit of God is a two-way transaction, where both parties give to the other. He gives anointing and gifting to us. He wants us, in return, to give our

bodies to Him in total surrender. We have sometimes emphasised the first, while ignoring the second. But Acts 1:8 will not
permit that, with its two promises. Neither will Romans 12:1–
2, quoted in the story above. The fully genuine spiritual
transaction involves not just a communication of power
from Him to us. It also involves a transfer of ownership from
us to Him.

One grave danger in the Church is that we swerve from
extreme to extreme, finding balance – the middle and comprehensive position – hard to embrace. It is true that some who
rush out to evangelise the world would have done better to
have waited for 'power from on high'. But equally it is also
sadly true today that in those sectors of the Church where
there has been such discovery and joy in the work of the Holy
Spirit, there has also been far too little emphasis on the second
promise: '...*and you shall be witnesses to Me in Jerusalem, and in
all Judea and Samaria, and to the end of the earth.'*

And this, as we have seen above, was the heart of the battle
in the early Church. The early Church in Jerusalem did start
out in obedience to the second half of Acts 1:8, but they
stopped too soon. They wanted to reach out in Jerusalem, but
they did not want to go to the ends of the earth.

It had in fact been a battle with them in this way before Jesus
ascended into heaven, before He spoke those words in Acts 1:8.
In Acts 1:6, gathered with Jesus after all the Resurrection
events that had so impacted and revolutionised their lives,
the disciples are seen to be on the wrong agenda:

> *'Therefore, when they had come together, they asked Him,
> saying, "Lord, will You at this time restore the kingdom to
> Israel?"'* (Acts 1:6)

Brought up in the Old Testament, they carried over a limited
view of the purposes of God. One writer comments:

> 'The hope of "the day of the Lord" grows gradually in the
> Old Testament (Amos 5:18). Different aspects of the end
> time hope were that the Gentile nations would recognise
> the Jews as God's chosen people, Jerusalem as God's
> chosen city and the non-Jews would come to Jerusalem

to learn of Yahweh and His law (Zechariah 8:7–23). Such an idea lies behind the disciples' question in Acts 1:6.'[14]

But the response of Jesus was unambiguous:

> *'And He said to them, "It is not for you to know times or seasons which the Father has put in His own authority. But you shall receive power when the Holy Spirit has come upon you; and you shall be witnesses to Me in Jerusalem, and in all Judea and Samaria, and to the end of the earth."'*
>
> (Acts 1:7–8)

As the writer above observes:

> 'Jesus' response is to reverse their expectation: they are to go from Jerusalem to the ends of the earth to tell of Jesus (Acts 1:7–8). Do we expect non-Christians to come to our church to hear about God, or do we take Jesus' command seriously and go out to them?'

Even before Pentecost so impacted them, the early Church needed a major reversal of their thinking. Their view involved their sitting in a state of spiritual blessing in Jerusalem, whilst the nations flowed to them. Jesus' view was that of servants of His kingdom who were to leave Jerusalem and go to the nations, just as He had left heaven and come to us. This view of our role as servants who 'go out' is intrinsic to mission.

The early Church thus had to surrender their mindsets to God's Word. It was not true that they had no responsibility to the nations. Neither was it true that their responsibility was only to care for those of the lost who came to find them. So in our day those same (or similar) faulty concepts, which cause us to avoid going out to the lost in the right way, also need to be surrendered. The fact is that these wrong ideas are alive and well today. They manifest in at least three ways in our modern church life.

The first manifestation is what I call, **the 'come to me' mentality**. We may unconsciously be living in Acts 1:6 and not in Acts 1:8. In other words, we are expecting the world to flock to our church doors. We see no need to go out – at least not very far out. That may be because we expect others to come so that they can be taught how to emulate our success – in worship, in evangelism techniques, in cell groups, in hermeneutics, in gifts of the Spirit or a host of other things. While that may be good and legitimate, yet it should never take the place of our people going to a dying world, a world that will never come to our conferences, because they do not even know they are happening. Unless we go out, even the unreached on the next block will never be reached.

In Singapore, where I live, there has been over the last number of years a very exciting move of God. The church that I attend (very occasionally, because I am almost always travelling or preaching elsewhere) has grown to about 8,000 in number in one decade. The pastor (an ethnic Chinese) is not yet 40. The average age of the church members is about twenty-two. There are people saved every week in every main service. The commitment is thrilling and challenging. But the reality is that when I walk out in the evening to pray by the sea in the beautiful East Coast Park, the fruit-sellers, the soft drink sellers and the hawker-stall owners that I chat to in Chinese – or in English – have never heard of that church, though it is only about two miles from where they work. They have never heard either of the even bigger 10,000 member church, which is probably only one mile away. If those who live within a few miles of our churches find it hard to hear, how will those in different lands ever hear – unless at least some of our membership are released to go and tell them.

The second modern expression of Acts 1:6 is what I would call **'the Holy Spirit will do the work'** theology. There are those who believe that if we reach a certain place of holiness or the manifest Presence of God, the world will beat a path to our door. They will see something that will so attract them that they will flood to our churches and be saved. There may be an aspect of real truth in this. But we have to avoid replacing one truth with another by imbalance. The will of God in our generation will never happen without us doing it in the way that God said – going to the ends of the earth. No amount of manifest blessing will avoid that reality. The reason is obvious

– how will the vast majority of the world, almost all of whom live outside our cities or communities, ever know what is happening unless someone goes and tells them?

A phrase from a well-known and otherwise excellent worship chorus is worth considering in this light:

'Let Your glory fall in this room
Let it go forth from here to the nations.
Let Your fragrance rest in this place
As we gather to seek Your Face.' [15]

Unless there is another hidden meaning, the implication seems to be the glory of the Lord should flow out to the nations from our worship meetings, whilst we stay in the warm Presence of the Lord! The problem is that He did not order His glory to go out (theologically it fills the world already). He told us as His people on earth to go out to the ends of the earth – and to leave those warm meetings, as Jesus left the warmth of the Father's Presence.

The third version of the Acts 1:6 phenomenon is **'the four-stage view of Acts 1:8'**. Some who hold this view argue that they are called to focus on their Jerusalem only. They feel that their church should labour on until they have won a significant number in their Jerusalem to Christ – until it is 'fully reached'. Only at that point will they advance out to their 'Judea'. When that stage is completed, and their Judea is reached, their 'Samaria' may then be targeted. And finally, at some point in history – perhaps – the ends of the earth might be considered.

If we adopt this four-stage view, however, the ends of the world folk, a whole generation of them, will die before we ever get round to reaching them. It took the church I attend in Singapore a full decade to reach 8,000. The pastor, a friend and respected man of God, told me that he could not spare people, because they are all needed for the work of his local church – it was growing so fast. So how long will we wait until even Judea and Samaria hear if we embrace the four-stage view? They will die in their sins waiting for us first to finish building our local church.

It is therefore manifestly obvious to me, that God calls His people simultaneously to Jerusalem and Judea and Samaria and the ends of the earth – to all four stages at once. This 'exocentric progression', as it has been called, is God's idea for getting the job done and He certainly does not believe in any four-stage theology! Paul was called, directly and sovereignly, to serve the Gentile church. He made it clear from the beginning that he wished to leave the responsibility for Jerusalem to others, that he might respond immediately to his call to the nations.

> *'But on the contrary, when they saw that the Gospel for the uncircumcised had been committed to me, as the Gospel for the circumcised was to Peter (for He who worked effectively in Peter for the apostleship to the circumcised also worked effectively in me toward the Gentiles), and when James, Cephas, and John, who seemed to be pillars, perceived the grace that had been given to me, they gave me and Barnabas the right hand of fellowship, that we should go to the Gentiles and they to the circumcised.'* (Galatians 2:7–9)

Has God changed? What of the modern Pauls today, who on the day that they experience salvation are called to serve in distant lands? How will they obey God if we embrace a false four-stage theology? And what of the 'Gentiles' that those Pauls are called to reach – those would-be new believers who today would like to rejoice in their new life because 'Paul' has been released to come to them:

> *'And the disciples were filled with joy and with the Holy Spirit.'* (Acts 13:52)

What of those who would consider the Word if they could but hear it, and do not have enough of their lifetime left to wait until we have finished our Jerusalem plans?

Paul's own position was actually the very reverse of the four-stage position. In Acts 13:45–49, when the Jews saw the multitudes, *'they were filled with envy; and contradicting and blaspheming, they opposed the things spoken by Paul.'* Paul did not get hung up on an unresponsive people.

'Then Paul and Barnabas grew bold and said, "It was necessary that the Word of God should be spoken to you first; but since you reject it, and judge yourselves unworthy of everlasting life, behold, we turn to the Gentiles. For so the Lord has commanded us: 'I have set you as a light to the Gentiles, That you should be for salvation to the ends of the earth.' " Now when the Gentiles heard this, they were glad and glorified the word of the Lord. And as many as had been appointed to eternal life believed. And the Word of the Lord was being spread throughout all the region.'

Paul moved on quickly to the Gentiles, because he was primarily called to them and because they were responsive. Our modern Pauls need to be given the encouragement and the freedom to do that.

Indeed, as we look at the four stages – at Jerusalem, Judea, Samaria and the ends of the earth – we may consider them as four stops on a journey. In that light, it is not unreasonable to ask ourselves where our personal or church journey ends? Which of them is our own perceived final destination? Where do we get off? If it is short of the final stage, the 'end of the road', it is also short of the purposes of the God whom we serve.

The first and vital element of the Antioch Factor is therefore that we embrace Acts 1:8 for all that it is worth, and not for just half of it. That requires that we understand that our Heavenly Father does not just issue blessing for us to squander in selfish ways, but to enable us to be equipped to do His will.

There is a powerful prototype of that in the Old Testament book of Ezra. At a time when the city of Jerusalem was in ruins, and the people of God were only beginning to return from the exile that their continued disobedience to God had brought upon them, we read these words:

'Then the prophet Haggai and Zechariah the son of Iddo, prophets, prophesied to the Jews who were in Judah and Jerusalem, in the name of the God of Israel, who was over them. So Zerubbabel the son of Shealtiel and Jeshua the son of Jozadak rose up and began to build the house of God which is in Jerusalem; and the prophets of God were with them, helping them.'   (Ezra 5:1)

The prophets prophesied encouragement. They helped them in every sense. The result of that encouragement was not just a general increase of warmth and well-being amongst the people of God, real though that was – previous to that ministry they were defeated and demoralised, seeing the Temple and the wall in ruins. The real fruit and the ultimate test of the prophetic ministry was that:

> '...*Zerubbabel the son of Shealtiel and Jeshua the son of Jozadak rose up and began to build the house of God*...'

They rose up and began to build. They did more than embrace a genuine feel-good factor. They turned good feelings into observable service to build up the work of God.

Later, in Ezra 6:14, there is a gloss that defines that prophetic momentum:

> '*So the elders of the Jews built, and they prospered through the prophesying of Haggai the prophet and Zechariah the son of Iddo. And they built and finished it, according to the commandment of the God of Israel, and according to the command of Cyrus, Darius, and Artaxerxes king of Persia.*'

The prophets prophesied; the people heard, were encouraged and challenged. Then they rose up and built – and finished the building. That is also what Acts 1:8 is all about. That is why there are two halves to the verse – the feel-good experience half and the rise up and build to the ends of the earth half. Acts 1:8 has to produce tangible results – and not just in Jerusalem. Essentially then Acts 1:8 is a prophecy, just as much as the words of Haggai the prophet and Zechariah the son of Iddo in Ezra. Jesus said 'You shall receive ... you shall be witnesses.' The words are actually more prophetic than mere promise alone. And if they are prophetic words, they have to be 'lived out' to be fulfilled – to the ends of the earth.

Closer to the present day, we have a classic example of this in John Wesley. He wrestled with the opinions of his day, which in their own subtle way tried to prevent him from obeying God and setting out to win England to Christ. The blessing he received when he met God had to be turned into external obedience, but it was not easy for him.

> 'As a young man Wesley was ordained into the Church of England, but after his heart was "strangely warmed", his evangelistic fervour resulted in him becoming ostracised by many members of the clergy and excluded from the pulpits of a large number of parish churches. He was then faced with the choice of either giving up preaching or preaching in the marketplaces and fields. His biographers say that when confronted by this possibility he went through a torment of soul that is impossible to describe. To his ordered and reverent mind there was something vulgar about taking worship out into the open air. The idea offended him deeply, but he knew that this was the only course left to him. When a friend remonstrated with him and appealed to him not to take his ministry to the public places on the basis that he ought to have some respect for his good name, Wesley replied: "When I gave my all to God I did not withhold my reputation." He took to the open air, saying: "I consented to be more vile."' [16]

The easy thing would have been for Wesley to accept the limited in-church ministry offered to him, or to give up entirely. He might have accepted the view that 'proper people' did not preach in the open air. But those views were short of the will of God. So, in spite of the pain and rejection, he risked all for God. Wesley himself gave a simple explanation of how he lived and ministered for Jesus. 'I set myself on fire,' he said, 'and people come to see me burn.'

God wants to set His people on fire by His Holy Spirit, not just so that we can arrange church firework displays to entertain the saints, however spectacular they may be. He wants us to share the warmth of that fire with a dying world.

The early Church had no plan to do that outside of Jerusalem. They apparently mistook the fact that God was blessing the work for His approval of them in every area. But partial obedience and tunnel-visioned zeal were not what God was after. A 'cosy huddle' in Jerusalem was never going to reach the world. Thus the next chapter shows how drastically God invaded their party – and how drastically He may invade ours – if we do not heed the lessons of the Antioch Factor in the early chapters of Acts.

Chapter 4

Why, Lord?

'Whensoever Tanna turns to the Lord and is won for Christ, men in after years will find the memory of that spot still green, where, with ceaseless prayers and tears, I claimed that land for God in which I had buried my dead (my wife and baby child) with faith and hope.'
(John Paton,
missionary to the New Hebrides Islands)

The previous chapter outlined how, from the beginning of the book of Acts until the first half of chapter 6, the early Church experienced a period of almost uninterrupted growth. In those early days in Jerusalem the church grew strong both spiritually and numerically. They did experience some strong attacks and even seeming reversals, yet even those apparent setbacks quickly turned to gain and expansion. Opposition and persecution (Acts 4); discipline (Acts 5); an internal dispute and division (Acts 6) – all these things, under the leadership of the Holy Spirit, seemed only to result in further growth. Indeed it could be argued that problems worked for them rather than against them, and served only as new opportunities for growth.

But in the next section of the narrative, starting from Acts 6:9, the early Church experienced a huge and devastating setback. The brightest and possibly best of their young men, Stephen, was martyred – cut down unjustly in his prime by evil and prejudiced men. Here we need to face Scripture honestly and realistically, not simply in a romantic manner. The impact on the early Church must have been devastating. 'Why, Lord,' they must have cried. Acts 8 describes the reaction of Stephen's friends to his death:

> *'And devout men carried Stephen to his burial, and made great lamentation over him.'*   (Acts 8:2)

They *'made great lamentation over him.'* They were grief-stricken, struggling to understand what had happened and why God had allowed it. Maybe they even cried out for him to be raised from the dead. He was not. And so he was buried. To make matters worse, the next verse (Acts 8:3) shows that the reversal and devastation did not stop there. It was not an isolated incident. Worse was to follow. It triggered a season of unprecedented hostility and chaos – a real reversal for the young church.

> *'Now Saul was consenting to his death. At that time a great persecution arose against the church which was at Jerusalem; and they were all scattered throughout the regions of Judea and Samaria, except the apostles.'*   (Acts 8:1)

The events concerning Stephen had not started that way. In Acts 6:5 Stephen was chosen as a deacon (though the text bestows no title; 'servant' would be a better word) along with six other young men in the new church. From there he went out into the city of Jerusalem 'full of faith and power', preaching the risen Jesus and performing miracles under the power of the Holy Spirit. Even when opposition arose against him, they could not resist his anointing of wisdom from God.

> *'And Stephen, full of faith and power, did great wonders and signs among the people. Then there arose some from what is called the Synagogue of the Freedmen (Cyrenians, Alexandrians, and those from Cilicia and Asia), disputing with Stephen. And they were not able to resist the wisdom and the Spirit by which he spoke.'*   (Acts 6:8–10)

It seemed at first as if it was more of the same – the earlier pattern of every event turning to evangelism and growth, even when opposition arose. They were not able to resist his words. Their opposition could not stand in the way of the spread of the Gospel of life. But now, between Acts 6:11 and 7:60, events changed dramatically. Wicked men, using religion as a cloak for their prejudice and their violence, seized him and brought him for trial before the Jewish religious council:

> *'Then they secretly induced men to say, "We have heard him speak blasphemous words against Moses and God." And they stirred up the people, the elders, and the scribes; and they came upon him, seized him, and brought him to the council.'*
>
> (Acts 6:11–12)

Stephen responded by sharing a historical review of the Jewish people, which was more an indictment against his accusers for their rebellion to the purposes of God than it was a defence of himself. The impact of his message was that they took up stones and stoned him to death. Stephen saw the heavens opened and had a face-to-face vision of the Lord Jesus Himself (Acts 7:56). And so he died.

Even with the encouragement of Stephen's manifest entry into the Presence of God, this event must have triggered a huge reaction in the early Church. Stephen clearly was a future leader in the church. In secular terms, having been chosen as the first of the selected young men in Acts 6, it is surely likely that he was seen as 'a future CEO of the church'. Equally, his evangelistic boldness was seemingly almost unparalleled even in the early Church. Its loss was a severe setback in the advance of the Gospel in Jerusalem.

Now he was gone, cut down by wicked men. The early Church faced both the loss of a beloved friend and a season of profound danger to themselves. There must have been great fear in some quarters. We are too romantic at times, not seeing that the early Church was not filled with supermen and superwomen. They sometimes struggled as we would. Some of them would have found it difficult to understand how God could allow such a devastating event, and equally would have lived in real personal fear of a similar fate happening to them, given the explosive burst of persecution under Saul and others:

> *'As for Saul, he made havoc of the church, entering every*
> *house, and dragging off men and women, committing them to*
> *prison.'*   (Acts 8:3)

This time the pattern that had so far prevailed – of all events, good or bad, leading to church growth – was broken. Stephen was dead, the church was being scattered. It must have seemed as if the honeymoon from Acts 1:8 through 6:7 was now shattered, and the church would face decimation and even decline. There seemed to be no gain this time, just accumulating loss. The community was broken up, connection with the leaders and with one another in Jerusalem was removed. It must have been very hard to accept and understand.

But then, with equal surprise and suddenness, in Acts 8:4 the narrative changes again. It reverts to the tone that had prevailed before Acts 6:7 – one of triumph and advance for the Gospel and the Church. Philip travelled down to the city of Samaria and preached Christ there (Acts 8:5). God's Word was proclaimed, miracles were released into the attentive audience (Acts 8:6). It was just like old times in Jerusalem! Men and women heard the Gospel and saw the love of God manifested through healing miracles, and there was 'great joy in that city' (Acts 8:8).

> *'Then Philip went down to the city of Samaria and preached*
> *Christ to them. And the multitudes with one accord heeded the*
> *things spoken by Philip, hearing and seeing the miracles which*
> *he did. For unclean spirits, crying with a loud voice, came out*
> *of many who were possessed; and many who were paralyzed*
> *and lame were healed.'*   (Acts 8:5–7)

Even when occult opposition arose, God's power continued to be released with great authority over Satan's deceptions and counterfeits. A new church was born in the area.

And so the narrative continues, one triumph following another. Philip goes into the wilderness and meets the Ethiopian cabinet minister (Acts 8:26 and following). In Acts 9, Paul is converted, and a whole new saga of Church history is ushered in. The great advance was back on track.

Why then did God allow this short and savage interlude in the middle of the growth chapters? Why was there such a severe reversal, with the death of Stephen and the huge persecution that sprang up against the Church, sandwiched between these long sections of advance and increase in 1:1–6:7 and then chapters 8 and following?

The answer to that question is one of the most vital statements that is made in the entire New Testament. It is also a core element of the Antioch Factor. We should be careful not to see Acts merely as a historical narrative. It is equally a book of teaching and of revelation concerning the purposes of God. Especially, it is designed to give evidence to the staggering lengths to which God will go to achieve His purposes. An understanding of that reality is foundational to the Antioch Factor.

In Acts 6:7 we observed two key words – 'in Jerusalem'.

> *'Then the Word of God spread, and the number of the disciples multiplied greatly **in Jerusalem**, and a great many of the priests were obedient to the faith.'*   (emphasis mine)

That verse tells us that although the Church was exploding in the first period of growth, both in quantity and in quality, yet also it is clear that everything happened only in Jerusalem. It was in effect a progressive resistance to the overriding mandate of Acts 1:8 – *'to Jerusalem, Judea, Samaria and to the end of the earth.'* That mandate was being ignored. All was 'in Jerusalem' and Jerusalem alone.

Acts 8:1, the historical gloss that follows the martyrdom of Stephen, contrasts this with a most incredibly revealing statement. Acts 8:1 tells us that whilst the persecution that arose over Stephen occurred 'at Jerusalem', yet it scattered all but the apostles *'throughout the regions of Judea and of Samaria'*.

> *'Now Saul was consenting to his death. At that time a great persecution arose against the church which was at Jerusalem; and they were all scattered **throughout the regions of Judea and Samaria**, except the apostles.'*
>
> (Acts 8:1 – emphasis mine)

It is impossible to over-exaggerate the importance of this statement. In one swift act of persecution God forced obedience on His Church, compelling them to move out to Judea and Samaria – the second and the third target areas of Acts 1:8.

Pointedly, deliberately, the Holy Spirit uses the rest of Acts 8 as the fullest chapter on the ministry of an evangelist in the New Testament. Where does Philip go? To Samaria, the third geographical sphere of Acts 1:8, referred to in the last chapter. Then he moves into the ends of the earth (sphere number four) through the Ethiopian cabinet minister. Although the latter was probably a Jewish convert, who had visited Jerusalem for a Jewish Feast, yet the nation to which he returned was a Gentile nation. And the results of that carry through to this day in Ethiopia.[17]

The statement that the Spirit of God is making in Acts 8 is enormously powerful. In its simplest form it is twofold. Firstly, it says that God will have His way. He will see the nations reached no matter what. The Great Commission will happen. It may be through the voluntary obedience of His Church. Or it may not. But He will obtain obedience to His Word in one way or the other – and that includes permitting martyrdom and persecution.

Secondly, because that is so radical, it may well be that our reaction is the same as the early Church. As the events unfold, we may experience some form of the 'great lamentation' of Acts 8:2. It is more than likely that we will not understand, that we will struggle even to begin to comprehend why God could possibly allow certain things to happen – our 'Stephens' taken in their prime.

It is an awesome thought that our thinking can be so much linked into Doctor Ryland's thinking that even when God gives a course correction, we interpret it as some form of failure on His part, rather than on ours. If ever the Scripture in Isaiah were true, it is here:

> ' "For My thoughts are not your thoughts, nor are your ways My ways," says the LORD. "For as the heavens are higher than the earth, so are My ways higher than your ways, and My thoughts than your thoughts." '   (Isaiah 55:8–9)

Yet the astonishing truth is that, if we stand back from the emotion caused by the death of Stephen, we can see that it probably resulted in more obedience to the Great Commission than almost any other single event in the post-Resurrection New Testament. It is fully in line with the events before it – that everything that happened served for the spread of the Gospel. It was just that the required break-out from Jerusalem took something more severe and dramatic than had been required up to this point. But it was effective. From that death, and the subsequent scattering under severe persecution, there occurred at least three major world-changing events.

Firstly, as we have just observed, most of the church was thrust out of Jerusalem, and spilled out into Judea and into Samaria. With them went the preaching of the Gospel. Fifty percent of the target areas of Acts 1:8 were thus reached through that persecution and scattering that followed this one single event. It was enormously profitable for the spread of the Gospel.

Secondly, Stephen's martyrdom was a major factor in the conversion of the man who was to become the most significant missionary of all time, Paul. Twice in the narrative of the death of Stephen the writer refers to Saul (later to be the apostle Paul). Acts 7:58 tells us that Stephen's murderers laid down their clothes at Saul's feet. Acts 8:1 tells us that Saul was consenting to Stephen's death. Saul, the young up-and-coming Pharisee, witnessed these events. There is no doubt that they had a powerful impact on him. He believed that Stephen was a heretic, because Saul's understanding of the Old Testament was that God could not have a Son. But there must have been at the same time a struggle in his mind. He would surely have expected to witness Stephen dying in agony, in devastation, or cursing his murderers – something quite common in the region. Instead, Saul saw Stephen die as he had lived, lost in the Presence of God. He heard him, battered by those cruel rocks, praying that his murderers should be forgiven (Acts 7:60). He saw him manifestly experience Jesus in his hour of most desperate need.

There is no way that Saul could have easily passed over these events. They must have haunted him. In my opinion, when Jesus appeared to Saul in Acts 9, the expression in verse 5 (*'it is*

hard for you to kick against the goads') refers at least in part to
Saul's theological inability to explain how Stephen could have
died in this way, so full of the Presence, love and grace of God.

A second result, then, of Stephen's unjust death was to set in
motion the events that would lead to the salvation of Saul.
This cold-hearted witness to extra-judicial murder was the one
who later was so miraculously transformed into Paul, the
apostle to the Gentiles, the man who more than any other
pursued obedience to the Acts 1:8 mandate to take the Gospel
to the ends of the earth. In a real sense, he in effect took over
the mantle of Stephen, that of aggressive reaching out to the
lost. But the sphere was to be quite different. It was not just to
Jerusalem, but now to the ends of the earth.

The third result of the death of Stephen comes in Acts 11:19.

> *'Now those who were scattered after the persecution that arose
> over Stephen travelled as far as Phoenicia, Cyprus, and Anti-
> och, preaching the word to no one but the Jews only. But some
> of them were men from Cyprus and Cyrene, who, when they
> had come to Antioch, spoke to the Hellenists, preaching the
> Lord Jesus.'* (Acts 11:19–20)

Christians fleeing the persecution that arose in Acts 8 as a
direct result of his martyrdom fled as far as Phoenicia, Cyprus
and Antioch. They preached Jesus in the city of Antioch,
reaching not just Jews but also Gentiles. There these ordinary
believers, running for their lives with only the clothes on their
backs, proclaimed the reason for their suffering, the cross of
Christ, to the people of the city. The result was that a church
was born in Antioch. As we shall see, it grew rapidly, its stature
and influence also growing with its size. Most importantly, it
was Antioch that sent out Paul in Acts 13 on his missionary
journeys to plant churches amongst the Gentiles, the ends of
the earth peoples.

Stephen's death, savage though it was, was then the direct
cause of the Church reaching out to Judea and Samaria. It was
also at least the indirect cause of the salvation of the apostle to
the ends of the earth, Paul, and of the birth of the Antioch
church. These three results were totally revolutionary, totally
invaluable, to the work of the early Church. The direct result of

the martyrdom of Stephen was that the history of the early Church was turned upside down, and the unwilling believers were thrust out, at last, into the fullness of the divine mandate.

Therein lies the message hidden in these events that is both awesome and fearful. The message is that God will allow anything to happen in order to obtain His purposes of reaching the lost. It tells us that if Jesus was willing to come down to reach those who have never heard, then we also must be willing to 'go'. The cost should be measured for us on the scale of the cross of the Lord Jesus Christ, and the price that He paid there.

The message is that God is not primarily committed to successful ministries (like Stephen's), nor even to church growth (if it is not in the place where He wants it to be), nor yet to great churches. He is primarily committed to the Great Commission. He is willing to go to any lengths to achieve His ends – up to and including allowing the death of the brightest and the best, Stephen.

God believes in hell. He believes in it enough to have sent His Son from the hidden comfort of heaven to the degradation of a fallen world, 'to seek and to save the lost'. He believes in it enough to have given His only Son to die in a most awful manner, physically and spiritually, on the cross. He believes in it enough to want to teach us that we have to live in the same way, with that same motivation and lifestyle.

If we will not go, if we do prefer rather to rest in the confines of our 'Jerusalem' comfort zones, God has but two alternatives. The first is **persecution**, to drive us out. The second is **substitution**, to find some others elsewhere who will do what He wants. That is the awesome truth of the Antioch Factor – that nothing is secure, nothing is permanent, nothing is guaranteed to own God's favour, even though it seems to be His building and to have His anointing. Only that which obeys His deepest commands can be assured of His continuing favour.

Why is Paul's life so comprehensively described in the New Testament, second only to that of Jesus? Because Paul saw and understood this aspect of the Antioch Factor and lived by it. Paul is intended to be a role model to us in terms of his values and priorities. The Great Commission was paramount to his thinking. It should also be to ours.

> *'And so I have made it my aim to preach the Gospel, not where*
> *Christ was named . . . '*   (Romans 15:20)

History has been blessed with other Pauls. John Paton was one of them. Paton grew up in Scotland in a three-room cottage with his parents and ten other children. The front room served as bedroom, kitchen and parlour. The rear room was his father's stocking-making shop. The middle room was a closet where John's father retired each day for prayer and Bible study. The sound of his father's prayers through the wall made a powerful impression on young John. John then responded to an appeal by the Scottish Reformed church for missionaries to go to the South Pacific islands. When he asked his parents for their advice and counsel, they told him that he had been dedicated to foreign mission before he was born. How powerful was the impact of the values of the parental home on the young Scotsman. Acts 1:8 was real in the small Scottish cottage.

Paton sailed from Scotland on 16th April 1858, arriving in the South Pacific New Hebrides islands in November 1858. There he worked amongst cannibals. He was in continual danger.

> 'They encircled us in a deadly ring and one kept urging the other to strike the first blow. My heart rose up to the Lord Jesus; I saw Him watching all the scene. My peace came back to me like a wave from God. I realised that my life was immortal till my Master's work with me was done.'

The turning point came when Paton decided to dig a well to provide fresh water for the people. The islanders, terrified at bringing 'rain from below', watched with deepest foreboding. Paton dug deeper and deeper until finally, at thirty feet, he tapped into a stream of water. Opposition to his mission work ceased, and the wide-eyed islanders gave him their full respect. The chief, Mamokei, accepted Christ as Saviour, then a few others made the daring step. On 24th October 1869, nearly eleven years after his arrival, he led his first communion service. Twelve converted cannibals partook of the Lord's supper.

'As I put the bread and wine into those hands once
stained with the blood of cannibalism, now stretched
out to receive and partake the emblems of the Redeemer's
love, I had a foretaste of the joy of glory that well nigh
broke my heart to pieces.' [18]

On the surface there is an Acts 1:8 to 6:7 ideal example here.
The godly praying parents; the responsive son. His courage,
faith, perseverance and endurance leading to a breakthrough
permeated with the glory of God, as men and women turned
from darkness to light. The kingdom of God breaking through
in salvation's glory, as a man dares to go, to risk his all for the
Gospel's sake.

But there were other events in Paton's life that were nearer to
the Stephen events. There, on a distant station of Tanna in the
New Hebrides, his wife died in giving birth to a son, and
seventeen days later the baby died too. Paton dug their grave
with his own hands, not far from the house, and despite his
breaking heart he covered it with coral blocks and made it as
beautiful as he could. Did God provide him with grace in such
a wilderness? Consider what he said:

'I was never altogether forsaken. The ever-merciful Lord
sustained me, to lay the precious dust of my beloved ones
in the same quiet grave dug for them close at the end of
the house. Whensoever Tanna turns to the Lord and is
won for Christ, men in after years will find the memory of
that spot still green, where, with ceaseless prayers and
tears, I claimed that land for God in which I had buried
my dead with faith and hope.'

There is no easy answer to such pain and suffering, no simple
triumphalism that can provide slick answers. I have sat with a
former China Inland Mission worker and watched him well up
with tears of pain as he told me how his son had died twenty
years before in China – because he was serving the Lord in a
place where he could not get medical help. Had he been in the
States, events would have been different, the son would in all
probability have still been alive.

There is pain in these events, whether it happens because we have gone out in obedience, or because we have not gone and must be encouraged to do so by Stephen-like events. Both are possible. But the common thread is the promise of victory to those who will go and will keep on going through the valley of the shadow of death. How precious does Paton's faith in danger and in grief appear to us today:

> 'I realised that my life was immortal till my Master's work with me was done ... Whensoever Tanna turns to the Lord and is won for Christ, men in after years will find the memory of that spot still green, where, with ceaseless prayers and tears, I claimed that land for God in which I had buried my dead with faith and hope.'

The deep pain of such loss only makes sense when we see that the Lord's ultimate priority is to reach those islanders, or their modern equivalent, with the Gospel of Jesus Christ, that they might turn from death to life. When we do see such events in that light, they begin to make sense. God deals with eternity as the ultimate, and if we name the Name of Christ, we must do so too.

Will that Stephen interruption happen again in our generation? Very possibly. It may be in terms of the decline of the influence of dominant churches who refuse to use their resources of finance, people and prayer to reach the nations, who refuse to see eternity as the only ultimate reality. It may be in terms of churches from new nations (South America, Asia, Africa or elsewhere) rising up to take over the mantle of Church leadership in our world today. Or it may be in terms of apparent tragedy, of the loss of precious and seemingly irreplaceable servants of God. Or savage and seemingly senseless persecution and devastation of the Church – for a period of time. All is possible. The only certainty is that the God who inspired Acts 1:8 will have His way, just as certainly as He did in early Church times. How could we presume to say that Stephen's martyrdom is acceptable in those early days, but that such things could or should not happen in our day.

The Church in China serves as a classic example of this principle. In the early 1970s a leading Asian newspaper stated that the Church in China was by then non-existent, or almost so, given the horrendous ravages of the Cultural Revolution in the 1960s and 70s. But the years that followed saw almost unparalleled growth in the Chinese Church, as literally millions of men and women turned to Christ. The period of severe persecution was clearly linked to the subsequent period of amazing growth. The first dark period purged and prepared the Church, and indeed some in the nation, to seek for the God Who is real and Who loves men and women, not the modern ideological god-man of Marxism who offered so much and delivered so very, very little. If, as I believe, the Church in China is the fastest growing part of the Church in the world, we have to acknowledge that that growth has flowed out of the darkness of the Cultural Revolution. Such events in our lives, or in anyone else's, are never pleasant or welcome. But they are best endured when we see that there really was and is only one underlying purpose for which God sent His own Son, and that that purpose must today be used as our key to understanding God's interventions in human history:

'For the Son of Man has come to save that which was lost.'
(Matthew 18:11)

The test then is not whether the events are good or bad, pleasant or not. The test is whether they serve the purposes of God, indeed even hasten them, in reaching a dying world with the one item of news that can help it. That perception will radically change our view of past history and of today's events, in the same way as it offers the key to understanding how God could have allowed Stephen to be martyred and the Church to be scattered.

How then does the Church get from Acts 6 to Acts 8, from a 'Jerusalem only' vision to a commitment that includes Judea, Samaria and the ends of the earth? I suppose that the choice is ours. The Antioch Factor shows that the 'in Jerusalem' route is a painful one. Our task then is to take Acts 1:8 seriously. Ultimately, our generation of believers must decide for itself.

God will write the script. He will have the nations reached. Just as He seamlessly moved from Acts 6:7 to the sudden and devastating death of Stephen, and then back again to growth under Philip and the others, He can and will do it again today.

He can write a seamless history to get His will done. The only issue is whether we as Christians and as churches in our generation choose to be willingly involved – or to pass unwillingly through the valley of events similar to Stephen's death.

Chapter 5

The Whole Nine Yards

'And in that day there shall be a Root of Jesse,
Who shall stand as a banner to the people;
For the Gentiles shall seek Him,
And His resting place shall be glorious.'

(Isaiah 11:10 – emphasis added)

In the last chapter we observed a drastic intervention by God into the life of His Church, which He deemed necessary in order to achieve the mandate of Acts 1:8. The death of Stephen and the subsequent scattering of the believers through persecution served to fulfil, not thwart, the purposes of God to reach outside of Jerusalem with the Gospel. In this chapter we need to study a second initiative of God into the life of the early Church, which, though it was very different from the first, yet was perhaps even more dramatic in its effect. We shall see that God took two further steps to enforce His purposes of mission on the Church. Firstly, He raised up the 'late-born' apostle Paul to spearhead the work, which the Jerusalem team could or would not do. Secondly, He took away the initiative from the Jerusalem church because of their unwillingness to go out to the Gentiles and gave it to another – the church at Antioch.

It is not that the church in Jerusalem exactly **rejected** the ends-of-the-earth mandate. It is just that the believers were so consumed with their local vision (obedience to the first stage of the mandate if you like) that they neglected the rest of the package. And that, sadly, as it always does, had exactly the same effect. Touching 'ends of the earth' people in Acts 1:8 terms did happen, but only incidentally – for example in the spontaneous encounter between Philip and the Ethiopian cabinet minister in Acts 8. The problem was that there was no full strategy or plan; it was a negative rather than a proactive item on the church's agenda (see the embarrassment rather than delight with which Cornelius' conversion was greeted in Acts 10 and 11). There was no clear and specific commitment or programme to obey God in this matter. How parallel that is to much modern church thinking. It is not that we are opposed to mission, to reaching the ends of the earth. If someone in the church has such a burden, we will probably give them some help. But far too often there is no 'business plan' from the elders or other leaders. If it happens, it happens – maybe! Of course there are some wonderful exceptions, but they do not represent the majority of cases.

Those down the ages who have made an impact on the nations, however, did not do so by accident, while they were on their way to do something else, as it were. They did so because they heard God on the matter and made mission their main priority. Robert Morrison of Scotland was such a man, a God-given example of the kind of vision and determination that it will take to achieve these wider purposes of God.

Robert Morrison was born in 1782. Like Carey, he was a plodder.

> ' . . . His schoolmaster uncle viewed him as an average student with a high degree of determination. He became a Christian at age 15 and joined a praying society that met every Monday night in his father's workshop. Robert spent weekends studying the Bible, applying his brand of determination to Christian growth. He redoubled his academic disciplines, moving his bed to a corner in his father's workshop so that he could study in solitude through late evenings. He later wrote, "The happiest abode (so far as the house goes) was my father's workshop, swept clean by my own hands of a Saturday evening, and dedicated to prayer and meditation on Sunday. There was my bed, and there was my study."
>
> By 1801 he felt he could only be happy by entering the ministry, and in preparation, he began taking Latin. As it turned out, he discovered a gift for languages, and he

began thinking about missionary service. His mother, hearing of it, was alarmed. She was not well, and felt she could not part from him. Robert agreed to stay by her side as long as she lived.

She died the next year, and on November 24th, 1802 Robert applied for admission at a preachers' college in London. Two years later he sought duty with the London Missionary Society. His father's protests broke his heart but not his determination. He pursued further training, then boarded ship and sailed from Britain on February 28th, 1807, becoming the first Protestant missionary to China.

His plodding, vicelike determination served him as well in China as it had in England, for he witnessed no breakthroughs for seven years. Finally he baptised his first convert. He persevered another 18 years, encountering staggering difficulties and seeing fewer than a dozen others follow Christ. At his death there were very few native Christians in the entire Chinese Empire. But he significantly helped to open the door, and today there are millions of Chinese believers.'[19]

Morrison succeeded in the purposes of God for His life. But it was not easy. He was one who faced unusual discouragement from family, from long and seemingly fruitless labours, and from opposition within China. His success lay in the fact that he embraced God's plan for his life, set his face to obey it, planned accordingly, and did not pull back. And so his life made a difference – he pressed through for the great nation of China, and the rest is history. Like Carey, the challenge he brings to us is that of seeing a vision, and then of 'selling his all' for the sake of that vision in obedience to the Lord Jesus. Churches and individual Christians today cannot offer less.

When Robert Morrison sailed as a missionary to China, the captain of the ship on which he sailed was very sceptical of his vision. As Morrison was leaving the ship, the captain said, 'I suppose you think you're going to make an impression on China?' Morrison replied, 'No, sir, but I believe God will!'[20] It is that passion, that commitment to the purposes of God that will make a difference – and that alone. There are all too few

Morrisons in mission history. How God must yearn that we would consider their examples, their courage, but, above all, that we would embrace their vision to give our all for the nations. They had plans born out of vision; and they carried them out. Did not Jesus Himself say:

> *'Again, the kingdom of heaven is like a merchant seeking beautiful pearls, who, when he had found one pearl of great price, went and sold all that he had and bought it.'*
>
> (Matthew 13:45–46)

If Jesus would lay down His all to seek and to save the lost, that pearl of great price, should not we do the same for the billions of people alive today who have not yet heard? It will not be done accidentally; it will only be done by those who lay hold of God's Heart and His vision for the lost in the nations, as Morrison did.

The early Church had no more excuse in this matter than we do. Acts 8 had brought a clear statement of the purposes of God. As we saw in the last chapter, nowhere is that more powerfully stated than in the contrast between verse 3 and verse 4. Verse 3 looks backwards to the difficulties and trauma that the people of God faced:

> *'As for Saul, he made havoc of the church, entering every house, and dragging off men and women, committing them to prison.'*   (Acts 8:3)

The atmosphere there is of a defensive church, on its heels, scattered, on the retreat. Verse 4, however, switches track completely, almost without reference to what has gone on before:

> *'Therefore those who were scattered went everywhere preaching the Word.'*   (Acts 8:4)

Those who were scattered, far from hiding in caves, *'went everywhere preaching the Word.'* The example that we looked at in the previous chapter – that of Philip the evangelist – is merely a specific example of a general activity. It is also a most extraordinary illustration of the Heart of God. It is as though in inspiring these verses, the Lord of the Church was repeatedly saying: 'How can I get these readers to see what really matters to Me, which is reaching a dying world with the Gospel.' God's Heart is always for the nations, for those who are not yet being reached – for the ends-of-the-earth people.

Samaria now had an indigenous Church in its midst. Significantly, Peter and John, representing the most senior leadership of the Jerusalem church, came down there and inspected the work in Samaria that Philip had established (Acts 8:14–25). They brought improvement to the work and apostolic insight concerning Simon the sorcerer, discerning that his purported intent to follow Jesus was not real. They also brought approval by Jerusalem of the new and significant work amongst these Samaritan people.

But once again there was a problem. Once more the temptation was to fall back into that frame of mind that characterised the Church before the death of Stephen. Before Acts 6:7, the mental attitude was an 'in Jerusalem' attitude. God shattered that, as we saw in the last chapter, with the death of Stephen and the explosion of the church outwards to Judea and Samaria. Now, with that large increase in the church's geographical sphere of operation, there was a danger of settling for the wider region, but still not for the ends of the earth. It was, after all, three quarters of the whole. But God would not tolerate that. Because of this fact, in effect, in the section that lies between Acts Chapter 9 and Chapter 11, God wrested away from Jerusalem the leadership mandate in the church, and gave it to a church that had not even been born up until this time. And He did that to my mind, for one single reason – that Jerusalem still refused to go to the ends of the earth. That was His priority, but it was not theirs.

We must see the focus of God in these events. That fourth circle, the Gentile nations, the ends of the earth people, actually represents the vast majority of the population upon the face of the earth. God's intent at this point in Acts is to make clear His overwhelming desire that men and women from that vast unreached sector of the world's population should have opportunity to hear the Gospel. Now therefore between Chapter 9 and Chapter 11 there runs a powerful and

consuming contrast. It is the contrast between the efforts of
the Jerusalem church to obey God in this matter, and God's
alternative plan to bypass the people and the climate of the
Jerusalem church.

On a parallel with the death of Stephen these events make an
extraordinary statement regarding God's intention of running
His Church according to His agenda. The reality is that
Jerusalem, for all that it was His original choice and for all
that it was the centre of Christianity in the world at that time,
would lose its place because it failed to respond to the purposes
for which it had been given the status, its divine destiny.
Leadership on a corporate or individual level is a gift of God, a
stewardship from Him, which is permitted only because it is
given to achieve His purposes. If those purposes are rejected, or
merely neglected, then the cutting edge of His anointing may
be lost, by church and individual alike. He will never leave us,
because He loves His people. But our significance may decline,
even as Jerusalem's did.

God thus needed to bring into being two 'weapons' to reach
the Gentiles. The first weapon was a man, the servant of God
who carried that vision with the fierce and focused determination to obey. That man was Paul.

Secondly, God needed a community willing to support the
man with the vision. That community was the church in
Antioch. Acts Chapter 9 details the first element; Acts Chapter
11 details the second element. But incredibly, as part of the
divine contrast, in the middle section, from Acts 9:31 and on
through Chapter 10, we see a powerful contrast as the Jerusalem church struggles to come to terms with God's will for the
nations. As Jerusalem struggles to obey, outside of Jerusalem
God builds the people and the institution that He needs to
fulfil His purposes. Once more, the contrast is deliberate, not
accidental.

Jerusalem could not manage the kind of commitment and
reception of vision that was required in this period of church
history. Perhaps they were never supposed to. I do not know.
I only know that God broke in once more with massive
authority to take the agenda away from Jerusalem and to make
sure that His will was done. The easiest way of illustrating that
is to break the narrative of Acts 9–11 down into four building

blocks, two of which detail God's wider agenda, two of which are concerned with the Jerusalem church. I believe they are deliberately set in contrast, as key elements of the Antioch Factor, key components of the hidden message of the book of Acts. If we know how to read it, the book of Acts is an amazing piece of literature, revealing the purposes of God by contrasts and by models within history. It is history (His-story) in the fullest sense of the word.

The four blocks are:

1. **Acts 9:1–30:** the birth of the Antioch Factor apostle, Paul, and his early steps on the Antioch path.

2. **Acts 9:31–43:** a contrasting picture of the Jerusalem church, happy still in Jerusalem and Judea – and a little bit of Samaria.

3. **Acts 10:1–11:18:** God's attempts to jump-start the Jerusalem church into caring for the ends of the earth.

4. **Acts 11:19ff:** God's final decision to abandon His first plan and to start again with Antioch.

We must now look at those four stages in detail.

1. Acts 9:1–30: the birth of the Antioch Factor man, Paul, and his early steps on the Antioch path

In Acts 9, we see God bursting amazingly into the life of the Church's chief opponent, critic and persecutor, and saving him. Saul, or Paul, was a man who ran totally with the vision that he held – whether that vision was truth or error. Salvation and revelation would now reprogram him with a vision from God, not from hell. That zeal that had set itself to destroy the Church is now employed to take its message to the ends of the earth, to the Gentiles. I assume that the events of Chapter 9, astonishing as they are, are familiar to most of my readers. I simply want to observe here the elements of God's working in Paul's life at this time.

Firstly, the issue of the 'who' was settled. The pre-conversion Paul of course believed that faith in Jesus was a heresy, that it was in direct contradiction to the Old Testament. Thus the first issue to be settled was the Lordship of Jesus, the fact that He was indeed the Son of God. In answer to Paul's question in verse 5, 'Who are you, Lord?', there comes a clear and categorical reply: 'I am Jesus.' Once established, that position never altered in Paul's life. For him to live was Christ, and to die was gain – because it meant even more of Jesus than living did.

Secondly, once the 'who' had been settled, then the 'what' needed to be delivered by God into Paul's life. The 'what' is the calling of God, the purpose for which Paul had been created. The issue is dealt with immediately, in the dust of the Damascus Road:

> 'So he, trembling and astonished, said, "Lord, **what** do You want me to do?" Then the Lord said to him, "Arise and go into the city, and you will be told what you must do."' (Acts 9:6)

Verse 15 clearly identifies what that meant for Paul.

> 'But the Lord said to him, "Go, for he is a chosen vessel of Mine to bear My name before Gentiles, kings, and the children of Israel.' (Acts 9:15)

Paul was not to reject his own people, the Jews. But his categorical call was to the Gentiles. That element is repeated again and again in the New Testament. On the two other occasions where Paul shares his testimony and it is retained for us in Scripture, he equally emphasises this key element:

> 'Then He said to me, "Depart, for I will send you far from here to the Gentiles."' (Acts 22:21)

In Acts 26:17 the same categorical statement is made:

> 'I will deliver you from the Jewish people, as well as from the Gentiles, to whom I now send you . . .'

'The Gentiles to whom I now send you.' The 'what' in Paul's life manifestly and clearly is the Gentile people, the ends of the earth people. Paul never deviated from that conviction:

> *'Therefore, King Agrippa, I was not disobedient to the heavenly vision...'*
>
> (Acts 26:19)

In Acts 9:16, Paul is given a third element, the 'how' to add to the 'who' and the 'what'. He is told clearly how much he must suffer for Jesus and for the call to the Gentiles. Suffering, as he himself clearly teaches, is an integral part of the calling:

> *'For I will show him how many things he must suffer for My name's sake.'*
>
> (Acts 9:16)

Paul's call is then complete. The vision would burn within him for the rest of his life – to reach the ends of the earth peoples with the Gospel of Jesus Christ. There is of course much more to it than that. His writings in Romans and Galatians are manifestly written as theological proclamations of the right of the Gentiles to come to Christ without first becoming Jews. But the heart of it all was the single reality of Romans 15:

> *'Therefore I have reason to glory in Christ Jesus in the things which pertain to God. For I will not dare to speak of any of those things which Christ has not accomplished through me, in word and deed, to make the Gentiles obedient – in mighty signs and wonders, by the power of the Spirit of God, so that from Jerusalem and round about to Illyricum I have fully preached the Gospel of Christ. And so I have made it my aim to preach the Gospel, not where Christ was named, lest I should build on another man's foundation, but as it is written: "To whom He was not announced, they shall see; And those who have not heard shall understand"'*
>
> (Romans 15:17–21)

2. Acts 9:31–43: a contrasting picture of the Jerusalem church, happy still in Jerusalem and Judea

The Lord made Paul's vision for the nations clear to the Jerusalem church when Paul visited them in Acts Chapter 9:

> *'And when Saul had come to Jerusalem, he tried to join the disciples; but they were all afraid of him, and did not believe*

that he was a disciple. But Barnabas took him and brought him to the apostles. And he declared to them how he had seen the Lord on the road, and that He had spoken to him, and how he had preached boldly at Damascus in the name of Jesus. So he was with them at Jerusalem, coming in and going out.'

(Acts 9:26–28)

But Jerusalem, far from embracing the vision, responded by two contrasting moves. They sent Paul away without really embracing his vision from God. At the same time, they themselves continued doing what they had done before. The passage that follows is deliberately designed, in the hidden message of the book of Acts, to show how strongly God's initiative for the Gentiles was being resisted, and therefore how hard it is for Him to break into the Church with His Antioch agenda. And if it was so then, might it not also be so for us today?

Paul was then despatched 'to the provinces', to the place where he was born, far away and out of harm's way!

'And he spoke boldly in the name of the Lord Jesus and disputed against the Hellenists, but they attempted to kill him. When the brethren found out, they brought him down to Caesarea and sent him out to Tarsus.'   (Acts 9:29–30)

Far from being received, he was filed under 'pending'. The private church record may have read: 'Troublesome visionary, likely to disturb hard-won church peace. Send home and leave there.' Out of sight, out of mind! There is after all no evidence that the Jerusalem church ever intended to free him up from Tarsus!

Secondly, Acts 9:31 and the rest of the chapter show us where Peter and the majority of the Jerusalem church were happiest – working with the newly established churches in Samaria, Judea, and Galilee, the familiar territory that Jesus had opened up during His ministry. Peter moved amongst them with anointing and grace, seeing Aeneas healed and Tabitha raised from the dead. Many were saved (Acts 9:35, 42), many were comforted and encouraged in their faith. It is good solid, church building ministry amongst the Jews and perhaps also the Samaritans.

There is nothing wrong in this activity in itself. It is just that it does not reach far enough. There is no evidence of any movement beyond those borders, or of any plan or intent to do so.

3. Acts 10:1–11:18: God's attempts to jump-start the Jerusalem church into caring for the ends of the earth

Acts Chapter 10 therefore abruptly contrasts with the end of Chapter 9 by revealing a new initiative by God. The Lord breaks into the Jerusalem lifestyle and their familiar ministry pattern with two visions – one to Peter and one to a Gentile. God comes uninvited with a vision to Peter, designed to show the Jerusalem leadership that God is not a respecter of persons (Acts 10:34). But though Peter eventually accompanies the Gentile strangers to preach Jesus to a Gentile audience, he is reluctant to receive the full implications of the vision. Though Peter opened the Gospel to them, the whole tone of Chapter 10 may be summarised by the word 'reluctantly'. I do not believe that Peter was unwilling to obey, but I believe that he and those with him (verse 45 specifically refers to those of the circumcision) struggled through without the benefit of fully embracing God's vision. It was a responsive obedience, rather than an empowered destiny.

Peter's language is resonant with reluctance. In verse 28, as soon as Peter begins his message, he makes a statement that is almost insulting:

> 'Then he said to them, "You know how unlawful it is for a Jewish man to keep company with or go to one of another nation. But God has shown me that I should not call any man common or unclean.'
> (Acts 10:28)

It is in these terms that he and his party approach this matter – an unwilling heart struggling with ethnic or theological tensions in their positions. Some even argue that he was unwilling to make a conclusion to his sermon, which is then interrupted by the Holy Spirit Himself giving evidence of God's love for the Gentiles by coming directly upon them in love and power. This evokes a remark by Peter: *'In truth I perceive that God shows no partiality.'* But behind that still is 'reluctance'. Sometimes when we think we are being culturally generous (embracing the Gentiles), we are in fact perceived as being culturally arrogant or condescending. God-given vision burns that out of men and women, replacing it with a passion and love, which can only come from Him. If this burned in Paul, it did not burn in Peter or his group. Again, in verse 47, Peter says, *'Can anyone forbid water.'* That sentence in many senses sums up the whole tone. Peter and his group do have obedience, but it is an obedience that senses it is walking through a minefield, and thus counsels caution and care, whilst instinctively slowing the work down by imposing tests at every point. That is not the work of vision. That is obedience struggling with deep and sometimes unrecognised opposition.

Worse is to follow. In Chapter 11, Peter, fresh from the unique experience of the outpouring of God's love on the Gentiles, returned to Jerusalem, and described all that God had done for him and for his party. He pulled no punches. He declared openly to the Jerusalem leadership that the Gentiles had also received the Word of God:

> *'Now the apostles and brethren who were in Judea heard that the Gentiles had also received the Word of God.'* (Acts 11:1)

The reaction from at least one part of his audience in Jerusalem was clearly hostile. Without any pause, in the very next verse (verse 2) they begin to contend with him.

> *'And when Peter came up to Jerusalem, those of the circumcision contended with him, saying, "You went in to uncircumcised men and ate with them!"'* (Acts 11:2–3)

In the end (verse 18) the result is positive. Their conclusion was that God had *'also granted to the Gentiles repentance to life.'*

> *'When they heard these things they became silent; and they glorified God, saying, "Then God has also granted to the Gentiles repentance to life."'* (Acts 11:18)

They accepted the activity of God amongst the Gentiles. But the rest of Acts shows that there was never a reduction of opposition from some quarters of that community, nor therefore the capacity to rise as a community to the challenge of reaching the Gentiles.

In strict legal terms, if the Jerusalem church were to be asked whether it had achieved the task of reaching the fourth circle, the ends of the earth people, its answer would have been 'yes'. However in real terms, in terms of passion, in terms of vision, in terms of a cause for which to live and to die, their honest answer would have to be 'no'. There was no plan, no strategy to work out obedience to this aspect of the will of God.

4. Acts 11:19ff: God's decision to abandon His first plan and to start again with Antioch

At this point it is clear that the urgency of the task demanded another plan. This new plan from God immediately manifested itself. Paul has been raised up as the apostle to the Gentiles, the ends of the earth people. Antioch is now raised up as the church that will serve that vision and that visionary in place of Jerusalem. Acts Chapter 11, with one of those stark and deliberate contrasts that Acts displays, moves straight in to show how God chose others to reach the Gentiles, others from outside Jerusalem doing exactly what Jerusalem struggled so hard to do. But even there the change was not easy. It required two distinct stages before it came to pass.

> 'Now those who were scattered after the persecution that arose over Stephen travelled as far as Phoenicia, Cyprus, and Antioch, preaching the word to no one but the Jews only.' (Acts 11:19)

This scripture tells us that these persecuted believers, scattering across the then-known world, held a theological mindset that is almost impossible for us to understand. Coming into Antioch, they *'preached the word to no one but the Jews only.'* Antioch was a mostly Gentile city, and it is almost inconceivable that they should ignore all but a minority of people in the city, that they should assume God only wanted to save a small selected minority of the people. Jerusalem's tentacles were strong, continuing to permeate the Church with the view that only Jews could or should be saved. They ignored the evidence concerning Peter and the Gentiles – unless their fleeing from the persecution in Jerusalem meant that they had not heard the news of these recent events at Cornelius' house.

But some of those folk preached to the Hellenists (verse 20).

> *'But some of them were men from Cyprus and Cyrene, who, when they had come to Antioch, spoke to the Hellenists, preaching the Lord Jesus.'*   (Acts 11:20)

The context here is clearly not that of Greek-speaking Jews, but of Greek Gentiles. And as soon as they did this, as they opened God's heart and His love to the Gentiles, many believed.

> *'And the Hand of the Lord was with them, and a great number believed and turned to the Lord.'*   (Acts 11:21)

It was a moment of Church destiny. The church at Antioch, which we shall look at later in more detail, was born. From there, in Acts Chapter 13, God sent out Paul and Barnabas on the first missionary journey. Acts Chapter 14 sees them return. Acts Chapter 15 sees Paul go out again from there, though this time without Barnabas. Antioch became a model community as it stood with Paul in his epic endeavours to take the Gospel to the unreached.

But for now it is enough to emphasise one element. The men and the women who broke the church tradition of preaching only to the Jews in verses 19–20 **were not from Jerusalem**. 'But some of them were men from Cyprus and Cyrene, who, when they had come to Antioch, spoke to the Hellenists, preaching the Lord Jesus.'

They were from Cyprus and Cyrene. God needed something and someone new, who could break the shackles of disobedience to the truth of Acts 1:8, indeed to the sovereign command of the Lord of the Church, Jesus.

Again, when God wished to call Paul and send him out, he did it from Antioch, not from Jerusalem. Indeed, in Acts 11 Barnabas had to rescue Paul from Jerusalem's sentence of returning to Tarsus. Jerusalem after Acts Chapter 9 perhaps admired Paul, but it never could come to terms with the man or his gifting. He did not fit into Jerusalem's vision. Their most effective technique was therefore to remove him to a far away place, a kind of distant admiration that would not rock their boat. There is evidence to say that a sector of the Jerusalem church continually harassed him, and certainly Galatians Chapters 1 and 2 clearly emphasise the battles that Paul continued to face with them.

The reality is that to get obedience to His clear command, God had to go to Antioch and not to Jerusalem. From this point in church history Jerusalem ceases to be the world focus of Christianity. Antioch in this period becomes the main teaching Church of the New Testament times. It is financially stronger than Jerusalem, in the sense that in Chapter 14 Paul and Barnabas take a financial gift from Antioch to Jerusalem. It is there, and not in Jerusalem, that Paul finds a home and a place to learn (Acts 11:25–26).

There is much more that needs to be said later in this book concerning the church at Antioch. But for now the message is clear. It is that 'Jerusalem churches' even today, originally chosen, richly anointed, full of New Testament teaching, experiencing amazing miracles, basking in rich worship, may yet face an uncertain future. The key is whether or not they are willing to embrace the Great Commission, to go all the way with God. The birth of the Antioch church shows us that God can move to other people and to other places. Obedience to His purposes is the only way to be assured of His continued favour. That is not because His best comes by works, but because He is intent on finding a people who will obey His will.

What does that say to us? Surely the message is that prominence, growth, success, ministry models, anointed worship – none of these evidences of His anointing – guarantee God's continued favour. Only a determination and a vision to complete the final purposes of God, the Great Commission, will do that. The reality is that if our church, its doctrines and its stature, becomes our vision, it will not last beyond a second or a third generation. The first generation is hungry and is willing to pay a price. They see the church established, they see a reputation and genuine teaching and training flowing out of the church. But then gradually they turn inwards in pride and see themselves as those to whom others should come to learn. The next generation generally exhibit a 'we have it all' arrogance. The arrogance is most easily seen not in their leaders, but in the people of the second and third generation who pick up the unspoken attitudes of their leaders. Because there is no vision beyond their own standing, there is nowhere to go – but backwards.

Those with a vision for the Great Commission are a different people. Generation after generation they run with the vision. No matter what they achieve, they have never arrived, because there is another people beyond them that needs to hear of Jesus, another young church that cries out for help.

Where then does that leave us today? In trouble, unless God can find in us an Antioch heart for the ends of the earth, not just a Jerusalem attitude. Much church planting is like Peter in Acts Chapter 9, moving into familiar territory, adding little Jerusalems to our bigger Jerusalem. It is good; but it is just not enough.

Consider again Acts 11:19:

> *'Now those who were scattered after the persecution that arose over Stephen travelled as far as Phoenicia, Cyprus, and Antioch, preaching the word to no one but the Jews only.'*

They were good people, sacrificial people, beyond what most of us have known. They were New Testament people, who might have heard Peter and John preach and seen them heal the sick and even raise the dead. But for all that they were deeply and seriously wrong, trapped in a biblical understanding that made nonsense of the express commands of Jesus, reaching only the Jews and not to all of those on whom God was now focusing His love.

Have we become like that? If it could happen to New Testament believers, how much more could it happen to us. It is time to change. And that will not be easy. But the heart of the decision is a simple one: do we want to be children of 'Jerusalem' or children of 'Antioch'?

Chapter 6

Hard Choices

We have considered the transition away from Jerusalem, because Jerusalem failed to reach outside of itself and its own people, the Jews. In its place, as we have seen, God raised up a church, the Antioch church, and a man, the Apostle Paul. Did that really make any difference? Is there anything that we can learn from God's dealings in that way – anything that is relevant to us in the 21st Century, with our different world-view?

The answer to those questions lies in Acts 11:19–26, the passage which, more than any other in Scripture, lies at the heart of the Antioch Factor. In this chapter we shall study in detail this seminal passage, and as we do so, we shall observe two major principles of the Great Commission flowing out of it. The first principle is that God can use mightily any (whether that is individuals or churches) who set themselves to obey His ends-of-the-earth mandate. The second principle is that obedience, and with it the power to bring significant spiritual and material change for good in our world, only comes through radical and custom-breaking adherence to the Word of God. It will happen because we, as churches and as individual Christians, choose to go with the minority, with the cutting-edge few who dare to be different because they are trying to obey exactly what God says to His Church.

To illustrate these two vital principles, we shall consider a one-legged Scotsman and a radical Englishman.

The first principle: God is willing to use any who embrace the Great Commission vision

The one-legged Scotsman illustrates this first Antioch principle. God used this unusual and in some ways unimpressive man, because he wanted to reach the lost in China. His name was George Stott and he was a missionary with the China Inland Mission. In 1868, he entered the city of Wenzhou in China. Wenzhou was a port on the South-eastern coast of China, and was largely given over to idolatry. There was probably no Christian presence there. The political atmosphere of the time was also hostile to his missionary work. Stott faced a daunting task. He did however manage to rent some simple accommodation and also to open a small school. Slowly, the atmosphere softened. A few years later, as some citizens of Wenzhou turned to Christ, a small church was planted. To the one-legged Scotsman was added a partly paralysed young Chinese worker, who walked with difficulty. He became the first native Chinese evangelist in Wenzhou. It could hardly be described as a very auspicious beginning – a one-legged Scotsman and a part-paralysed Chinese lad. But God looks on the heart of the man, not on his physique. Of the events that followed, Tony Lambert has written the following: [21]

'The Gospel spread, and a decade later the China Inland Mission built a large church capable of seating several hundred in the centre of the city ... In the summer of 1997 [over 100 years later] I visited Wenzhou ... The former CIM church was still in the centre of the old city, overlooking a busy street-market where farmers sold every conceivable kind of fresh meat, fish and vegetables. A Bible verse (John 3:16) inscribed on the wall was a witness to the teeming passers-by, as was a large red cross gracing the traditional Chinese roof. I walked inside a rather dilapidated courtyard to attend the Sunday morning service to find over a thousand Chinese crowded into the main worship hall .... The pastor, quite a young man, invited me to stay for lunch. He told me the church had been reopened in 1979 after the debacle of the Cultural Revolution. Today, in the entire Wenzhou Municipality, which has 6 million inhabitants, there are more than 600,000 evangelical Protestants – 10% of the population! Wenzhou, which only three decades ago was an "atheistic zone" is now popularly known among Chinese Christians as the "Jerusalem of China".

Today Wenzhou has over one thousand church buildings officially open for worship. In addition there are over 1,100 registered "meeting-points" which are more simple venues for worship, often in rural areas, but also usually attended by hundreds of people. There are also many unregistered house-churches, which meet more clandestinely. In less than two decades there has been a positive explosion of Gospel witness across the entire region...

It is in the rural areas that the revival is most apparent ... In the main township of Yongjia, a satellite county which is part of the Greater Wenzhou municipality ... a gigantic church towered above the other modern blocks of flats, offices and shops. Large Chinese characters over the entrance gate proclaimed "the Gate of Salvation" – the name of the church ... with pews and a gallery to seat 1,000 people. The church was beautifully built in marble-like stone ... Over the next four hours driving through the region I must have seen more than a dozen churches, and doubtless missed as many more, in every village and hamlet we passed through. Nearly all appeared to have been erected in the past decade. Just as remarkable was the open Christian witness of many of the local inhabitants who had pasted Bible verses and crosses over their doors. Some modern blocks of flats had "Emmanuel" engraved in large Chinese characters on their fancy tiled facades ... Yongjia County with a total population of 730,000 has a registered evangelical Christian (adult) population of 130,000 souls. This does not include children under eighteen, nor, presumably, many unregistered house-church believers. The implications are staggering – here in the lush, southern Chinese countryside on the outskirts of a modern, port city, 18% of the population are officially recognised to be Bible-believing Christians!'

Tony Lambert concluded his description of revival in the Wenzhou area with the comment:

'Who could have imagined in their wildest dreams that
the seed originally sown by a one-legged Scotsman and a
paralysed Chinese boy would over a century later bear
such fruit?'

Who indeed? But the message is that even the 'despised of
this world' can make a significant difference if they go for God
to the nations in their generation. That kind of initiative of
God through His willing servants is at the heart of the Antioch
Factor. So the challenge, succinctly put, is that churches
should be willing to take in the 'one-legged Scotsmen' of their
generation, to train them and then to release them to the
mission calling that beats in their hearts. That in turn involves
embracing their vision for the people to whom they are called,
often a strange and different people. It is not easy to embrace
the 'one-legged Scotsman', with all his quirks and foibles
(missionaries by definition are different and even difficult
people!). Nor is it easy to put church resources behind them
to reach a people we may never have met and of whom we
understand little if anything. But the result can be awesome.
To think that men and women of God in our local churches
could be involved in reaching into distant communities that
do not know the Saviour and in seeing them changed – just as
Wenzhou in China was!

Paul saw that same process in the book of Acts. It was hard
but it was glorious. Acts 17 gives us a little cameo of how God
used Paul in so many towns and cities to bring the light and
love of Jesus with transforming power into many lives:

> *'Then the brethren immediately sent Paul and Silas away by
> night to Berea. When they arrived, they went into the synagogue
> of the Jews. These were more fair-minded than those in
> Thessalonica, in that they received the Word with all readiness,
> and searched the Scriptures daily to find out whether these
> things were so. Therefore many of them believed, and also not a
> few of the Greeks, prominent women as well as men.'*
>
> (Acts 17:10–12)

Of course there was much suffering for Paul on the way. But
in Berea and a host of places the Word went forth, men and

women were saved, and churches were born. What had been darkness became light. And Antioch, because they had sent him out, got to feast at his table. Acts 14 depicts a time of blessing and encouragement for both Paul and Antioch, as he and Barnabas returned from the first missionary journey. It must have been a rich time, as Paul encouraged them with the unusual results of their sending and their praying for this first outreach to the Gentile peoples:

> *'From there they sailed to Antioch, where they had been commended to the grace of God for the work which they had completed. And when they had come and gathered the church together, they reported all that God had done with them, and that He had opened the door of faith to the Gentiles. So they stayed there a long time with the disciples.'* (Acts 14:26–28)

Today's churches are making a choice, whether they realise it or not. The potential of the one-legged Scotsman is there. We can be like Antioch, or like Jerusalem. Antioch took in Paul (who though he had both legs was by no means a normal man!) and then sent him out, accompanied by their leader Barnabas, to reach the nations. That is the heart of the Antioch Factor. When Jerusalem would not take him in, Antioch did. When Jerusalem would not send him out (they had sent him home indefinitely to Tarsus), Antioch again did. They 'owned' his vision for the ends of the earth people, and in so doing made it possible.

Will we, can we, change enough to take in and to send out, so that the nations may be reached? That is what God is calling His people to do in our generation. New George Stotts need releasing; new Wenzhous are now waiting. How will we respond?

The second principle: change is difficult, and only happens when we are determined to make it

If there is the potential there to make such a difference, to have so profound an impact on the nations of the world, why do we not see it happen more often? Why are not more churches engaged in this?

The answer to that question lies in the second principle from Acts 11 referred to above. The truth is that effectiveness – that power to bring significant spiritual and material change for good in our world – only comes through radical and custom-breaking obedience to the Word of God. It can be illustrated by a radical Englishman, a man by the name of Hudson Taylor. The answer he gives us to that question is that we have to dare to be different, to embrace change in our churches and ministries, if we are truly to impact the world. We will not do it by following the majority, by doing what churches usually do. We will only do it by radical and unusual obedience. It will not happen automatically.

The mission with which the one-legged Scotsman worked, the China Inland Mission, was founded by that radical Englishman. But the core fact here is that in order to found the China Inland Mission, Hudson Taylor literally had to walk away from the church norm and dare to be different.

'While in England on leave from his work in China, Hudson Taylor was attending a church service on the south coast of England, in a town called Brighton. Before returning to England from China, Taylor had been asked by his first full-time Chinese co-worker, Brother Ni, why, if Taylor's nation had known the Gospel for centuries, they had not told the Chinese about this most fundamental truth of the universe. Why had Ni's father sought for truth in China for twenty years, but had died without ever finding it? Why had no one come to tell him about Jesus? The question that Ni had put to him and the burden for China's lost millions lay heavily on him. But this was apparently not the case for many of the other believers who worshipped God in that church on that significant Sunday morning. They seemed largely unconcerned for the world's lost. Taylor walked out of the meeting before it had finished – not out of rebellion or anger, but because of his burden for China. He walked on Brighton beach, not for the benefit of the sunshine (remember he was in England!) but lost in deep in prayer with the Lord. He cried out to God to provide him with twenty-four willing and able workers to go with him to

China. His response was a specific one – and so was the Lord's. Indeed the small group of men and women that the Lord raised up in answer to prayer became the nucleus of the China Inland Mission (CIM), one of the greatest missionaries organisations there has ever been. The CIM was to reach deep into many parts of China with the good news of Christ.'[22]

Hudson Taylor had to walk the lonely road of radical difference and so must we in our day. Every initiative of God to reach the lost amongst the nations has begun in that way, with that step of faith, in one way or another. Every such initiative has involved going 'against the tide'. What will it take to do these things in the new millennium? The answer is obedience, equally as radical as that of Hudson Taylor, with all that it will cost us in change and in the courage to be different.

Sometimes the process of change is most easily measured in contrasting sample statements from different generations. The change in values regarding the matter of the Great Commission in the mind of the average Christian or church today can be seen in this way too. Charles Hadden Spurgeon, perhaps the greatest English-speaking preacher of all time, and one who as much as any man reflected the values of his own now long-gone age, said of mission:

'If there be any one point in which the Christian Church ought to keep its fervour at a white heat, it is concerning mission. If there be anything about which we cannot tolerate lukewarmness, it is in the matter of sending the Gospel to a dying world.'

White heat and an intolerance of lukewarmness? Contrast that with the following, written by a friend a few years ago, which I believe very accurately describes the attitude of some modern believers:

'The biggest surprise in all of this has been what He has quietly revealed to us about ourselves, our attitudes, and our perception of "missionary-types". We believed them to be somewhat of an oddity, a throw-back of church history (even if we saw them as Christians), who were certainly more "spiritual" than other people. (We believed that) missionaries were religious kamikazes determined to crash themselves into the powers of darkness in some remote and irrelevant God-forsaken jungle. We admired their dedication to the kingdom of God, but questioned their sanity!

After all, what people in their right minds would want to move from the familiar comforts of their own culture, to risk health, financial potential and even possibly their lives, to minister to strange and perhaps dangerous heathen? Like many others with a call to full-time service, we would dodge the thought that God might send us to any far away place. Fear – the enemy we all seem to have to face!'

If that is a commonly held position – and from much experience I believe that it is – a radical change is needed. In Acts 11:19–26, the passage that outlines the birth of the Antioch church, we can observe three fundamental areas of change that we need to embrace. They are all changes that need to take place in our perceptions. The first is in the way we see the peoples of the world; the second is in the way we see our role in the church; and the third is in the way we see the Great Commission.

1. Change in the way we see the peoples of the world

The first change that occurred in Acts 11:19–26, when the work in Antioch started, was a most significant one. It was nothing short of a revolution in the way those unnamed believers viewed the world and the sea of humanity that lives in it. It is a change that many Christians need to embrace in our generation.

To understand how dynamic it was, let us look again at Acts 11:19:

> *'Now those who were scattered after the persecution that arose over Stephen travelled as far as Phoenicia, Cyprus, and Antioch, preaching the Word to no one but the Jews only.'*

We have already considered this verse in the last chapter. Yet I have to say that no matter how many times I look at it, I never cease to be amazed and stunned by those words, muted and played down as they are in the scripture. Up to ten years after Acts 1:8, with a clear mandate by Jesus to preach to Jew, Samaritan and Gentile alike, those who emanated from the Jerusalem church were **still** only preaching to their own people. They preached '... *to the Jews only.*' Yet Jews were only a minority of the population! The city of Antioch had been founded by Seleucus Nicator in 300 BC and had, in the beginning, an entirely Greek population. But it was to become the capital city of Syria, and Syrians became the majority of the population as the city grew. Later came the Jews, many of whom were descendants of colonists imported from Babylon. They possessed equal rights with the Greeks and maintained their own synagogue worship. The Jews were therefore the latest to arrive and the fewest in number. How could anyone seriously consider preaching Jesus **only** to that minority people, the smallest group who had arrived last?

But that is the nature of exclusive thinking. It does not realise how absurd it looks to history. And we still do the same today. It is as ludicrous as having some Billy Graham of our generation visit the United Kingdom and say that he was only willing to witness to the Welsh, but not to the Scots, the Irish, the English or anybody else! It would also be like some Asian evangelist in Singapore saying that he was not willing to preach to any of the population except the 10% who are of Indian origin, this ignoring the majority Chinese and other sectors of the population.

But there were **some** in that foundational period of the church in Antioch (significantly they were non-Jerusalem people) who tried a different approach. They witnessed to **non**-Jews:

> *'But some of them were men from Cyprus and Cyrene, who, when they had come to Antioch, spoke to the Hellenists, preaching the Lord Jesus.'*   (Acts 11:20)

And the result of this preaching Jesus to the Greeks (Hellenists) in the city as well as to the Jews was, to say the least, dramatic.

It was as if God had been waiting for that step of obedience, waiting for His people to give the Gentiles a chance to hear:

> *'And the Hand of the Lord was with them, and a great number believed and turned to the Lord.'*   (Acts 11:21)

In that change of mentality by those who planted the church, Antioch became an inclusive, rather than an exclusive, church. It did not exclude people from the right to hear of the love of Jesus because they were not Jews, or for any other ethnic or social reason. That is part of what Paul meant when he declared in Galatians 3:28:

> *'There is neither Jew nor Greek, there is neither slave nor free, there is neither male nor female; for you are all one in Christ Jesus.'*

It is not just inside the church that there are to be no racial or social distinctions. All outside the church alike are candidates to hear of the grace of God. The fledgling church at Antioch tackled that issue at its inception with great courage. No wonder we read a few verses later:

> *'And the disciples were first called Christians in Antioch.'*
> (Acts 11:26)

For the first time people understood that this new teaching about Jesus was not from the Jews only to the Jews – some new form of Judaism. They saw it was for all men, Jew and Gentile alike, and therefore they called it Christianity, essentially the religion of Jesus and not of Judaism. So in doing what they did, these anonymous Christians changed the Church's view of the world. From now on there was no 'one special group' who alone had the right to hear the Gospel. The Church had a debt to every group now. It was 'open season' on the whole world for the Gospel.

David Shibley in his book on mission entitled *Once In A Lifetime* gives an example of a pastor who almost missed God's opportunity precisely in this way – because God's opportunity, when it arrived, did not come with a designer label that fitted his social perceptions; it came in a most unattractive package. A youth pastor in the 1960s befriended some hippies in the United States. One day, as a result of his ministry, thirty of the hippies arrived to attend a Sunday evening service. They sat at the front of the church. 'The conservative church sat in dumbfounded, judgmental silence as long-haired boys in sandals shuffled down the aisles with their arms around girls in halter tops and cut-off jeans.' The pastor, who was about to preach from God's Word, reacted. He later said: 'I was one sentence away from telling our ushers to escort these hippies out of the building for being disrespectful to God's house!' But God challenged the pastor from the title of his own message, which was 'Christ is the answer'. God's intervention was a simple one: 'Is He (Christ) the answer for the hippies?' The pastor repented and lovingly delivered the good news of the Gospel. As a result of the events that followed this incident, 1500 teenagers found Christ through that one church alone.

How many times is that battle happening, only on a much bigger scale? How many times does God bring us a package that is seemingly unattractive, seemingly disturbing and distracting to the 'important work of the church'? The fundamental problem is a stark one. If that pastor had been asked by God, 'Would you like Me to add 1500 young people to your church?' of course he would have gladly agreed. But that is not how the offer comes. It is still in its original package, which, like the hippies on the surface, is both unattractive and difficult to handle.

The essential question, then, that we have to ask ourselves is simply this: Is everybody, of whatever background, colour, race or social status, welcome in our church? And is our church ready to send people to the ends of God's world to reach them, as He leads? Put the other way round, does the Lord have the right to redirect us to any group that may be on His Heart? Some have settled in comfortably with their original group, and find it harder and harder to grow, because they are exclusive and not inclusive.

The text of Acts 11:20 still leaves one further question in my mind. As we have seen, the Christians coming into the city broke convention and preached to more than just the Jews.

They preached to the Hellenists, the Greeks. Exciting though
that is, and great though the resulting move of God was, there
is no mention of them preaching to the Syrians, who were
probably the majority by that time.

Does that mean that they still stopped short of the largest
people group in the city, the Syrians? I do not know. But at the
very least it comes as a powerful warning to us to reject any
church tradition that falls short of God's view of every person
in this dying world having an equal chance to hear the Gospel.
It will take courage to make that change.

2. Change in the way we see our potential and our responsibility in the church

The second radical change that took place in the Antioch
church was in the way in which the believers viewed their roles
and spheres of service as Christian men and women. The
easiest way to define this aspect of the Antioch model is to
look at Barnabas. He set a matchless example.

> *'Then news of these things came to the ears of the church in
> Jerusalem, and they sent out Barnabas to go as far as Antioch.'*
> (Acts 11:22)

When the news of the salvation explosion at Antioch
reached Jerusalem, they decided to send Barnabas down. It
was a pivotal moment. Up to now, not only had the Gospel
been preached almost always only to the Jewish people (Acts
11:19), but even when Gentiles had accepted the Lord, the
common practice was that they had to become Jews before
they became Christians.

So when Barnabas came to Antioch, it was as though heaven
and earth held their breath, waiting to see how he would
approach these new converts in the city. The answer is a
thrilling one:

> *'When he came and had seen the grace of God, he was glad,
> and **encouraged** them all that with purpose of heart they
> should continue with the Lord.'*   (Acts 11:23)

Astonishingly, Barnabas ignored entirely the battle that had taken place a few verses earlier over Peter's ministry to Cornelius in Acts Chapter 10, where strong voices had demanded that Cornelius' household had to be Jews before they could be Christians. He saw and recognised the grace of God in saving these Greek people through the cross of Jesus, and affirmed that that was enough. It is impossible to over-estimate the radical courage of that step, nor the profound impact on the future of the church that followed from it. Barnabas' heart was for these people, simply desiring them to grow in Jesus. That was all he wanted – to encourage them all to follow Jesus. His role as leader was to help the new believers become like the men and women who had led them to Christ – mature enough to walk into a city and church plant. How did he do it? The answer lay in one word – he **encouraged** them. He also initiated a change that was as enormously significant as that of those who had preached the Gospel to the Gentiles as well as to the Jews. He declared that the Cross, the finished work of Jesus, was the sole and sufficient grounds of salvation. These people did not **need** to become Jews as part of the package of believing in Christ. At the same time, he established a model of the leader as servant, who is there not for his position, but for those he serves, that they might know Jesus better.

Barnabas shows us that one man who has the courage to obey radically the Word of God can bring very significant change, both locally in his church and also way beyond that into history.

The result was dramatic:

> '... *And a great many people were added to the Lord.'*
>
> (Acts 11:24)

Many more were added to Jesus. This is one test of leadership – does it draw many more to turn to Jesus, because it is encouraging and not judgmental or dominating?

But this Barnabas, this servant leader, was not finished yet. He now saw the new Antioch church as a resource for the training and releasing of other young leaders. So he went down to Tarsus and released Paul from the 'prison'[23] into which that the Jerusalem church had put him:

'Then Barnabas departed for Tarsus to seek Saul. And when he had found him, he brought him to Antioch. So it was that for a whole year they assembled with the church and taught a great many people.'   (Acts 11:25–26)

Barnabas went out, found Saul and then gave him a place of training and mentoring. He saw his position as 'senior leader' in that work not as his own personal possession, but rather as a resource with which to serve the purposes of God in others, to release the potential that lay in them. That is the heart of Antioch leadership. It judges not by the scope of its own leadership territory, but by the amount it can release others into their calling. It thus follows Jesus' pattern, not the world's (see Matthew 20:25–28). Churches either perceive their members and their younger leaders as elements to be used in their own master plan (or even empire building) or as valuable individuals under their stewardship to be released into the purposes of God. Jerusalem struggled with Paul because he did not fit the norm, so they sent him away. Barnabas gave a new definition to Antioch's purpose and identity. He went and looked for Paul, brought him into the middle of what God was doing in Antioch, letting the former Pharisee breathe the oxygen of grace for a whole year – then he was ready to be released into his calling.

There are good churches around with good programmes, which settle down as they mature and cannot venture on with God when the next 'wave' of His moving crashes on the shore. But a key factor in Antioch was that when Paul came in to their midst they were willing to embrace the whole package. That was to involve a move of God through him that exploded both him and Barnabas out of the church to the nations, with all the disruption and change that that would entail. It was both glorious when it happened – and very demanding. Yet Antioch could handle it.

Antioch had the capacity and the willingness to take in the missionary, to embrace Paul, to make space for the apostolic. At first sight that might seem easy to do. Paul after all made Antioch famous and very few of us, whether we admit it or not, are allergic to fame. But that is to view the matter with hindsight. At the time of taking Paul in, it is the risk rather than the reward that is more evident – the reward only comes later. At the beginning that embracing, that receiving of the one who carries a missionary burden and vision, seems to offer loss and cost. It does not fit, it is not appropriate for our local plans. Our instinctive reaction will be to reject it. Like any genuine Christian act of significance, it is by faith and not by sight. That is what makes it so hard to do. That is why most churches today miss their Pauls. That is also why the Barnabas model, that of the embracing servant leadership, is such a hard and radical one. Few churches manage to attain it.

3. Change In the way we see the Great Commission

Antioch brought also a third significant change. It was a change in the way Christians saw the Great Commission. In Antioch, obedience to that mandate was not a second or third place activity on the church's agenda. It was at the top of the list. This can be seen in Acts 13, another core Antioch passage.

> *'Now in the church that was at Antioch there were certain prophets and teachers: Barnabas, Simeon who was called Niger, Lucius of Cyrene, Manaen who had been brought up with Herod the tetrarch, and Saul. As they ministered to the Lord and fasted, the Holy Spirit said, "Now separate to Me Barnabas and Saul for the work to which I have called them."'*   (Acts 13:1–2)

As the church leaders met to pray and seek the face of God, the Holy Spirit spoke to them. In effect, He said to them: 'Give Me the best two men that you have, and let Me take them away for mission to the ends of the earth. You have no guarantee that you will ever see them again. You will also get nothing out of it yourself, except the loss of the two men you feel you most need.' What an impossible offer!

But they accepted it. Why? Because they also accepted that the church, the whole Antioch 'empire', belonged to Jesus as the Lord of the Church and not to them. And so they did exactly what He asked.

> *'Then, having fasted and prayed, and laid hands on them, they sent them away. So, being sent out by the Holy Spirit,*

they went down to Seleucia, and from there they sailed to
Cyprus.'   (Acts 13:3–4)

It is an awesome record of Scripture. What it says is that the
believers at Antioch accepted that Jesus had the right to
demand of them any resource that He chose for His ends-of-
the-earth priority – and that meant people, prayer, finance or
whatever. They also accepted His definition that mission was
not low on the list of priorities. It was top. So it had to have the
best they could offer.

While Jerusalem stayed within the city walls, Antioch
accepted that the world was its parish, the ends of the earth
its target area. And therefore everything and everyone had to
serve that vision. That too is a hard place to come to. Perhaps
that is why so many of us prefer to live in Jerusalem rather
than in Antioch.

Out of these radical changes in their view of the world, of
their roles and of the Great Commission, flowed great blessing
– the one-legged Scotsman principle! But it was only because
they were willing to make these changes that they came to
enjoy the blessings. That principle is just as true today. But let's
face it – it is not easy.

Some churches simply do not want that. They just want to
try to touch their Jerusalems and leave it at that. For the rest,
they are content to disobey three quarters of Acts 1:8. Other
churches begin the Antioch way and they press through to
know some degree of success leading to maturity. But sometimes maturity then becomes immobility. Then they cannot
and will not embrace any more change. Antioch was not like
that. How about our church? Are we capable of welcoming
change, or are we so 'mature' that we cannot really change?
How often churches, as they mature and grow, adopt a 'we
have it all' attitude and cannot move on any further, because
they are expecting others to come to them and listen to them –
despite the fact that they themselves find it hard to hear God
in a radical way any longer. The church at Antioch had the
capacity to continue obeying and embracing the will of God,
even after they had become mature.

Antioch, then, had the capacity to hear God, and to allow
Him to redirect. It was not just in its birth that the Antioch

church embraced radical change. As it pressed through each stage of its growth towards maturity, it still sustained the ability to hear God and change direction. Only thus could Antioch do what it was called to do – become a sending church that reached the nations.

In this respect there are only two models in the Bible, the Jerusalem church and the Antioch church. We have to be one or the other. The choice is ours.

Chapter 7

The First Antioch Secret: the Ordinary People of God

If our heart is set on making a difference in the world in which we live, it is not enough simply to embrace the truths that we have observed so far – that God raised up a man (Paul) and a church (Antioch) so that He could reach the nations with the good news of His Son Jesus. Nor is it enough to pass the test of the two principles that we considered in the last chapter. It is necessary to take a further step, which is to consider what specific elements are required to build Antioch churches today. What do we need to have in place to engage successfully in the great calling to world mission? The next four chapters will therefore consider what we need to build into our churches to make them 'Antiochs', each chapter revealing one key element.

The Scriptures provide the model for what we need in this and every area of life. It will therefore be necessary to continue to focus on the core passage concerning the church at Antioch, the one that reveals its foundations, which is Acts 11:19–26. Antioch is a vivid example of biblical balance. It was a church of anonymous men and women; it was also the church that was home to Paul, the most significant man in the New Testament outside of the Lord Jesus Himself. The Bible is a book of such balances, which can only be held together by divine revelation and application. They are deliberately beyond our capacity to perfect, so that we are forced to depend on God and not on our own resources.

Here, in this chapter, we shall consider the first factor that formed the bedrock of this world-changing church. It is the place of the laity, the ordinary men and women of God.

'Now those who were scattered after the persecution that arose over Stephen travelled as far as Phoenicia, Cyprus, and Antioch, preaching the Word to no one but the Jews only. But some of them were men from Cyprus and Cyrene, who, when they had come to Antioch, spoke to the Hellenists, preaching the Lord Jesus. And the Hand of the Lord was with them, and a great number believed and turned to the Lord.'   (Acts 11:19–21)

The incredible reality of this passage is that the most significant church of this period was founded by anonymous men and women. We do not know the names of any of those mentioned in Acts 11:19–20. We only know that they went into those three cities, including Antioch, and preached Jesus. We know some at least of them were from Cyprus and Cyrene, but that is all. Not one single name is mentioned.

The Holy Spirit is making a powerful point here. Antioch was not born from the evangelistic ministry of some famous apostle or evangelist. It was not a monument to one man's ministry. No one man's name was written over the front door of the church. Antioch's genetic structure contained a vital core element – it was the church of the ordinary people. Nobody took the credit, but each one had space to be what they might be in God. It was born out of anonymous men and women who had little to distinguish them except for one key factor – they loved Jesus and wanted others to love Him too.

They also believed that He would use them – just as they were. So the amazing truth is that these nobodies, working in a potentially hostile environment, gave birth to a world-changing church.

The first key to building an Antioch church is then to recognise ordinary believers, to find a place for them and to give them the space to bring change, to do exploits for Jesus in their own land and overseas. Antioch was a church that proclaimed release not just for the sinner at the cross, but also for the believer into his or her God-appointed place of ministry, service, and effectiveness.

I am aware that most successful churches are built round the ministry of one person, usually an anointed leader who is probably a gifted preacher of the Word of God. Sometimes that may broaden out into a core ministry team, with different

expressions of gifting from the Holy Spirit. I have seen many
examples of that, not the least in Singapore where I live, where
such ministries have been richly used of God to build churches
where many have come to Christ. But, as I have stated above,
Scripture is full of balance. And the balance here is that no
matter how powerful and anointed the ministry of such a
leader may be, there must be the place of release for the
'ordinary believer'.

Selwyn Hughes, with his usual instinctive and Spirit-led
insights, said this:

> 'We of this generation ought to be quietly thanking God
> that we are alive to witness one of the greatest revolutions
> that has taken place in the Church over the past 2000
> years – that of seeing the laity coming into its own. I
> know some churches and denominations still have a long
> way to go, but those who resist these changes will, I'm
> afraid, be left behind. The future of the Church belongs to
> the laity – the one people of God ... I cannot help but feel
> that if the Lord delays His coming, church historians in
> the future will look back at this generation and see it as
> one of the turning points of the whole church age.' [24]

'The future of the Church belongs to the laity.' This is a very
powerful statement. It is also one that anyone who has a
position of church leadership would do well to consider. The
danger we face is that we see 'the ordinary men and women',
the laity, merely as material for our programmes. Their usefulness lies in the fact that they can provide the troops we need
for our battles. There is truth in that, because Luke 16:10–13
makes it clear that each must learn to serve first and foremost.
But there is a balancing truth to that. It is on the one hand a
fact that ordinary men and women in the church should offer
themselves to their leaders. It is also true however that leaders
should equally offer themselves to their people in return by
seeking to release them into their destiny.

In men's eyes, Edward Kimball could have been considered a
nobody. But he was also a determined nobody – he was
determined to win the Sunday school class that he taught to
Christ. One teenager tended to fall asleep on Sundays in

Kimball's class, but Kimball, undeterred, set out to reach him at the lad's place of work. His heart was pounding as he entered the store where the young man worked. 'I put my hand on his shoulder, and as I leaned over I placed my foot upon a shoebox, I asked him to come to Christ.' Discouraged, Kimball left the store thinking he had botched the job. The truth was quite the opposite. The fact is that young man's name was Dwight L. Moody. Later that day, after Kimball had shared his heart and departed, Moody left the store a new person in Christ. Moody eventually went on to become the most prominent evangelist in America.

On June 17th, 1873, Moody arrived in Liverpool, England, for a series of crusades. The meetings went poorly at first, but then the dam burst and blessings began flowing. Moody visited a Baptist chapel pastored by a scholarly man named F.B. Meyer, who at first disdained the American's unlettered preaching. But Meyer was soon transfixed and transformed by Moody's message. At Moody's invitation, Meyer toured America. At Northfield Bible Conference, he challenged the crowds saying, 'If you are not willing to give up everything for Christ, are you willing to be made willing?' That remark changed the life of a struggling young minister named J. Wilber Chapman. Chapman went on to become a powerful travelling evangelist in the early 1900s and he recruited a converted baseball player named Billy Sunday. Under Chapman's eye, Sunday became one of the most spectacular evangelists in American history. His campaign in Charlotte, North Carolina, produced a group of converts who continued praying for another such visitation of the Spirit. In 1934 they invited evangelist Mordecai Ham to conduct a city-wide crusade. On October 8th of that year Ham, discouraged, wrote a prayer to God on the stationery of his Charlotte hotel: 'Lord, give us a Pentecost here ... Pour out Thy Spirit tomorrow...' His prayer was answered beyond his dreams when a Central High School student named Billy Graham gave his heart to Jesus.

And Edward Kimball thought he had botched the job.[25] He had not. Rather, he became a significant part of a chain of people and events that ushered literally millions into the kingdom of God, all the way from Moody and Sunday to Billy Graham. All because a 'nobody' obeyed God and took responsibility for a sleepy young Sunday School member. Such is the power of a 'nobody'.

What a vision that ushers into our lives. A vision for leaders to see their 'nobodies' as men and woman of destiny, so that the chief call of a leader is to release 'nobodies' into their calling to be 'somebody' in Christ, to be richly effective for Him. And for 'nobodies' themselves to gain more than just a fleeting glimpse of what God can and will do through them – even them!

Recently an old friend called me. He has laboured faithfully in a good church for some years in its local church eldership. Now in his fifties, he was making an interesting observation. He felt that there should be a change of season in his life, a new ministry direction, but he did not know where to turn. Once the single track within the church where he has laboured seemed to draw to a close (partly by his choice, partly by that of others), he did not know what to do. His question, slightly tongue in cheek because he knows and loves Jesus, was: 'Am I finished at 50 years of age?' He referred to another close friend of ours, who planted and raised up a church in the area, but who now has moved on to another town. Though busy in his local church, John also felt that frustration of not knowing where to go in his fifties to serve God more effectively.

The problem in such situations is often that the leadership they work under may be more concerned with their programmes for the church than with finding the destiny of the 'ordinary' people. Obviously there are personal factors involved, but I believe such cries from the heart also reveal one of the dangers that a successful church faces. That danger is that the church has grown into the habit of referring most questions to the demands of its own programmes for growth, rather than to the destiny and calling of its people. An Antioch church does not do that. It realises it is only there because of ordinary men and women, recognises the resource that those 'nobodies' represent, and seeks to release them into their God given destinies.

These men and women who birthed Antioch, these anonymous soldiers and saints, are therefore well worth considering. What does a leader need to do to produce an anointed laity? What do ordinary Christians need to seek for God to do in their lives, that they might even go into cities and plant churches? The Antioch saints manifested at least five characteristics which are worth our consideration. They are the soil on which Antioch was built. [26]

(i) They were undaunted by persecution

One extraordinary fact about these men and women who birthed the church at Antioch is that they themselves walked into Antioch while they were under much pressure, fleeing from persecution. They did not arrive in a convoy of Mercedes, clutching credit cards, brandishing name cards that spoke of prosperous businesses or ministries. They basically had only the clothes on their backs and whatever personal possessions they could carry. But they were not intimidated. They were not silenced by what had gone before, nor by Antioch, which was by no means a friendly city.

Their message was then a most extraordinary one. Their message, simply stated, was: 'Following Jesus has cost us all that we have – our homes, our jobs, our secure environment. But His love and His grace in our lives are worth all of that and more. We therefore invite you to follow Him with us.' And the incredible fact was that '... *a great number believed and turned to the Lord'* (Acts 11:21).

Powerful is the testimony of the one who has been set free from the fear of persecution. My wife and I have for many years had a friend from Mainland China, who came to faith in Jesus in the UK. For the first few years of her Christian life she was too frightened to testify of her faith openly to other Mainland Chinese. On one occasion she helped set up a showing of the Mandarin version of the 'Jesus Film', but left before the other Mainland Chinese non-Christians arrived to view the film. She was frightened to tell them she was a believer. But God met her powerfully through His Word and His Spirit and set her free. Now she is one of the most effective witnesses to her own people that I have ever met – often telling me of chance encounters in supermarkets with Mainland Chinese, and seeing them changed by the power of her testimony to the Gospel of Jesus Christ.

If leaders desire to plant and build Antioch churches, they will need to spend time with the ordinary believers in their churches, helping them to find the power of God – and not just in church meetings where there is little or nothing to fear. They must experience Him in the streets of hostile cities and towns. A people undaunted by persecution will plant Antiochs.

Wang Ming Dao, the famous house church leader in China, who was imprisoned for two decades for his faith and specifically targeted for many years, said to me that he considered amongst the many fears we carry 'the commonest is the fear of man.' He himself is eloquent testimony to the reality of God's power to overcome fear in our lives. In his early imprisonment he in effect denied the Lord, but he then repented and stood firm again, thus having to face many more years of imprisonment.

(ii) They were unsullied by their environment

F.F. Bruce comments that Antioch was well known for its immorality, to the extent that a Roman poet wrote about the moral sewage running from Antioch down to Rome. But these unknown Christians brought light into that darkness, light from the Lord Jesus. They were not influenced by the darkness.

Antioch churches have the capacity to produce ordinary brothers and sisters who make a difference in the dark world around them. They refuse to allow its darkness to embrace them. Perhaps their model is that of Peter and John in Acts 4:

> 'Now when they saw the boldness of Peter and John, and perceived that they were uneducated and untrained men, they marvelled. And they realized that they had been with Jesus.'
> (Acts 4:13)

(iii) They were not compromised by other religions

As has been mentioned above, there were other religions already existing and entrenched in Antioch. The Jews were but a minority. Most people believed in Greek or Syrian religions. But these ordinary men and women proclaimed Jesus uniquely and faithfully. How else would so many have known to turn to Christ. There was no universalism in their message, no statement that all religions are equal. They were not ashamed of the Gospel.

They indeed adhered firmly to the statement of the Lord Jesus in John 14:6:

> *'Jesus said to him, "I am the way, the truth, and the life. No one comes to the Father except through Me."'*

They did not offer Jesus as one among many roads to heaven. They said what He had said, that He was the only one. That was the undaunted position of the early Church:

> *'Nor is there salvation in any other, for there is no other name under heaven given among men by which we must be saved.'*
>
> (Acts 4:12)

If we differ from them today, it is because we have strayed from the Word of God. We are not wiser for our eclectic compromising. We are the weaker for it. They changed Antioch. We will not change our culture if we do not believe that Jesus is the only way to God. It is the heart of the Bible, of the Antioch message.

(iv) They were uninhibited by their position

They were lay people. They were not even deacons, far less apostles. But they believed that God could use ordinary men and women. They acted on their belief, with powerful consequences.

Interestingly, they did not wait for permission from Jerusalem before venturing into this new city. They did not have telephone or email to do that. They just went ahead and walked into a city, and then preached Jesus. I believe in accountability and correct submission to leadership, but I believe that Antioch people need to have the capacity to change cities because they believe that change is not brought about by position, but by Jesus. How many today wait in the line at the base of the pulpit steps, longing to preach, or feeling that if only they were given titles and position in the church they could make a difference? Titles do not change anyone, for the better at least, but possibly for the worse. Believing that God uses ordinary people, with or without position and titles, is what makes the difference.

(v) Finally, they were not bound by tradition

The church had a tradition, which we have already observed in Acts 11:19, that they only preached to Jews, and so they did not preach to Gentiles. These people knew that that was a wrong tradition, that it was in disobedience to the Word of God. So they discarded the tradition and exalted God's command, and thus changed the city. How many of us today labour under our church traditions, the book of rules, which may or may not coincide with the Word of God? Antioch people do not do that.

One writer puts it this way:

> 'The Cypriot and Cyrenian believers who preached at Antioch departed from the general exclusive procedure of their fellows by preaching to Greek Gentiles. Luke's comments here during this period of transition emphasised the exceptions rather than the usual procedure of preaching.'

It is time we found more ordinary brothers and sisters who can run with godly exceptions rather than with accepted procedures.

There are no doubt other factors than the five that I have mentioned above. At the end of the day, what these ordinary men and women possessed was a first love for the Lord. That first love for the Lord drew them into the city and then changed the city.

Pastor and leader, as you read these pages, do you see the ordinary men and women in their tens or hundreds or even thousands, who look at you from their seats each Sunday? Have you ever allowed God to break you with a vision of their extraordinarily significant potential – as it sits there before you – potential for change in homes, communities, towns and cities, and the nations of the earth.

If you who read these pages consider yourself as an 'ordinary brother or sister in Christ', let me challenge you as well. I spoke recently in Vancouver, Canada, to a fascinating congregation. I had preached elsewhere in the morning in Mandarin Chinese, to a more defined group. But this second congregation asked me to speak in English and translated it into Cantonese. There were folk from many nations there. Into my heart God dropped a thought to challenge and inspire them. It was simply that Jesus made a difference wherever He went, and so could and should they!

> '...God anointed Jesus of Nazareth with the Holy Spirit and with power, who went about doing good and healing all who were oppressed by the devil, for God was with Him.'
>
> (Acts 10:38)

If we follow Jesus and walk with Him, then we also will make a difference in our world. It does not matter how 'ordinary' we are. It will just happen, if we stay close to Him. Have you stopped to consider that Jesus in you will make a difference? He wants to use you.

In the first chapter of this book I referred to William Carey. What a powerful example of this principle he is – that failed schoolmaster, mediocre teacher, laborious preacher. He himself gained this confidence. When he plugged into his God-given destiny, he walked out of mediocrity and failure into a calling that was powerful enough to bring change to a nation and effect many who followed after him.

I also mentioned Moody at the start of this chapter. Moody was described by the old Encyclopaedia Britannica as leading over one million people to faith in Jesus Christ. But the amazing fact was that he had none of the modern apparatus of audio-visual equipment that we enjoy today. What an amazing achievement. And yet at the heart of Moody's ministry lay a seminal event in his early life. From it, he himself picked up this confidence in the willingness of God to use ordinary men and women.

When he began his ministry, he applied to be a Sunday school teacher. He was rejected, on the grounds that there were more teachers than there were classes to teach. Instead of feeling rejected, Moody trusted God, went to the streets of Chicago, rounded up some children, taught them God's Word by the Great Lakes, and then took them to the church with him, saying: 'Now I can be a teacher; I have brought my own class to church.' That is Antioch, raw Antioch – folk who believe that God uses nobodies. When these folk cannot even make it on to the church roster, they create their own rosters!

England in the Seventeenth Century was blessed with an 'ordinary woman' who was like that:

> 'What a difficult life. She was the twenty-fifth child in a Dissenter's family. Though brilliant, she procured little education. Though strong-willed, she lived in a male-dominated age. She married an older man and bore him 19 children. Nine of them died. Her house burned up, her barn fell down, her health failed, and she lived with a wolf at the door. Samuel and Susanna, married in 1689, began pastoring in dreary little Epworth in 1697. They served there 40 years, enduring hardships like these:
>
> • Samuel's salary was so small (and he was so incapable of managing it) that he was thrown into debtor's prison, leaving Susanna to fend for herself.
>
> • The two were strong-willed and argumentative. Samuel once prayed for the king and waited for Susanna's "Amen!" She didn't say it. "I do not believe the prince of Orange to be the king," she said spiritedly. "Then you and I must part," replied Samuel, "for if we have two kings we must have two beds." They separated, to be reunited only after the king's death.
>
> • They also disagreed about Susanna's ministry, for her Bible lessons drew more listeners than his sermons.
>
> • Susanna gave birth to a daughter during the election of 1705. The nurse, exhausted by overnight revelry, slept so heavily the next morning that she rolled on the baby and smothered it.
>
> • Susanna herself was often bedfast, having to delegate home duties to the children. But several of her chil-

dren were so wayward that she called them "a constant affliction."

- Her brother, having promised her a sizeable gift, disappeared mysteriously and was never heard from again

- Finally, on July 21st, 1731, Susanna described an accident in which her horses stampeded, throwing Samuel from their wagon and injuring him so that he was never well from that day.

A difficult life. And yet ... and yet the parsonage at Epworth was destined to become the most celebrated in English history. Her name was Susanna Wesley, and from her house came two of the greatest evangelists of all time, John and Charles Wesley. And the mother who raised them shook the world through them.'[27]

What a difficult life, but what a fruitful life. God will use struggling people, seemingly fearing people, if they trust Him and do what He says! It was ordinary people who birthed Antioch. It was not the apostles from Jerusalem, nor even the deacons.

'The future of the church belongs to the laity.' It is ordinary people who will birth new Antiochs, just as they built the original Acts 11 one. They will add to the record of faith in Hebrews 11 in our generation, if we can work with them to do that. They will also reach into the nations and do wonders there. If we wish our church to be an Antioch church, and not a Jerusalem church, we must find a broad place for these 'nobodies'.

Chapter 8

The Second Antioch Secret:
No Barnabas; No Paul

The Bible is a book of wonderful balances, of which Antioch is a vivid example. In the last chapter we looked at how it was founded by a group of anonymous men and women. Now we need to consider that it was also a church with significant leaders. Having looked at the 'nobodies' who were really 'somebodies' in the last chapter, we now need to look at the other half of the balance – the significant leaders. The first of these, the subject of this chapter, is Barnabas. His gifting and contribution is the second element that is needed to build an Antioch church.

One clear characteristic of the Antioch Factor is life – explosive life, which gives birth to vibrant fast-growing churches through ordinary people. But no church can sustain that kind of spiritual activity without other kinds of gifting being in place. The first is the Barnabas ministry, the caring pastoral gifting, the ministry of encouragement. This is the manifestation of Christ's care for His people through gifted and anointed individuals, men and women whose lives confirm afresh to those on the edge that God cares for them. This Barnabas ministry is the glue that holds Antioch churches together.

There is a powerful example of this in the Old Testament in the life of David. On one occasion, when David was on the run from the vindictive and jealous King Saul, he experienced a major reversal at the hands of the Amalekites, who invaded Ziklag, where he and his men were based.

> *'Now it happened, when David and his men came to Ziklag, on the third day, that the Amalekites had invaded the South and Ziklag, attacked Ziklag and burned it with fire, and had taken captive the women and those who were there, from small to great; they did not kill anyone, but carried them away and went their way. So David and his men came to the city, and there it was, burned with fire; and their wives, their sons, and their daughters had been taken captive.'*   (1 Samuel 30:1–3)

The attitude of David's men was unusually hostile. It placed David in danger of his life.

> *'Now David was greatly distressed, for the people spoke of stoning him, because the soul of all the people was grieved, every man for his sons and his daughters.'*   (1 Samuel 30:6)

David faced both physical danger and deep loss himself – his own wives had been taken prisoner. His answer to the situation was challenging, to say the least:

> *'But David strengthened himself in the Lord his God.'*
> (1 Samuel 30:6)

David knew how to lay hold of God for Himself, hear God, and see the deliverance of the Lord. It is classic biblical faith, the man who knows His God personally and individually.

But even David sometimes needed more than that. On another occasion (when he was in mortal danger from King Saul) he experienced a different kind of deliverance and help:

> *'Then Jonathan, Saul's son, arose and went to David in the woods and strengthened his hand in God. And he said to him, "Do not fear, for the hand of Saul my father shall not find you. You shall be king over Israel, and I shall be next to you. Even my father Saul knows that." So the two of them made a covenant before the Lord. And David stayed in the woods, and Jonathan went to his own house.'*   (1 Samuel 23:16–18)

It is a remarkable example of the selfless ministry of encouragement. In encouraging David that he would be king,

Jonathan was taking an amazing stance, since he himself, as Saul's son, should have been king. If David was to become king, Jonathan would have to stand aside. The ministry of encouragement flows out of choice servants of God like that, who simply want their brothers and their sisters to know that the Hand of God is on them for good. They desire that others should walk in the assurance that His promises will not fail and that God is good – even if that involves the encourager himself paying a price to make it happen.

It is not within the scope of this book to analyse the balance between these two sources of encouragement in God – that of our finding it directly from Him and that of our finding help through the ministry of encouragement from another. The end result is the same, of course, since it brings us back into the security of God Himself. But the fact is that all of us, even the Son of God Himself, need to hear the words 'Well done' from some source, if we are going to be able to keep going. The Gospels record for us three times at crucial points in His life when Jesus received the Father's affirmation (Matthew 3:17; 17:5; John 12:28) and God is surely ready to give the same to us today. Nevertheless let us observe here that, one way or the other at some time in our lives, we shall all almost certainly also need the help that Jonathan offered to David.

This latter is the contribution that Barnabas brought to Antioch. Without it, we will not build Antioch churches. The reality is that missionaries are people who often live 'on the edge', and who therefore experience pressures far in excess of the average Christian. They sometimes feel lonely, misunderstood or just plain ignored and rejected. They need encouragement through the Barnabas ministry. In this chapter we will see how that ministry functions.

Barnabas first appears in the Acts of the Apostles in Chapter 4. The reference is brief, yet powerfully definitive of the life of the church in Jerusalem in the early days:

> *'Now the multitude of those who believed were of one heart and one soul; neither did anyone say that any of the things he possessed was his own, but they had all things in common. And with great power the apostles gave witness to the resurrection of the Lord Jesus. And great grace was upon them all.*

> *Nor was there anyone among them who lacked; for all who*
> *were possessors of lands or houses sold them, and brought*
> *the proceeds of the things that were sold, and laid them at the*
> *apostles' feet; and they distributed to each as anyone had need.*
> *And Joses, who was also named Barnabas by the apostles*
> *(which is translated Son of Encouragement), a Levite of the*
> *country of Cyprus, having land, sold it, and brought the money*
> *and laid it at the apostles' feet.'* (Acts 4:32–37)

Into this Jerusalem church came Barnabas. The striking fact is that he earns a mention in an environment of such high quality. Perhaps it is that the Holy Spirit wants to make the statement that he was a giant amongst men. Yet little is said about him. That contradiction is at the heart of the Barnabas ministry. Those who exercise it are giants. But the fruit of their anointing points to others, not to themselves. Its results are seen primarily in the lives of others. How many missionaries are there today who will stand if they can find a Barnabas to care for them, but who will fail if they cannot? The modern Barnabas thus measures his 'success' in whether others stand or fall, not in his own exploits.

A few years ago in Singapore a distinguished missionary brother working in the region came to see me. He had tried to make contact several times, but I had been busy and not expecting him, and we had not connected. Finally we met on a Saturday morning. He shared his heart, basically saying that he doubted that his wife and he would be able to carry on their work as missionaries. The battle was too tough, and some factors were weighing them down. I struggled hard with what he said after we parted, because I personally knew the church that had sent him out from a Western country. Indeed, I had preached there and they had told me that they were experiencing revival. What kind of revival could it be, I asked myself, that left those they sent out to the front line of mission neglected, tired and searching for someone to talk to? Where was the Barnabas in that church when he was so badly needed?

Barnabas is one of the most defined cameo portraits in the New Testament. That makes it easy to see what he did and how powerful those actions were.

Firstly, recognising the goodness of God in his own life, he laid down his family property and surrendered his money to the church leadership (Acts 4:36–37). Before ministry came relationship with Jesus as Saviour and Lord – he surrendered all to Him.

> *'And Joses, who was also named Barnabas by the apostles ...*
> *having land, sold it, and brought the money and laid it at the*
> *apostles' feet.'*   (Acts 4:36–37)

Secondly, in terms of his own ministry and destiny, even in a church which was experiencing 'great grace', he was specifically recognised as having unusual grace in the area of encouraging others, and he was given the name 'Son of Encouragement'. Obviously he was well taught in the Old Testament and in the ways of God, because he was a Levite. But on this foundation of the law was built an unusual anointing and capacity to encourage others.

One amazing factor is that the state of the church at the time was excellent, yet they still needed men like Barnabas:

> *'And with great power the apostles gave witness to the resur-*
> *rection of the Lord Jesus. And great grace was upon them all.'*
> (Acts 4:33)

Significantly, even when church life prospered internally and externally they still needed encouragement, and they needed specific anointing in believers like Barnabas to manifest it. What an observation. If such ministry is needed at the best of times, how much more it is needed in a struggling church community.

Hebrews 3:12–13 powerfully defines the reason for that:

> *'Beware, brethren, lest there be in any of you an evil heart of*
> *unbelief in departing from the living God; but exhort one another*
> *daily, while it is called "Today," lest any of you be hardened*
> *through the deceitfulness of sin.'*   (Hebrews 3:12–13)

The word 'exhort' is more accurately translated 'encourage' – that is the margin translation of the NKJV. So the verse more properly reads: '... *encourage one another daily, while it is called*

"Today," lest any of you be hardened through the deceitfulness of sin.'

The awesome truth of this scripture is that we need encouragement **daily**. Much like a vitamin, it gives us a boost of energy and renewed hope, but its effectiveness is only for a day. The next day we need another dose. And if we do not find it, this passage tells us, we may become 'hardened through the deceitfulness of sin'. The power of criticism is such that it can affect us for a life-time (how many of us can recall in fine detail unkind things said to us even in early childhood). But sadly encouragement is only effective for a day – that is the force of these verses. How urgently then, this ministry of encouragement is needed!

There are many who used to run with anointing for Jesus, but who are now far from God. Could this factor – the lack of encouragement – be one reason for that?

The famous artist Vincent van Gogh, who was the son of a Dutch pastor, was once a very promising young evangelist working first in the slums of London, then in mining communities in Belgium. He had an unusually tender heart for the poor and longed to do more for them, both practically and to reach them with the Gospel. However he began to show signs of mental instability and both his church and his missionary society withdrew their support. He turned to painting as a means of supporting himself, while continuing to help the poor. While there is strong evidence to suggest he did not reject his faith, nevertheless he did become acutely depressed and landed up in torment, leading to despair and eventually to suicide. Anyone who knows his art, which was not even recognised for what it was until after his death, will be able to discern the anguish there, especially in his self-portraits. How painful, then, for us to realise how he started out as a young man and what might have been, had there only been a Barnabas in his life, instead of those who criticised or at least failed to affirm him!

The ministry of encouragement is utterly indispensable for healthy life. Aside of course from Jesus Himself and the Holy Spirit, Barnabas stands in Scripture as the chief dispenser of encouragement. It is my contention from the record in Acts that his exercise of this ministry was so vital to the Antioch process, and to Paul in particular, that without Barnabas there would have been no Paul as we know him and no Antioch church as we know it. It is that critical an ingredient to the Antioch Factor.

Barnabas next appears in Acts 9. Saul has now been saved. He is however on the run, having escaped in a basket over the wall from the city of Damascus, as enemies of the Gospel sought to kill him for his bold testimony to them of Jesus as the only Son of God.

> *'Now after many days were past, the Jews plotted to kill him. But their plot became known to Saul. And they watched the gates day and night, to kill him. Then the disciples took him by night and let him down through the wall in a large basket.'*
>
> (Acts 9:23–25)

Obviously some of the Jews were incensed that the chief Jewish persecutor of the church had now become the chief propagator of the resurrection of Jesus. As so often happens, if man cannot stop the message, he will try to stop the messenger. So they determined to kill Paul.

Paul then arrived in Jerusalem to a very dubious welcome. The last time that Jerusalem had seen him he had been assenting to the death of Stephen and fervently arresting Christians. Now he was arguably the most celebrated new disciple of these New Testament times. Why should they believe him? Was this not just a trick to gain access to the inner leadership of the church, the better to arrest them? Those familiar with the church in the former Eastern European Communist lands, or in China today, will know of the regular practice perpetrated by Communist regimes of controlling the church by placing in its leadership those who are working for the Communist Party, not for Jesus. The main role of such people in the church is to arrange for the arrest of leaders, and generally to oppose and control any element that might lead to growth of the church and the up-building of the people of God. A number of China's Christians have spent years in prison betrayed by their fellow 'believers', who were – and sometimes still are today – in reality 'wolves in sheep's clothing'. I know of one faithful servant of God who spent 20 years in prison in

China – a sentence that resulted directly from his betrayal by a pastor in his own church.[28]

Even if Saul was genuine, he still represented a real danger to the Jerusalem church. The triumph of his testimony of salvation and grace had to be set against the fact that he threatened to bring more trouble to the church, given the hostility of the Jews. The religious authorities were angry at this significant defection from their ranks. And so the early Church in Acts 9 hesitated to receive Paul.

But Barnabas did not. The Son of Encouragement stepped into the gap, stood with Paul, and introduced him to the leaders of the early Church at Jerusalem:

> *'And when Saul had come to Jerusalem, he tried to join the disciples; but they were all afraid of him, and did not believe that he was a disciple. But Barnabas took him and brought him to the apostles. And he declared to them how he had seen the Lord on the road, and that He had spoken to him, and how he had preached boldly at Damascus in the name of Jesus. So he was with them at Jerusalem, coming in and going out.'*
>
> (Acts 9:26–28)

This was so strategic. Paul, who had been called by God to be the apostle to the Gentiles, needed recognition of that calling from Jerusalem, the apostolic centre of Christianity at that time. The first two chapters of the book of Galatians show this clearly, detailing how important it was that the apostles who were called to the Jews should recognise that Paul was called to the Gentiles.

Barnabas' role in Paul's life at this time was strategic. But it is very clear that this was not an easy ministry for Barnabas. It was an action that risked his freedom, even perhaps his life. In order to facilitate Paul's entry to the Christian community in Jerusalem, Barnabas risked everything. If Paul were, in fact, to have been a traitor and infiltrator, the reality is that Barnabas would have been one of the first to have been arrested. Or at the very least he would have significantly lost his credibility with the remaining Christians for his huge mistake in opening the door to Paul. But he took that risk. In so doing he also gave Jerusalem the opportunity to acknowledge Paul.

The next major contribution of encouragement that Barnabas makes to Paul begins in the same chapter of Acts. Paul, having gained access to Jerusalem, preached boldly in the Name of Jesus. Once more men from a hard-line Judaistic background attempted to kill him. The reaction was the same as it had been in Damascus. They were angry that the chief prosecutor was now chief evangelist right there in Jerusalem – in their back yard. It must have been hard for them to understand what power had so radically changed Paul.

> '*And he spoke boldly in the name of the Lord Jesus and disputed against the Hellenists, but they attempted to kill him. When the brethren found out, they brought him down to Caesarea and sent him out to Tarsus.*'   (Acts 9:29–30)

The church leadership responded by sending Paul back to Tarsus, the city of his birth and previous residence. There was of course logic in this. They had real fears of another Stephen incident. Acts 9:29 suggests that Paul, who had assented to the death of Stephen, was now preaching in the very synagogue in which Stephen himself had preached. Paul had moved in the eyes of the Jews from being one of their own to being a significant enemy. The tables are now turned on Paul as he becomes the target of vicious persecution. Thus the church's decision to send him to Tarsus was perhaps an attempt to prevent Paul suffering the same fate as Stephen, which in turn would have led to another major persecution for the church in general. But because he was uncomfortable to have around, there must also have been just a small element of expediency in the decision to send him there!

But it was short sighted and could well have resulted in great loss for the future of the church. It relegated Paul from Jerusalem, the spiritual hub of the day, to Tarsus, a relative backwater. And that in turn set up a contradiction. On the one hand, Paul, as one under authority to the church leadership, would remain under their authority and would not seek to leave Tarsus. It is important that we understand Paul's upbringing, and indeed his understanding of spiritual leadership. Many modern readers might point out that God had spoken to Paul directly (which He certainly had). They would state that there was therefore no further need for spiritual accountability to others, and that he should just do what God said. But Paul did not perceive personal guidance and submission to spiritual leadership as conflicting elements in quite that way. Some today may well find this hard to understand. But Paul was nearer to biblical conduct than many of us are today. Be that as it may, the contradiction lay in the fact that he was called to go to the Gentiles in the nations, who by definition were not by any means confined to Tarsus! Paul thus faced a dilemma – should he obey men and stay in Tarsus or obey God's call and go to the ends of the earth?

Barnabas resolved that conflict for Saul in Acts 11. As we have already seen, Barnabas travelled from Antioch to Tarsus specifically to look for him:

> *'Then Barnabas departed for Tarsus to seek Saul. And when he had found him, he brought him to Antioch. So it was that for a whole year they assembled with the church and taught a great many people. And the disciples were first called Christians in Antioch.'*   (Acts 11:25–26)

Finding him he brought him back to Antioch, and then ministered together with him for more than a year. As we have seen, such was the impact of their ministry that the believers were first called Christians there (Acts 11:26).

Two direct results came from this activity of Barnabas in releasing Paul from Tarsus. Firstly, Paul was now free to leave Tarsus and to respond to the call of God on his life, which would come in Acts 13. Barnabas was an apostle from Jerusalem, and thus could release Paul out of Tarsus into his calling.

Secondly, that opportunity to work for more than a year directly alongside Barnabas had a life-changing impact on Paul. D.L. Moody observed: 'The grace of God is the soil out of which all great service for God grows and develops.' Where the Son of Encouragement was, there was grace. This was therefore the atmosphere in which Paul's leadership and ministry potential could be developed. As someone put it, Saul (meaning 'Demanded') became Paul (meaning 'The Little One'), the apostle of grace. Selwyn Hughes expressed the thought that up until this time Paul, the Pharisee of the Pharisees, was an ascetic, a man of perhaps over-severe self-discipline. Had he not been three years in the desert? The result of this was self-reliance. Therefore Barnabas' burden was for Paul to be exposed to the grace of God flowing at Antioch, and move in the sweetness of that atmosphere of God-reliance.

How significant for Paul was this work of Barnabas in Acts 11 to release and 'mentor' Paul into his calling. Once more, the Son of Encouragement was directly and immediately respons-ible for Paul being able to progress further into his destiny. Without Barnabas, there would not have been a Paul. Without Paul, there would not have been Christianity as we know it today. That is how vital the ministry of encouragement is in God's economy.

Before looking at the next way in which Barnabas assisted Paul through his encouragement, it is necessary to remind ourselves that this ministry was powerful enough to shape whole churches, not just individual lives and callings. We have already, in the last chapter, looked at the enormous effect that Barnabas had on the church at Antioch:

> *'Then news of these things came to the ears of the church in Jerusalem, and they sent out Barnabas to go as far as Antioch. When he came and had seen the grace of God, he was glad, and encouraged them all that with purpose of heart they should continue with the Lord. For he was a good man, full of the Holy Spirit and of faith. And a great many people were added to the Lord.'* (Acts 11:22–24)

How powerful is the statement that he was a 'good man'! It suggests that it is possible to be 'full of the Holy Spirit and of faith', but still not yet be a good man. The heart of the good man – or woman – is that he or she encourages men and women to go on with Jesus, laying down their own life that this might be so. We need to consider whether the enormous 'my ministry' emphasis of our generation is responsible for the lack of 'good' men and women today – those who really help us to press on with Jesus. Barnabas emphasised the calling of God in others, and not in himself. For the sake of others coming into their own, he was prepared to take great risks – here by not

requiring them to become Jews, but rather to follow the way of
Jesus only, the way of the cross. It was risky; he might have
faced Jerusalem's wrath. But it was also massively effective.
Those who were Christians pressed on; and at the same time
'. . . *a great many people were added to the Lord*' (Acts 11:24). How
powerful is the Barnabas ministry. It shaped Antioch, not just
Paul!

Barnabas was there for Paul once more in Acts 13. As the
Lord spoke, the Antioch church set aside its two chief servants
for the work of mission. Encouragement had also a major role
to play in the birth of Paul's missionary calling here. There is
no suggestion that Paul's calling to leave Antioch, to 'go' for
mission (as opposed to staying at home in support of those
who go) was also given directly to Barnabas. But Barnabas
embraced it for Paul's sake. He stood with him in this critical
early period. It is almost as though he was the first stage rocket
in a space probe, which would fall away only when Paul had
reached the orbit of God's destiny. Such is the ministry of
encouragement.

Their joint relationship thus begins in Acts 13:2 as 'Barnabas
and Saul'. But there is in the following few chapters a fascinating and gracious progression which takes us through
to 'Barnabas and Paul'; then 'Paul and Barnabas', and then to
'Paul' alone. Barnabas is there to encourage, to support,
to release his brother into his destiny. Then he moves on to
another rescue job (which we will look at below), his job with
Paul completed.

There is, however, one dramatic exception in Acts 15 to
this promoting of Paul's name to the fore. A group of men
from Jerusalem attacked Paul, claiming that Gentiles could
only be Christians if they first became Jews, and if they
accepted circumcision and the customs of Moses. In other
words, the whole process that lay at the heart of the birth of
the Antioch church in Acts 11 was being challenged once
more. Paul and Barnabas, together with the wider leadership
of the Antioch church, seeing the significance of this
theologically, decided that a delegation needed to go to
Jerusalem. It was necessary for them to meet with the leaders
of the Jerusalem church to seek a decision on this vital
question. It is not an overstatement to say that the future of

Christianity as we know it depended on the right resolution of this matter.

> 'And certain men came down from Judea and taught the brethren, "Unless you are circumcised according to the custom of Moses, you cannot be saved." Therefore, when Paul and Barnabas had no small dissension and dispute with them, they determined that Paul and Barnabas and certain others of them should go up to Jerusalem, to the apostles and elders, about this question. So, being sent on their way by the church, they passed through Phoenicia and Samaria, describing the conversion of the Gentiles; and they caused great joy to all the brethren. And when they had come to Jerusalem, they were received by the church and the apostles and the elders; and they reported all things that God had done with them. But some of the sect of the Pharisees who believed rose up, saying, "It is necessary to circumcise them, and to command them to keep the law of Moses."'
>   (Acts 15:1–5)

Twice in verse two the order is 'Paul and Barnabas'. Suddenly however verse 12 reverts to 'Barnabas and Paul':

> ' "But we believe that through the grace of the Lord Jesus Christ we shall be saved in the same manner as they." Then all the multitude kept silent and listened to Barnabas and Paul declaring how many miracles and wonders God had worked through them among the Gentiles.'
>   (Acts 15:11–12)

Barnabas had a good reputation and favour from his own time of service in Jerusalem. He had served there, Paul had not. Barnabas now uses that reputation once more to stand with Paul. Indeed it is not too much to say that the Son of Encouragement stood now between Paul and those who sought once more to destroy his calling to the Gentiles. Throughout the New Testament Paul's anointing seemed to have attracted bizarre falsifications of what he said and taught. Without Barnabas, who can tell what plans might have been raised against him in Jerusalem at this point? But Barnabas stood with him. And it was successful. The early Church agreed with the position that Paul and Barnabas were taking, and in so doing established the Church on the foundation of doctrine that we know today as accepted New Testament truth.

Yet another extraordinary definition of Barnabas' calling as the model of encouragement follows almost immediately after this incident. In Acts 15:35, Paul and Barnabas had returned from Jerusalem to Antioch, and were continuing to build up the church there. Then suddenly Paul and Barnabas themselves face division and dispute in their own relationship with each other:

> '*Then after some days Paul said to Barnabas, "Let us now go back and visit our brethren in every city where we have preached the word of the Lord, and see how they are doing." Now Barnabas was determined to take with them John called Mark. But Paul insisted that they should not take with them the one who had departed from them in Pamphylia, and had not gone with them to the work. Then the contention became so sharp that they parted from one another. And so Barnabas took Mark and sailed to Cyprus; but Paul chose Silas and departed, being commended by the brethren to the grace of God. And he went through Syria and Cilicia, strengthening the churches.*'
>
> (Acts 15:36–41)

Paul suggested that they should return to their missionary work, and revisit the churches that they had founded amongst the Gentiles, and also to plant new ones. Barnabas was happy with the idea, but wanted to take John Mark with them (Acts 15:37). Paul refused, for obvious reasons. Firstly, John Mark was Barnabas' cousin (Colossians 4:10), and there was perhaps some family prejudice there. But more importantly, John Mark had accompanied them on Paul's first missionary journey (Acts 13:4–5), but had deserted them when the going got tough:

> '*Now when Paul and his party set sail from Paphos* [in Cyprus], *they came to Perga in Pamphylia; and John, departing from them, returned to Jerusalem.*'   (Acts 13:13)

Paul was called to pioneer church planting. Front-line soldiers simply do not want to take with them one who could possibly turn back from the battle at a key moment. Barnabas, as the Son of Encouragement, had a different calling. He was more like the medical corps of the army, called to restore the fallen soldier. The division between Paul and Barnabas was so sharp that they separated and went on their separate paths, Paul with Silas and Barnabas with John Mark.

There is no need here to get lost in discussions on divisions in the Church. The reality is that Paul and Barnabas simply followed their different callings. Paul was called to take the Gospel to the Gentiles, to those who had not heard. Barnabas was called to be the Son of Encouragement, in this case to John Mark, as he had been in the past to Paul himself.

Barnabas and John Mark returned to Cyprus, which was Barnabas' home (Acts 4:36) and where, as his cousin, John Mark therefore also had relatives. It may be for that reason that John Mark had left Paul after they had departed from Cyprus on the first journey. (Perhaps the mission field proper was more than he had bargained for!) At any rate, Cyprus was the last place at which John Mark had worked with Paul. Barnabas took John Mark back to the place of failure. Restoration will always begin at that place.

We are not told what happened after that. The focus rightly remains on Paul and the taking of the Gospel to the Gentiles. But Scripture is not silent as to the results of the work of the Son of Encouragement in John Mark's life. Twice in his later writing Paul refers very positively to John Mark, saying that he had later become 'useful' to Paul, a compliment indeed after the dispute of Acts 15. He had even been restored to his place as Paul's fellow labourer:

> *'Only Luke is with me. Get Mark and bring him with you, for he is useful to me for ministry.'*   (2 Timothy 4:11)

> *'...as do Mark, Aristarchus, Demas, Luke, my fellow laborers.'*
> (Philemon 1:24)

How powerful then are the fruits of the labours of the Son of Encouragement in the early Church. Just as he had been there for Paul in Jerusalem and Antioch, so now he was there for John Mark in Acts 15 – for otherwise this young man would have been consigned to failure in man's eyes and even in the record of Scripture, rather than to the praise of being Paul's fellow labourer, 'useful to me for (the) ministry'. Barnabas' calling was never easy (he had to risk his friendship with Paul to rescue John Mark). But its results speak for themselves in rescued lives.

There is an increasingly desperate need for the Barnabas ministry in the Church of Jesus Christ today. Everywhere I go, sharing this message, I find a deep resonance. Christians in general, in the midst of busy programmes and product-orientated church life, long to find those who genuinely care for them.

In the late 1980s and the early 1990s it was my privilege to work closely with a man who was to me and to others a modern-day Barnabas. To encounter Harry Hughes was to be washed in the encouragement of God. There flowed from his life and ministry all the strengthening, the sustaining of vision and destiny, that comes from anointed encouragement. To spend time with Harry was to be the more convinced that my Father in heaven loved me, no matter how much the circumstances I was facing might seem to contradict that.

Towards the end of his life Harry needed major heart surgery. He wrote to me, saying that he did not know whether he would survive the operation, but that, in case he did not, he wished me to know that God had used my ministry to restore him in a very real way into further service for the Lord. I wrote back and told him that his major need was for a brain operation, not a heart operation! I told him that it was **his** life and **his** Barnabas ministry that had restored and strengthened and sustained me. The debt was the other way round; not from him to me, but from me to him! Perhaps it is simply that all real relationships of such mutual benefit leave us blind to our own contribution, such is our sense of debt to the other. Harry's life was to me perhaps the single most powerful example in human form of the Barnabas ministry that I have ever known. I know I am not alone in feeling that; there are many of us who feel a 'Harry-shaped hole' in our hearts, since he passed away a few years ago. The sad fact is that there are all too few Harrys around!

To further define the ministry of encouragement, I need to consider several more elements of Barnabas' life.

Firstly, it is no cheap or easy ministry. He paid a price to do what he did. As we have seen, in Acts 4 Barnabas laid down family property before the Lord, a sign of His surrender to the Lordship of Jesus. In Acts 9 he risked everything again to embrace Paul into the Jerusalem church. In Acts 11 he risked his Jerusalem position to travel to Antioch, not knowing what, if anything, he would find there. He left Jerusalem's security to serve in a place whose people he knew nothing about. Again, in Acts 11, he went to bring Paul to Antioch, thus jeopardising his own position in Antioch to Paul's superior apostolic anointing. In Acts 13 he risked losing Antioch to serve Paul's calling – risking so much for something that would not even benefit him. In Acts 15 he stood with Paul against those whose fight was more with Paul than with him. In Acts 15 again he was willing to jeopardise his long-standing relationship with Paul in order to rescue the fallen and rejected John Mark.

All these steps were so costly for him, bringing with them almost no personal benefit. He paid the price, others enjoyed the benefits. The cost of the Barnabas ministry, then, is that it will find its greatest effect in the release of another and not in personal gain. Is that why we find his ministry of encourage- ment so hard, why it is so rare in the body of Christ, and why there are so few like Harry Hughes today?

Secondly, although the Barnabas ministry of encouragement would be classically defined as a pastoral ministry, yet there is in it another rare and vital element that we need to observe. Though Barnabas was essentially pastoral in his gifting, he was also a Great Commission man. He had a heart for the lost of the nations as well as for the local Christians. There was no conflict between the two in his mind. Local care should result in the nations being reached. He did not shut out world missions; he positively encouraged it. There are many good pastors who are not Great Commission men. They simply care for their sheep, making sure that they have 'fresh water and green grass'. But they do not seem to care for those over the mountains, who are not yet in their fold.

This is a major element of the challenge of Barnabas. His life says that it is not enough for us to be pastoral in the sense of merely making the sheep comfortable for themselves. If we do that, we are engaged in a form of rebellion against the Lord of the Church, Jesus Christ. Barnabas concerned himself not just with loving the saints, but with co-operating with God, that the saints would find their destiny in reaching the lost amongst the nations. Barnabas' life carries a challenge to every pastor. Does our pastoral work help or hinder a vision for reaching the lost, even in our local neighbourhoods, let alone in the nations? Does it result in the encouraging of the saints to go out or does it make them so comfortable in the pews that they have no desire to move? Do they lose sight of those who are much worse off than they are, because they have not yet heard of the Saviour's love?

Thirdly, there is no place on the face of the earth where the ministry of the Son of Encouragement is so needed as it is in the lives of those who obey the call of Jesus Christ to front-line missions. The battles that these missionaries face are not just those that local Christians face in their own communities. In addition missionaries must battle with the pressures of strange cultures, strange weather, strange languages and strange peoples. And to that they may need on occasion to add one further sometimes crushing factor – the absence of anyone who cares for them enough to write or to phone or email or visit them to express their concern. Sometimes it boils down to empty post boxes, silent telephones and no 'you have mail' in their computer in-boxes. When that happens, nobody seems to be near enough to say to them: 'I am thinking and praying for you. I really do care that you have left the comfort of church, friends and family for the Lord's sake.'

Fourthly, world mission offers every Christian in every church an opportunity for service. It is for everyone, not just for a few. There are those who believe in the Great Commission, but who say that they have no idea how they could ever become involved. For reasons of their ministry call or their family or their health or whatever, they do not feel it is right for them to leave their own countries. I believe that many such people are called to be a Barnabas to missionaries on the field. That is how they can plug into the Great Commission. They are to be men and women of encouragement, who will by phone-call or letter or email or even the occasional visit bring a Hebrews 3 regular dose of encouragement and of care. Because they care, the missionary may grow strong again in the understanding that Jesus also cares. If believers in local churches could only get a vision for the power of the Barnabas ministry in the life of the modern-day Paul, what destiny many could find in such service today.

Later in this book my wife Christine will add a chapter on how we can practically be agents of the Barnabas ministry to those serving on the mission field. It is enough for me at this point to make a simple point again – if there had been no Barnabas, there would have been no Paul and no Church amongst the Gentiles as we know it today. That is how strategic Barnabas' ministry was. If his ministry was that important in the early Church, how important it must be today. You who say you cannot find your place in missions today, you can. You can by encouragement make a world of difference – literally! Without that, we will not build Antioch churches, and we will not reach the nations.

In closing this chapter, let me quote from a newsletter, just received, from one of our colleagues who serves with us inside China. She calls herself the 'Singapore Daughter' of the American believer about whom she is writing. He had just passed away when she wrote these words. I think they will speak poignantly for themselves:

> 'As I write this article, my heart grieves and yet rejoices because Clint has gone home to be with the Lord on 17 May 2000. I was really looking forward to having him stay at my China home for two months. Clint was planning to come to China in July to take care of a spina-bifida boy whom my company wish to sponsor for a club foot operation. His main responsibility was to take care of the boy after his operation and to train him to walk with a walker. To do this, Clint had to first learn the skills in the States so that he could apply the physio-therapy skills he had learned on the boy. Now that he has gone, we have had to postpone this operation till we have the right volunteer. As you can see, Clint was indeed one of the strong pillars in our work.
>
> More important, his love for us, especially his Singapore daughters, is something that words cannot express. With his bonus air mileage, he would travel to Singapore to

visit us. Not for sightseeing, but to see us. Clint would take every opportunity to care, love, help and esteem us whenever possible. And that's how we gave him the title of "Kentucky Dad". Clint's life was a real reflection of the good Samaritan man we read about in the Bible, who would go an extra mile for his neighbours. On our teams, he would always accompany me or bring back breakfast for the members in the morning. When he worked in the orphanage, he would voluntarily wash the dirty toilets that we would not want to be in, for even a second.

Because of such persistence and undying love, Clint brought many hearts nearer to God. His life speaks so much of love even though he may not have been able to articulate verbally, especially to the Chinese-speaking locals. On several occasions, he was interviewed and reported in the local China newspapers about his acts of kindness. What an example of Christ!

Clint, I will always have you in my heart and will continue to follow your excellent example of a good Samaritan man.

Chapter 9

The Third Antioch Secret: the Risk Takers

The first two building blocks of an Antioch church outlined in the last two chapters may seem to offer a fairly comprehensive package. A creative group of church-planters, cared for by a good and Spirit-filled pastor, offer more than enough to satisfy the hearts of many struggling churches. But that is the danger. If a church stops there, it will never be an Antioch church. The divide that separates us from the Antioch Factor is crossed only by taking the next step, which we must consider in this chapter. That step is the willingness to take risks by allowing 'Paul' to move into our midst, while at the same time releasing him to be all that God has called him to be – inside and outside the church.

This step is perhaps best summed up in an incident that I witnessed a few years ago. I was invited to attend the official opening of the new building of a good church. They had a fine leadership, good programmes and a growing group of believers. In the midst of the service for the dedication of the building, the Lord spoke through a prophetic word. I cannot remember it word for word, but it was to this effect: 'Many will pass through your doors; you will train them and build them up; but you will not keep most of them. Your front door will be wide; but so will your back door. You will minister to them as they pass between the two doors.' Obviously that is not the kind of word that most of us are looking for at such a gathering. We would prefer the word that says: 'I will build you up and make you by far the most successful church in the city, with unusual growth...' But I believe the word that came in that service is at the heart of the God of Antioch, hard though it was to receive. When I asked the pastor a few years later how the leadership had responded to the word, he said they had rejected it and ignored it. Whatever the rights and wrongs of that situation may have been, it has to be said that unless we are willing to take folk in, to give them all that we have, and then be willing to release them to the nations, we will never be Antioch churches. We will, ultimately, be Jerusalem churches. The Pauls of our generation will have to go elsewhere – to some other church that has caught the Antioch vision.

Can we and will we allow God to open our church doors and use all that we have to prepare men and women for a calling that may bring us no gain or credit?

The battle that lies at the heart of this matter is that when Paul arrives (remember the hippies in Chapter 6), he is wrapped in a most unattractive package. He has to be embraced by faith and not by sight. All the benefits were not on the table when Paul came to Antioch. What he actually offered was significant potential loss. Only later did Antioch get the benefits. That is the heart of the battle today for would-be Antioch churches.

As we have already observed, in Acts 11:25–26 Barnabas went to Tarsus to search for Paul.

> *'Then Barnabas departed for Tarsus to seek Saul. And when he had found him, he brought him to Antioch. So it was that for a whole year they assembled with the church and taught a great many people. And the disciples were first called Christians in Antioch.'*   (Acts 11:25–26)

It seems to be a good and profitable action. But we need to consider exactly how great a risk Barnabas took. On the surface the package was not a good-looking one.

First of all, Paul's recent track record hardly suggested that any sensible pastor should hurry to welcome him in. His first church experience had been in Damascus in Acts 9. He had created trouble. So much offence was caused through his bold preaching of the Gospel that the Jews wanted to kill him. The church responded by giving him a less than formal send-off.

> *'Now after many days were past, the Jews plotted to kill him.*
> *But their plot became known to Saul. And they watched the*
> *gates day and night, to kill him. Then the disciples took him by*
> *night and let him down through the wall in a large basket.'*
>   (Acts 9:23–25)

We are not told what happened to the Damascus church
after Paul left in such an ignominious manner. But it is
unlikely that their popularity rose sharply, particularly with
certain members of the Damascus community. Quite possibly,
there were some repercussions that the church had to face after
Paul's unusual departure.

Paul then travelled to Jerusalem for his second church
experience. Exactly the same thing happened there. He
preached boldly, but the Greek-speaking Jews or Hellenists
were upset, and trouble was quickly brewing again. Once more
they wanted to kill him.

> *'And he spoke boldly in the name of the Lord Jesus and*
> *disputed against the Hellenists, but they attempted to kill him.'*
>   (Acts 9:29)

The believers in Jerusalem responded in the same way as
those in Damascus had, except that this time Paul presumably
left by the front gate rather than in a basket over the wall, as he
had from Damascus! But if that was progress, it was minimal
progress in terms of the attitude of Paul's fellow believers. They
were not looking for trouble, and so they invited him to leave
again, as at Damascus.

> *'When the brethren found out, they brought him down to*
> *Caesarea and sent him out to Tarsus.'*   (Acts 9:30)

Again, there may once more have been repercussions in
Jerusalem after Paul left. However, in his absence, we do know
that there was a season of grace in the church:

> *'Then the churches throughout all Judea, Galilee, and Samaria*
> *had peace and were edified. And walking in the fear of the Lord*
> *and in the comfort of the Holy Spirit, they were multiplied.'*
>   (Acts 9:31)

The message of the early Paul was pretty clear to all – not the least to Barnabas, who was right there on site in Jerusalem and equally familiar with the Damascus events. This was the label on the package: he is a 'stirrer', and it would be better to steer well clear of him. Do not take him in, because this package attracts trouble as nectar attracts bees. If there is a season of peace to be had, it is when he is out of town, not resident in the church!

Paul's third and next venue was Tarsus. Admittedly that seems to have been more peaceful. But these realities must have been in Barnabas' mind when he came to consider his dramatic move in inviting Paul to Antioch.

As we have seen above, Antioch was a fast growing church. Both before Barnabas arrived and afterwards, Scripture is determined to point out that Antioch saw 'a great number' (Acts 11:21) followed by 'a great many people' (11:24) added to it. In other words, Antioch did not need Paul. Its numbers were impressive, and its growth was probably faster than that of any other church of this period. Barnabas thus took a major risk in inviting Paul in. In this early period of growth in Antioch, there is no suggestion whatsoever of any internal strife or external opposition and persecution. Indeed the followers of Jesus were for the first time recognised as Christians and not as Jews in Antioch at this point (Acts 11:26). Antioch had definition, it had growth, it had success. For Barnabas to invite Paul in at this stage was to risk that growth and new-found stability.

Whenever we embrace the embryonic missionary, the potential Paul, we take that risk. They are not comfortable people. They will rock our boat, they will disturb our peace. They will threaten our carefully crafted church growth plans. Of course they will bring benefit, but that does not seem to be in evidence at the beginning. Will we hear God, and take these rough-cut diamonds into our midst, polish and refine them, and then release them into the nations? Or will we do a 'Jerusalem' on them, and shut them up in Tarsus – and miss part of our destiny in God, not to mention theirs?

Secondly, Barnabas risked losing his leadership position in the Antioch church when he invited Paul in. Admittedly it was the early days, in terms of Paul's ministry, but the kind of

ministry that would church plant in Damascus, that could
rock Jerusalem, that could in the end write almost fifty per
cent of the New Testament, and open up the whole Gentile
world, was unlikely to have been hidden even at this point.
The ministry of Barnabas was defined, but he could not stand
beside Paul in stature. To invite Paul into his church was also
to invite a shift of the attention of the fast growing Antioch
church away from him and towards Paul. Barnabas readily
accepted the risk.

When a local pastor receives a 'Paul', thus taking in the
missionary and the mission vision in its totality, he takes a
risk, whether he knows that or not. It will disturb the comfortable focus on the local programme, and it may even distract
attention away from the pastor himself. In most local
churches, for example, the pastor is on the receiving end of
considerable respect from his congregation. He puts that at risk
when he invites in those with global vision. His own short-
comings may be revealed. But such decisions determine
whether he is a team man, a man who sees himself as part of
a greater whole, or whether his game plan is directed at
building something round himself alone.

Thirdly, the local pastor knows that whatever the benefits
are that he may gain from bringing in the Pauline vision, they
are at best only temporary. Acts 11:26 tells us that Paul and
Barnabas 'for a whole year ... assembled with the church.' We
might consider that a whole year sounds positive, but to many
local pastors it is not good news. After one year Paul is going to
leave, and in his leaving he will cause distraction. There will be
those who have caught his vision, and they may want to leave
with him, or their focus will be on him and his calling after he
has left. How distracting and difficult that is for the local
pastor. He sees week by week some in the congregation who
have seen a greater vision than his local concerns and who will
be constantly looking over his shoulder at a huge world that
he has not necessarily seen at all. Where is the gain in that
for him?

Fourthly, even while the missionary is still there in their
midst, the modern Barnabas knows that he is not really fully
there. He is often distracted. Like some computer that keeps
failing to respond to the keyboard because it is running

another programme in the background, he will be focused on a programme other than the local church one. In Acts 9 Barnabas had met Paul in Jerusalem. He spent time with Paul, he heard Paul sharing his testimony of how God had called him to the nations. Paul kept sharing it in the New Testament whenever he got a chance (Acts 22 and 26). How much more he would have done that with his friend Barnabas.

The cost must have been obvious to Barnabas when he went to get Paul from Tarsus. Even if Paul would come to work with him for at least a year, and thus bring benefit to his local church, Barnabas knew that Paul would not be fully focused on the local work. He would be waiting for the word of the Lord, waiting for that Acts 13 command to the church that would spring him loose into his call to the nations. Indeed, the nature of Barnabas' calling may well have suggested that it would be Barnabas who would finish serving Paul's call, rather than the other way round. And that is exactly what did happen!

Why then did Barnabas seek him out? Why should he have taken him in? The answer lies in Acts 11:24:

'For he was a good man, full of the Holy Spirit and of faith.'

It takes good men, full of the Holy Spirit and of faith, to take in Paul. Not just full of the Holy Spirit, but also full of faith. It takes the eye of faith to see that this in some ways unattractive apostle is full of enormous potential for the Church and for the kingdom of God. However, it takes more than faith alone; it takes 'a good man'. It may seem strange to say this, but it is very difficult to define what the words 'good man' mean here. Surely all Christians are supposed to be good! But it means more than that. It means 'good' in the sense that God was good when He sent His Son to die on the cross for us sinners. It means 'good' in the sense of God giving us the most precious possession that He had, His only Son, to come to earth. It means 'good' in the sense of my giving myself to His 'kingdom' (that which brings benefit to Jesus) rather than to my 'empire' (that which adds to my church portfolio alone, not to God's wider kingdom). Barnabas was that kind of a 'good man', and so he took in Paul.

What lies at the heart of this 'good man' battle? What is at stake? Logically, there are three areas of contention, three issues that can hold us back from taking in Paul, and embracing the Antioch vision. The issues are people, prayer and finance. These are the three contested and dangerous areas. How easy it is to think: 'If I take in Paul, he will siphon off my people, my money and my prayer.' In the prayer meetings, people will be distracted to pray for the ends of the earth and the lost that live there. They will start taking money that might have finished in the offering basket for local projects, and they will give it to the missionaries and to the mission work. People, young people and older ones alike, will start spending their summers on mission teams overseas. It is even possible that some young man or woman, the pride of the church's training programme, will suddenly announce that instead of giving their life to the Lord's work locally, they feel that they are now called to a life-time of service overseas!

When the issues are defined in black and white like this, most of us would throw up our hands in horror and say that we would never give way to such attitudes. But it does happen, again and again and again. Many churches never have a missionary weekend, never allow their missionaries to have decent pulpit time to share their vision and experiences with the people. These are real issues that I see as I travel around. Mission secretaries in the church know full well that whatever they say to the people will not be supported wholeheartedly by the pastor, and thus nobody really pays attention. There are missionary committees in churches that are staffed by diligent and praying people, but they are largely redundant because they have no direct access to the leadership of the church. Their decisions are largely irrelevant in the power circle of the local church. Pastors allow distinguished, successful missionaries to pass through their churches, never giving them opportunity to share with and challenge the congregation, because they are worried about what would happen to their money, their prayer and their people. It is understandable; it is also very wrong.

I have been there, and have sat on both sides of the fence. I have pastored a local church in the UK, and I have therefore experienced personally that concern about allowing 'para-church organisations' to come and take 'my' resources. I have also had churches treat me in that way, as I have travelled as a mission leader.

Sometimes, even when the pastor is willing to embrace the challenge of what world mission will mean to his church, the people are not. One pastor in Australia invited me to speak, and then apologised when only a few members of his congregation came to the meeting. He said that had happened before when a missionary came to share. He pointed out, however, that a few weeks before a prophet had come through and spoken to his people. He had not even advertised the prophet's Saturday night meeting, and yet the church was packed out, as folk queued for words that would bless them from the passing prophet. For the mission meeting, he admitted, not only did folk not come themselves, but they kept their children away, in case they should be called to mission! I have had the leader of a significant conference, when it was suggested that I should speak, say: 'But he's China, isn't he?' In other words, what relevance has a quarter of the world's population to his important conference? What relevance has mission to 'cutting-edge British Christianity'?

There are many exceptions, many great churches who are releasing their prayer, their people, and their finances for the work of the kingdom outside their local domain. But my point is a simple one. To do that, to take that risk, we have to be Barnabas people, those who are not only full of the Holy Spirit, but also full of faith. And not only full of faith, but dealt with by God so that we are 'good men' in the sense that Barnabas was.

Of course there will be a reward. Antioch became a remarkable church because it took Paul in. It was Paul, in part at least, that made it so. But that was not obvious when he came. Only later did the benefits roll in. When the missionary, lonely and unattached, knocks at my door, when the visionary offers his admittedly temporary services, the package is not attractive. It threatens to cause loss, not gain. The package threatens to a siphon off our resources. It offers no real long-term value-added services.

History now reveals to us that in the single act of taking in Paul, Antioch propelled itself from a church of local status to one of international reputation. Paul's coming assured them of a significant place in church history. The other Antioch factors that we are considering elsewhere were in themselves significant. But this one, the embracing of Paul into their midst, overshadows everything else like some colossus.

Firstly, he brought them the legitimate notoriety of having resident in their midst the most significant convert of the time. The strict Jew, who after being a bitter enemy of Christianity, became an important figure in its history, captured the attention and inspired the faith of the church (Acts 9:31). Any pastor or leader who does not admit that he would be thrilled to have such a man in his midst is probably being dishonest. How good it feels, as we chat at some conference about a significantly changed life, to be able to say: 'Yes, he attends my church; indeed we are close friends.'

Secondly, in theological terms, Paul's standing was significant, and he brought that standing to Antioch. He played a decisive part in extending Christianity's influence beyond the limits of Judaism, so that it might become a world-wide religion. As one writer has summarised it: 'Paul's lasting monument is the world-wide Christian Church. Though he was not the first to preach to the Gentiles, his resolute stand against the Judaizing party was decisive for future progress. It can be justly claimed that it was due to Paul more than anyone else that Christianity grew from being a small sect within Judaism to become a world religion.'

Thirdly, in terms of his impact on the canon of Scripture, and as a touchstone of early Church orthodoxy, Paul's standing is also immense. Antioch could bask in that standing. His surviving letters are the earliest extant Christian writings. They reveal both theological skill and pastoral understanding and have had lasting importance for Christian life and thought. His surviving letters were collected for general circulation. They quickly became a standard of reference for Christian teaching. For example, in the western (Latin) half of Christendom Paul had a lasting and profound effect upon the history of the Church through the writings of St Augustine. The Pelagian controversy concerning grace and free will turned on the interpretation of passages in Paul's letter to the Romans. The reformers of the 16th century were also deeply indebted to Paul. Martin Luther seized on the doctrine of justification by faith and made the distinction between faith and works the basis of his attack on the late medieval Church. John Calvin drew from Paul his concept of the Church as the company of the elect. Thus Paul's teaching came through the influence of Augustine to dominate the Reformation and its legacy in the Lutheran and Calvinist churches of modern Protestantism.

Paul thus propelled Antioch to significance as the major teaching church of the New Testament, a reputation that lived on through the centuries to come.

Fourthly, and by the far the most importantly, Paul's missionary vision extended Antioch's influence, as his sending church, way beyond its own local borders. It made Antioch's influence international, even global – an influence that extended way beyond its own time. Converted as he was only a few years after the death of Jesus, he became the leading apostle (missionary) of the new movement. In the 21st century, about one-third of the world's people claim the Christian faith, at least nominally. Christians thus constitute the world's largest religious community and embrace remarkable diversity, with churches in every nation. Christianity's demographic and dynamic centre has shifted from its Western base to Latin America, Africa, Asia, and the Pacific region, where more than half the world's Christians live. The tangibly real universal Church represents a new phenomenon in the history of religions. This is the fruit of mission. It is also a direct result of the life and vision that Paul brought through his theology, his writings, but most of all, through his missionary journeys. After all, on his numerous missionary journeys, the Apostle Paul showed a greater accomplishment in distances travelled than any known general of the Roman army, official of the Roman Empire, or trader of his time!

The missions and expansion of Christianity are among the most unusual of historical occurrences. Other world religions, such as Buddhism and Islam, also have raised a claim to universal validity, but no world religion other than Christianity has succeeded in realising this claim through missionary expansion over the entire world. Paul and Antioch were the launch pad for that movement.

Take, for example, Cyprus. It was the very first place that Paul visited on his first missionary journey. Historians say that undoubtedly the most important event for Cyprus in the Roman period was the introduction of Christianity. The Apostle Paul, accompanied by Barnabas, a native of the Cypriot Jewish community, preached there in about AD 45 and converted the proconsul, Sergius Paulus. By the time of Constantine the Great, Christians were numerous in the island and may have constituted a majority. Such was the impact of Paul's missionary journey on the very first place that he visited. But it was not just true of Cyprus. In AD 313 when the new Roman emperor Constantine declared the persecutions ended, Christians probably constituted 10 percent of the empire's population.

And the impact has continued through the centuries. The first seal of Massachusetts displayed an Indian with a beckoning hand and the inscription 'Come over and help us' – the words of the Macedonian who appeared to the Apostle Paul in a night vision (Acts 16:9).

One writer has assessed it in this way: 'Born on Jewish soil but quickly emerging from Palestine to cover the rim of the Mediterranean world, the new missionary faith made its first major transition. The Apostle Paul became the missionary to the Gentile world. With help from Barnabas and a local network of co-workers ... he evangelised Asia Minor and southern Greece and eventually reached Rome. When Rome destroyed Jerusalem in AD 70, Antioch became Christianity's centre in the Eastern Empire, and mission became one of Gentiles to Gentiles. Thus began the transition.'

To understand the totality of Paul's impact through his teaching and work as a missionary, consider this assessment of the book of Acts: 'The outline of Acts can be roughly divided into two parts: the mission under Peter centred in Jerusalem (Chapters 1–12); and the missions to the Gentiles all the way to Rome, under the leadership of Paul (Chapters 13–28).' In a sense it could be said that Paul, single-handedly under God, switched the whole focus and geographical content of the book of Acts. It revolves around him and his mission after Acts 13. And for that reason, Antioch, by embracing him in Acts 11, was propelled to leading status.

Consider again the end of the book of Acts. The book finishes with Paul imprisoned and sent to Rome, and we leave him witnessing openly and unhindered in the capital of the Empire. The book of Acts concludes with Paul's story, as an unfinished narrative, as if to say – watch this space, because where he is, there the action is also.

Of course no modern 'Paul' who comes into the life of our church is going to have an impact quite like that! But whenever the Pauline 'virus' has got into the inner heart of a man or a woman, something is going to happen! Why then is there a problem? The answer is that our taking in this third element of an Antioch church is a step of faith. At the time, it is a risk. Only later do the benefits flow.

Singapore, where I live, is called by some 'the Antioch of Asia'. I believe that is a dangerous and premature definition. We have not stopped to consider from these scriptures in Acts what that really means. It seems to offer gain and position. But in reality it will offer loss. It will cost prayer, people and finance in the task of world mission. It will upset local programmes. Perhaps we need to be more careful about the use of that title.

John Wimber summed it up in what he called a 'church-burial'. A large church in Central America had set itself to church plant, to pour itself out in running with the Pauline vision. The result was that they had planted fifty churches, but also that the pastor had died of overwork and the mother-church, the original sending church, had stripped itself of all its resources and was no longer viable. So the 'church-burial' consisted of the fifty or so new churches coming to bury, or to close down, the original church. How the glory of God was there! That is New Testament Christianity – that is the Antioch factor – in its purest form. I do not advise overwork to the point of heart attacks, nor being generous to the point of irresponsibility. But if we want to be Antiochs, we have to risk that happening. If we think that being Antioch means we are going to be famous without paying a real price, we have missed the point of the whole matter. It means doing what Barnabas did, and taking real risks for world missions.

When the unattractive package arrives at our door for the first time, nothing is obvious. We have to make a choice in the cold light of day, not in the bright light of Christian reputation and fame that might follow on later. But in that moment, in that choice, we will be able to know whether we are Antioch people or Jerusalem people. At the time the enormous implications of the choice, the results of taking the risk, are hidden from us. But that is the way of God.

And the 'bottom line' is clear. Without Paul, without this third element, we will not build Antioch churches.

Chapter 10

The Fourth Antioch Secret:
Keeping Nimble

This chapter will look at my fourth – and final – secret that helped Antioch to become a special church. I have called it 'keeping nimble'. By that I mean staying in the place of being able to hear God, to respond to His Word, and to change direction accordingly.

There are other qualities that I have not listed in these four chapters, important though they are. For example, the supremacy of the Lord Jesus, expressed through prayer, praise and the ministry of the Word. There are also the foundational elements of sacrifice and surrender to Him. These other elements are not unique to Antioch. They were also to be found in Jerusalem. I have chosen four secrets in this and the previous three chapters, which do seem to be defining elements of the Antioch church. I believe that these truths have a major significance to us today. They are secrets that are not too commonly found in our day, and are thus worth highlighting. They are only found on 'a path less travelled'.

In previous chapters we have observed throughout the early history of the Antioch church an unusual phenomenon. It is the capacity to hear God, to receive what He has said, and to change direction according to the word that He has spoken. I use the word 'unusual' not because this capacity to hear and obey should be uncommon in the Church of Jesus Christ today, but because experience shows it is not easy for us to emulate. Hard though it may be, its effect was so significant in the life of the Antioch church that we need to allow ourselves to be challenged by it. Antioch was Antioch because it was willing to find the time and the courage to hear the voice of God, and, in the hearing, it found fresh destiny and vision from God.

Lou Gerstner is credited with rescuing IBM in the post 1994 period from its era of huge decline. Around the time that he took over, this once great company was rated as having a negative value, an amazing fact when contrasted with a few years previously, at which time the company had 70% of the world-wide computer industry profits! Gerstner summarised the philosophy that enabled him to effect this rescue in the following words:

> 'My view is you perpetuate success by continuing to run scared, not by looking back at what made you great, but by looking forward at what is going to make you un-great, so that you are constantly focusing on the challenges that keep you humble, hungry and nimble.'[29]

Part of Antioch's success lay in its ability to remain 'humble, hungry and nimble' during these significant chapters of Acts. It remained entirely dependent on the Lord and continued to listen to Him. I do not know many churches or organisations that manage to stay hungry after they know a measure of success – hungry not to miss God when He moves again (perhaps in a way different from before), hungry to continue to make a real difference in their world. Too many churches are content to sit back and relax in their success zone after five or ten years. Antioch managed to stay nimble.

This is no more than the pattern of Jesus Himself, who manifestly stated that He only did what He saw and heard His Father doing. It was indeed a repeated statement of Jesus, emphasising that He did not minister in His own wisdom, but only as He received afresh the direction and leading of His Father.

> *'Then Jesus answered and said to them, "Most assuredly, I say to you, the Son can do nothing of Himself, but what He sees the Father do; for whatever He does, the Son also does in like manner."'*   (John 5:19)

'And He who sent Me is with Me. The Father has not left Me alone, for I always do those things that please Him.'
                                                            (John 8:29)

'Do you not believe that I am in the Father, and the Father in Me? The words that I speak to you I do not speak on My own authority; but the Father who dwells in Me does the works.'
                                                            (John 14:10)

Antioch to an unusual degree managed to walk in the Master's steps in this matter. It had, as one foundational key to being a world-changing church, the capacity to wait on God until He revealed His will for them. Antioch knew that its own plans almost certainly fell short of what God wanted for them. This 'hearing', though costly, was a vital key to Antioch's success in God. We urgently need to walk the same way ourselves. The willingness to listen to God and to obey Him may mean the difference between success and failure in fulfilling the destiny of God for our churches and ministries.

I believe that any significant work of God is born in such a way, with God speaking a defining word either to individuals or to communities. In 1984, whilst I was praying, God spoke a simple word to me: 'Take Derek Prince into China.' I had already been involved for a number of years in work amongst the Chinese. I also had a burden to serve the Chinese by helping to provide foundational teaching materials. I knew that God did not mean that I should take Derek in personally, but rather the ministry of the Word of God that had flowed from him for many years. As I write these words, God is helping us and as a result of that word to me from Him, we have by now printed and distributed some three million of Derek's books in Chinese to the Church in China. We have also done sixteen years of Mandarin and other Chinese dialect radio broadcasts into China. Through these and other ways, millions of lives have been impacted for the Gospel, and built up in the Lord Jesus Christ. It all flowed out of a word from God at a time when I had never even met Derek personally, nor was I in any way connected with him in ministry. But obedience to that word has blossomed into blessing for the

Chinese Church in a way that I could never have imagined, not the least through the team that God has raised up beside me for this work.

Isaiah 55:8–9 summarises Antioch's basic approach in this matter:

> ' "For My thoughts are not your thoughts, nor are your ways My ways," says the Lord. "For as the heavens are higher than the earth, so are My ways higher than your ways, and My thoughts than your thoughts." '

The disciples in Antioch knew that they had to wait on the Lord and hear Him to fulfil His destiny and purposes in them and through them.

We already referred to some instances of this, and a brief summary will suffice here. In Acts 11:19–20 some men and women left church tradition and obeyed the command of Jesus to preach to Gentiles. It is easy for us to miss the extraordinary courage that it must have taken to do that, because in effect it meant going against the general trend in Jerusalem and embracing the pattern that Peter had brought back from Cornelius' household (Acts 10:1–48). Essentially it involved the courage to be different, the courage to line up with the Word of God and not with the Christian thinking of the time. The Jerusalem church, or a part of it, had not accepted Peter's testimony of the word and will of God for the Gentiles (Acts 11:1–18; Galatians 1–2). These unknown believers needed to dig deep into Peter's words and the words of Jesus in Acts 1:8. This meant holding to the Word of God against the contrary practice that had already manifested itself in the Jerusalem church.

But it was this willingness to be different and to follow the revealed Word of God and the witness of the Holy Spirit that gave birth to the Antioch church. It was at this point, as we have seen, that God stretched out His Hand to save in power (Acts 11:19–21).

Without that willingness to be different through obedience, the Gentiles would not have heard the Gospel in Antioch, and would not have been saved. It is indeed a challenging place from which to begin – that the church was born not just by a leader hearing God and recruiting others to his vision, but by ordinary men and women who were willing to be different because God had spoken.

What a challenge! We live in an age when embracing any 'counter-culture' (whatever its moral and ethical values) is considered by many, especially the young, to be a positive virtue. Here Scripture tells us through these people that the real challenge is not just to be different for its own sake, but to be different because we decide to align ourselves with the Word of God. God's Word is the real counter-culture, the only one. That takes enormous courage. Few are willing to do it. But nations are changed by it. It brings insecurity, and sometimes great cost. But it also brings life and ushers in the power of God.

At the heart of it is the willingness to seek the Father's favour, not man's. Embracing the clear Word of God for the nations will cost us favour with men, because many leaders do not really believe in the Great Commission. If they did, they would build different churches.

Jesus summed it up powerfully:

> *'How can you believe, who receive honor from one another, and do not seek the honor that comes from the only God?'*
>
> (John 5:44)

The answer is that we cannot. We either seek favour from men, even fellow Christians, or from God.

My own nation, Scotland, saw revival through such men of the Word. The history of their extraordinary courage moves and challenges me as a Christian, as well as a Scot. They were willing to die for the Word of God, rather than live without it:

> 'Hamilton, Wishart, and Knox form a chain of names that transformed Scotland. The first man Patrick Hamilton was born about 1504 to a wealthy family near Glasgow. His mother told him stories of the Bible, and her lessons lived in his heart till the close of his life. His father, wanting a church career for Patrick, used his influence and money to secure his appointment to a church position when he was

but thirteen. That was in 1517, the year that Luther made his protest.

But Hamilton wanted nothing of church work, and he fled to the Sorbonne, the University of Paris, where he heard the sensational news of Luther's protestation. For an entire year, the Sorbonne studied little but Luther's writings. Hamilton graduated in 1520, returned to Scotland, and continued his studies in the University of St Andrews where, in time, he joined the faculty. The Scottish Parliament, meanwhile, condemned Lutheranism and announced that anyone possessing Reformation books or views was in jeopardy.

As it happened, Hamilton had adopted Reformation views. Archbishop David Beaton, rabid foe of Protestants, instantly sought his life. Hamilton fled the country. He travelled to Germany and spent time with Luther and the other Reformation leaders. His faith and courage deepened dramatically, and Hamilton determined to return to Scotland, heedless of danger, and preach salvation by grace through faith alone.

Great crowds flocked to hear him, and many were converted to Christ. Beaton promptly trapped and arrested him, tried him, and sentenced him to death. At high noon on February 29th, 1528, Hamilton walked to the stake with a quick, firm step. He handed a friend his copy of the Gospels and gave his cap, gown, and upper garments to his servant. The executioner chained him to the post and attempted to set the wood afire. The flame didn't burn well, and Hamilton suffered for six long, torturous hours. Finally when it appeared the fire was at last doing its work, he cried, "How long, O God, shall darkness cover this kingdom?"

His words did not fall to the ground.

Patrick Hamilton's dying words haunted George Wishart, only son of distinguished James Wishart of Pitarrow, Scotland ... In 1544 he began preaching in Dundee from the book of Romans. Among his listeners was a young man named John Knox ... (Knox's efforts) inspired Scots for years to come, and the Reformation triumphed in their land at last. [30]

Death was the reward for two of those three men, imprisonment and long years of toil for another. But a nation was changed, because they rejected disobedient religion for the living Word of God. These three men were Antioch people.

The second example of Antioch's capacity to be different because God willed it is, as we have seen, found later in the same chapter. In Acts 11:23 Barnabas breaks with tradition and allows Gentiles to follow Christ without first submitting to Jewish religious practices. The third example follows on immediately, in Acts 11:25–26. Barnabas by this time had become the Jerusalem-appointed leader of the fast growing Antioch church. If we view his status in our modern-day terms, he was in an extremely good position 'ecclesiastically'. He was now pastor or apostle over the fastest growing church in the world, one that was to become recognised for its leadership in teaching of the Word of God, for its prominence in its region and for its financial strength. The logical response by Barnabas towards this would have been to settle into comfortable and respected leadership, to attend with dignity the conferences for pastors of churches of over 1,000 people and so on. In short, to enjoy the trimmings and the trappings of his position. A travelling ministry, giving seminars on how to grow big churches, was a certainty for him, if we were to apply our modern practices.

But that is exactly what Barnabas did not do. Leaving Antioch temporarily, he went to seek for Paul and took him back to Antioch, as we have already observed. There he allowed Paul to work beside him for a whole year (Acts 11:25–26). This act by Barnabas was no more 'natural' for him than it would be for any of us today. It was the act of a man moving in accordance with the leading of God against his own self-interest. It was 'the Son of Encouragement' living up to his name. This unusual willingness to hear God according to his gifting was costly for Barnabas. But God directed Him to do it and he obeyed.

There now follows the most outstanding example of Antioch's ability to 'stay nimble' when God spoke. Some argue that the local church there numbered 25,000 people by this time. It was not only strong numerically; it was strong in almost every other way. Paul and Barnabas ministered there together for at least a year (Acts 11:26). It would be almost certain that others would have joined them in this exciting church as its influence and stature increased. And yet in Acts 13 some of the leaders (who are described as 'prophets and teachers'), including Barnabas and Paul, gathered together to seek the face of God. Scripture says that they ministered to God and fasted.

> *'Now in the church that was at Antioch there were certain prophets and teachers: Barnabas, Simeon who was called Niger, Lucius of Cyrene, Manaen who had been brought up with Herod the tetrarch, and Saul. As they ministered to the Lord and fasted...'*   (Acts 13:1–2a)

Why did they do this? What was the crisis that caused them to set time aside to hear God? We have absolutely no evidence of division or of any kind of split in the church. The church was not poor, because in Acts 14 it sent money as a gift to the church at Jerusalem. Nor was it in need of growth, because it was already growing fast. Nor did it seem to lack in the way of ministry, because Paul and Barnabas and others were ministering there.

Why then were they praying, fasting, worshipping and seeking the Face of God? My answer is that they felt God was doing something so significant in Antioch that they feared lest they should miss His wider purposes in it. They realised that the phenomenal growth and blessing that they had experienced up to that point must be for greater purposes than they had yet understood. And so they sought God's face to know His will.

During the Welsh revival at the beginning of the 20th Century, as the Spirit of God moved down the Welsh valleys in reviving power, saving many and filling churches, the Christians in one village noted that God was moving in the villages and towns around them. They called for a time of fasting and prayer in their village. The subject of their prayer was simple, 'God, as You move in power, please do not miss out our village. Visit us, don't skip us.' They had observed that there were some villages that seemed not to be touched by God's Spirit, and they themselves did not wish to be included on that 'missing list'. Assuredly, in answer to their earnest prayer, the Spirit of God visited them with grace and power and salvation, because that had been the cry of their hearts. God does not pass by such prayer meetings.

That was also Antioch's experience. They understood, with the father heart of Barnabas and the apostolic missionary heart of Paul, that there had to be more to this than just the blessing and the increase which they had so far received. And they wanted that 'more'.

And so God spoke, powerfully, clearly.

> '*As they ministered to the Lord and fasted, the Holy Spirit said, "Now separate to Me Barnabas and Saul for the work to which I have called them."*'   (Acts 13:2)

God answered them in essence by saying that what they had been doing to this point was good, but that they had not yet plugged into His fullest destiny for the Antioch church. More than anything their church was intended to be the sending church for the Great Commission outreach under Paul which would reach the Gentile cities and countries around them. The word of God, breaking into the midst of their worship and fasting, was this: 'Give me the best two people that you have in your church, to go to the nations that do not know My Son Jesus.' This was the work to which God had called them. This was the destiny of Antioch at that time.

Of course they knew that in principle. As we have seen elsewhere, Paul knew that at the time of his salvation and at his calling in Acts 9. With the friendship that existed between Barnabas and Paul, it would be clear that Barnabas knew it too. But there needed to be a release from God, a definition of His time of appointing for this to happen. There also needed to be that same word spoken into the church at Antioch, in order to confirm publicly the private word to Paul himself. That is what happened in Acts 13:1–3.

There are today many, many churches that have seen blessing. It may not be on the same scale as the explosion of grace at Antioch, but it is yet real blessing in terms of God's gift of salvation to a number of people and His provision of ministries to pastor, teach and lead them. But how many at this point begin to embrace Christian fame and approbation, and thereby miss their personal and collective Acts 13? They do not hear the Word of God. I believe that this matter of finding God's missionary destiny in an Antioch way for our churches is perhaps the single most crucial issue in our generation. It is not that there are not good churches. It is simply that there are so few churches who are hearing what God really wants to say to them in the way these leaders did in Acts 13.

What was Antioch's response? Incredibly, in verse 3, they responded positively to this challenge to give away their best two people:

> *'Then, having fasted and prayed, and laid hands on them, they sent them away.'* (Acts 13:3)

They fasted, they prayed, they laid hands on them, they sent them away. The full meaning of that is understood in Acts 14:26–28. When they returned, the church gladly gathered together to hear what had happened. That was because they had sent them out, had embraced them, and so later they took them back as their own.

How many churches pray for and serve into this work of Christian outreach to the ends of the earth? Antioch did – even though they personally gained absolutely nothing from it. In fact they lost much through it, because it took Paul and Barnabas away from them. They set us a model as a leadership and a people that were willing to surrender the best that they had for the sake of the lost in their generation. How did it come to pass? Because they waited on God, God spoke clearly, and they did what He told them to do.

But there is another core factor, perhaps the most important, in these events. In the examples listed above from Acts 11, we have observed that Antioch was at that time a young church. Everything was new to them. They had nothing, and therefore they had nothing to lose. But in Acts 13, they were already a large and famous church. They were successful. They had good ministry – preaching and leadership and teaching. They had a great deal to lose by this time.

It is so hard to change at this later time, in our Acts 13 period. It is one thing to change when we have nothing; it is quite another thing to change when we are already successful. But the measure of their stature is that they did manage to change during that period of major success. Viewed in that light, history may have a different verdict on some churches that seem to be successful – if, in their success, they simply settle down. Some seem exhausted by the first wave of hearing God and of living on the edge as 'pioneers'. They therefore choose to sit back as 'settlers'. Their future is not assured.

But that is where IBM's Lou Gerstner comes in:

> '...you perpetuate success ... not by looking back at what made you great, but by looking forward ... so that you are constantly focusing on the challenges that keep you humble, hungry and nimble.'

The Antioch church remained 'humble, hungry and nimble'. And so when in its success it heard God speak in Acts 13, it responded. It is a hard and challenging lesson to us all, especially the successful amongst us.

Out of the laity's obedience in Acts 11 was born the church at Antioch. Out of Barnabas' obedience in the same chapter was born the ministry of Paul. Out of the church's obedience in Acts 13 was born the missionary movement that drew tens of thousands into the kingdom of God, and planted churches throughout the then-known world. Out of that obedience the world was changed. Without it, none of that might have happened.

The truth is that Acts 11, the first phase, birthed an amazing and God-glorifying church. But it was the second phase, the Acts 13 phase, that birthed a world-changing church. The Acts 11 church is not the same as the Acts 13 church. Destinies can be missed if we will not change, or we will only change in our Acts 11 days.

> 'Lord, make us Antioch people and churches, ready to change in obedience to You. Make us, Father, humble, hungry and nimble in our generation – and do not let us settle back.'

Chapter 11

Where Do We Go from Here?

'Lord, send me anywhere, only go with me.
Lay any burden on me, only sustain me.
Sever any tie, except the tie that binds me to Thyself.'
(David Livingstone)

We must now address the most important question of all: is cross-cultural evangelism to the nations still required today? After all, Doctor Ryland denied its urgency in his generation. We have seen that the Antioch Factor is clearly evident in the pages of the book of Acts, but what difference does that make to Christians in the twenty-first century? Are our considerations in this book anything more than interesting historical insights? In a word, where – if anywhere – do we go from here?

Of course this issue has been covered in one way or another in various places throughout this book already. Yet our discussions would not be complete unless we now faced this central matter directly and clearly. The best way of doing that is to ask ourselves three very basic questions.

Question 1: Do we think that those who have never heard about Jesus should have the right to hear that He is the only way to heaven?

This issue is best considered in microcosm, by focusing on one small example. One of the missionary organisations with which I serve is working with a people group that numbers several hundred thousand people. As far as we know, there are no churches or pastors amongst them at all. Indeed, we do not know of one single born-again believer. That means that there are slightly under half a million people amongst whom there is not one Christian.

Focus your mind on them. Ask yourself this question: 'If I were one of them, surely I would hope that somehow I might hear, in a way that I could understand, that Jesus died for my sins. Would I not want to know how to find a place with the true God, my heavenly Father, for eternity?' If you know Jesus, there is only one answer to that question. Of course you would, just as surely as a drowning man would hope that someone would rescue him.

Question 2: What will it take for folk like this to hear the Gospel?

In the microcosm that we are looking at, the answer to this second question is simple. It will take someone who is willing to go and tell them. That would demand cross-cultural evangelism, because the language, customs and religious background of the one who goes will be totally different from those of the people he desires to reach with the Gospel. These people will not come to us, because they cannot – they are too poor. Nor do they have any idea that such a thing might even be necessary. Later, as God works amongst them, some from their midst will be saved, trained up and then will take over the work. But for now, the first step involves someone going to where they are to tell them. If no one is willing to go, they almost certainly will not hear.

The argument then is rather daunting. If I say 'yes' to Question 1 (should they have the right to hear?) then I have to, by sheer force of logic, say 'yes' to the issue of whether someone should go. It is a dangerous argument because that someone might be me!

My friend's testimony in Chapter 2 relates to this unreached people group which we are discussing:

'During my last trip to visit the X people, I had the powerful sense that our presence meant that God was in their midst. They needed to touch God through human arms, human smiles, human interaction. We gave them that in practical ways as we worked amongst them, as strangers who battled to make their lives better. In a sense, as they saw us helping them in that battle, they could say: "This is what God is like..."'

We are to be ambassadors for Christ, representing His kingdom to such people. Modern communications may help, but technology cannot take away the reality that a flesh and blood model is required to have a presence amongst them. Someone has actually to **go**.

Question 3: When someone does go, what is the aim of their work? What are they trying to do?

In my view, the aim of their work would be twofold: to share the Gospel with them in their own language; and to establish churches using their own language and culture.

Assuming you are a Christian, in what language did you first hear the Gospel? Most readers of this book will be Christians whose first language is English – otherwise you would not be reading it, or you would have read it in another language! The truth is that most of us heard the good news in our own first language, in our mother tongue. How much would you have profited from a presentation in French, or Tamil, or Mandarin Chinese? Even if you had understood it, you would probably have rejected it as foreign.

These people also have the right to hear in their own language. Not only must Christians go, but they must also learn their language.

When you went to church last Sunday, what language did you use in the time of worship, and what language did the preacher use to share from the Word? Again, the argument is obvious. We use our own language to worship God and to learn from His Word. And they must too.

The task of world evangelism will not be completed until every man, woman and child has had the chance to respond to the Gospel in their language of choice – their heart language. Nor is the job done until, once they have responded, they can worship God in that language.

I gladly acknowledge that this is the age of the indigenous church. The target of missionary work is to hand over the work of evangelism and church leadership to local Christians who use that mother tongue. But the reality is that huge sections of the world's population have no indigenous church or leadership. Until they do, missionaries must go. There are still millions of people alive today who have never heard the Name of Jesus. And there are many millions more who, even if they have heard of His Name, have never yet received a complete presentation of the Gospel. Given the massive explosion of the world's population, the reality is that the need now is far more urgent than ever it was when the book of Acts was written.

The Global Picture

The problem is that there are so many examples like this people group elsewhere in the world. Looking at one micro-cosm should not cause us to miss the wider picture. Mission is not needed because there are just a few people groups like this one that are still left unreached. It is needed because there are multitudes of them all over the world. However, the reality for many of us is that we cannot hear their voices or see their needs for ourselves. It is hard for us to maintain a sense of urgency in this matter. Yet the statistics have a voice of their own – a strong and clear voice – if we will but hear it:

Population

- There are reckoned to be some 6,250 million people living in the world today.
- 11% claim to be evangelical Christians. That means that around 89% still need to be reached with the Gospel.
- 15% of the 6,250 million are totally unevangelised. They have yet to hear the Gospel even for the first time.

Language

- Over 6,800 different languages are spoken in the world.
- Less than one third of these 6,800 languages have any portion of Scripture translated.
- The complete Bible is available in less than 300 of them.

- Over 4,000 languages are without any translated portion of Scripture.

- 1,000 of those 4,000 languages absolutely must have Bible translation but are still waiting.

- 2,500 on top of those 1,000 languages also probably need translation.

Missionary to unevangelised peoples ratio

- World-wide there is an average of twenty-four missionaries for every million non-Christians. That means one missionary is responsible for sharing the Gospel with 40,000 people who do not call themselves Christians.

- However the picture is not uniform. Many missionaries are concentrated in areas where there are already many Christians. This means that the most needy areas often have the fewest Christian workers living in them.

- Thus in parts of Asia there are just nine missionaries for every one million non-Christians; in the Middle East that figure is only seven.

Who are the unreached?

- The majority of the world's unevangelised people, around 85 percent, live within what is known as the 10/40 Window. This is the area of the world between 10 degrees north and 40 degrees north of the equator, and extending from Western Africa across the Middle East and Asia.

- An estimated 1.1 billion Muslims, 1 billion Hindus and 600 million Buddhists live within the 10/40 Window.

- Only 8% of the world's missionary force is currently working with the unreached within the 10/40 Window.

Bob Sjogren, addressing this issue, writes:

'Who are the unreached people groups of our planet? The 1,500 nomadic Chang-pa of Northern India, the twenty million Sundanese of Indonesia, the Engenni of Nigeria, the Wenki of China, the Gilyak of Russia, the Fulnio of Brazil – and about 11,994 more! ... For example, the country of India has about 3,000 distinct people groups within its borders, Irian Jaya has about 250, the Commonwealth of Independent States (formerly the Soviet Union) has more than 500 and Pakistan has 13...' [31]

Is world mission still needed? How can we even raise that question in the light of the overwhelming evidence in the world around us. Only by remaining steadfastly locked into our 'Jerusalems' could we ever begin to think that the needs around us are not urgent, nor the imbalances in the work of Christian ministry bordering on the criminal. As Frank Laubach has commented:

'Lord, forgive us for looking at the world with dry eyes!' [32]

Need alone – even though it is so obvious – should never in itself be our prime motivation. God's Word must be the reason for our involvement. It is therefore necessary to make two further observations about world mission. Firstly, we must engage in world mission because God told us to do it, from the beginning of the Bible to the end. Secondly, if we obey Him, we can expect to experience His blessing. The one who loves the Father does what He says; and the one who does what He says will experience more of the good Hand of His Father upon him.

Observation 1: World mission is commanded by God in Scripture, not just in the book of Acts, but from the beginning of the Bible to the end

Some believe that the Great Commission is just confined to a few verses in the New Testament. It is not. Bob Sjogren has presented very challenging material on this theme. [33] Writing about Genesis 12 (which as we know comes right at the beginning of the Bible) Sjogren says:

'Most believers think Jesus first gave the Great Commission. Actually, Jesus reviewed the Great Commission. The Great Commission was given to Abraham several thousand years earlier in Genesis 12. Abraham was commissioned to

reach all the nations on the face of the earth ... The Great
Commission is the foundation for the story of the Bible.'

In other words, Jesus did not invent the message of going to
the ends of the earth in Acts 1:8 or in the Gospels. The message
is there right from the beginning of the Bible. The Great
Commission in Matthew 28 was not an afterthought by Jesus.
It is a restatement of one of the most original principles of the
Bible, which is first presented at the very beginning:

> 'Now the Lord had said to Abram:
> "Get out of your country,
> From your kindred
> And from your father's house,
> To a land that I will show you.
> I will make you a great nation;
> I will bless you
> And make your name great;
> **And you shall be a blessing.**
> I will bless those who bless you,
> And I will curse him who curses you;
> And **in you** all the families of the earth shall be blessed."'
>
> (Genesis 12:1–3 – emphasis mine)

Sjogren writes:

> '...Abram (soon to be renamed Abraham) was to be
> blessed and to be a blessing to every people, tongue, tribe,
> to every distinct group ... This message was given to
> Abraham in two simple parts in what we'll call the "top
> line" and the "bottom line". The top line refers to God's
> blessing of Israel. He wants to bless His people. The
> bottom-line responsibility reveals that He wants His
> people to not only enjoy that blessing, but then to turn
> around and be a blessing to all families on the face of the
> earth, resulting in His greater glory.'

Sjogren's point is that God did not just tell Abraham that he
was to be blessed (the 'top line'). He also told him that he was
to take that blessing and share it with all the nations around

him (the 'bottom line'). Abraham had a specific responsibility
to the nations around him:

> 'If you count the number of groups listed in Genesis 10,
> you'll find that after the tower of Babel confusion of
> languages, there were approximately seventy groups
> of people on the face of the earth. God maintained His
> intention of being glorified through a diverse creation that
> was to return honour and praise to Him.'

Abraham's blessing could not be complete without those
other seventy nations being blessed. It was never intended to
be some kind of private party, attended only by Abraham and
God. All seventy of the nations around him were supposed to
get an invitation to the blessing.

It is exactly the same format as Acts 1:8. There is the top line
(*'You will receive power when the Holy Spirit comes upon you'*); and
there is the bottom line (*'and you will be My witness ... to the end
of the earth'*). Interestingly, the bottom lines of Genesis 12:3
and Acts 1:8 are both promises, just as much as the top line in
each place is also in the form of a promise:

> *'And in you all the families of the earth shall be blessed.'*
>
> (Genesis 12:3)

> *'... and you shall be witnesses to Me in Jerusalem, and in all
> Judea and Samaria, and to the end of the earth.'* (Acts 1:8)

If both the 'bottom lines' are promises ('shall be blessed';
'shall be witnesses'), rather than just commands, it confirms
that the blessing that God wants to lavish on us, just as He did
on Abraham, is not complete until we do our part to fulfil the
bottom line. Just receiving the top line blessing is not enough.
Think of that – **if we do not engage in being a blessing to the
nations, in reaching out to the ends of the earth, then we
will miss out on part of the blessing that our Heavenly
Father wants to give us.** Churches that do not engage in
world mission miss something that God wants them to have.
Without world mission, we will never manage to get all the
blessing God has for us.

To further prove the point that the whole Bible is permeated with Great Commission thinking, Sjogren has an interesting review of the ministry of Jesus in the Gospels. He writes: [34]

'How many themes do you think Jesus would have to address in order to do justice to all of the Scriptures? If I were to quiz you to name a major theme that Jesus would have to address, what would you say? Grace? Mercy? Love? And how many major themes would He cover? Ten? Thirty?

Interestingly, Luke tells us that Jesus broke down all the Scriptures into two central themes. Now, let's be honest. If Jesus can take the entire Scriptures and break them down into two central themes, you and I need to be intimately acquainted with those themes, and should be teaching them to those around us.

Jesus says in Luke 24:46, "This is what is written: 'the Christ will suffer and rise from the dead on the third day.'" That's the first theme: suffering, rising from the dead on the third day. He's speaking of the forgiveness of sins, about a relationship we can have with our God. And then He explains in verses 47 and 48 that "repentance and forgiveness of sins will be preached in His name to all nations, beginning at Jerusalem. You are witnesses of these things." The second theme is that His name should go to all the nations on the face of the earth.

Sounds a bit familiar, doesn't it?

That He should suffer and rise from the dead on the third day to provide salvation seems to refer to the top line. And that "repentance and forgiveness of sins should be preached in His name to all nations" refers, of course, to the bottom line of the covenant. We can thus say that Jesus broke all the Scriptures down into two central themes: top line and bottom line.'

The Great Commission is at the heart of the Bible, from beginning to end. It is not a peripheral theme of the Scriptures, nor something that Jesus thought up in His last days on earth. It is the will of God, from beginning to end in the Old and the New Testament.

Observation 2: It is possible for ordinary people and churches in our generation to make a real difference when they engage in world mission

If the 'bottom line' offers blessing to us, then that surely means that many of us can find real fulfilment, experiencing God in a deeper way, so long as we obey the Great Commission. Because God's promises are true, many today are experiencing that.

There is a need for many different types of people with many different giftings on the mission field. The amazing thing is that God really can use anyone. However weak and feeble we may feel, He can use us. If we find it virtually impossible to learn a foreign language, He can use us. If our primary skill is as a cook, a teacher, a doctor or nurse, a mechanical engineer, a secretary, a lorry driver or a builder, He can use us. There is a place for everyone, because God created us as we are for a purpose.

Belinda and Lisa are ethnic Chinese from outside of Mainland China. They have a burden for the unreached people groups of China. The Lord has led them to an area of China where several Muslim groups live. Belinda and Lisa cannot stand on a street corner and share the Gospel, but they can demonstrate the Lord's love to these needy people in practical ways.

They have brought groups of overseas Christians to work with the children in the local orphanage. Each summer they organise camps for these neglected children. They have arranged for Christians overseas to sponsor individual children, so that their most basic needs are met. One local area has no access to clean water and villagers have regularly to walk several miles to buy water in. So Belinda and Lisa have arranged for water storage tanks to be built. Now they are helping to build a small school for the local children. When local people ask why they are doing this, Belinda and Lisa want to share about the love of God that motivates them. Their work is breaking down barriers to the Gospel and they trust that in God's timing they will see folk coming to trust in Him for themselves.

John and Mary have a burden for another unreached people group. This people group are Buddhists and there are virtually no Christians among them. Open preaching of the Gospel amongst them is forbidden. Yet John is a computer expert. His skills are much needed as the people of this land seek to improve their economic conditions. As John works for a local business, he makes friends with other employees. As friendships grow, it is natural for the couple to share their faith. They are also able to meet with some of the small number of local Christians to encourage them.

Brian was called to a remote tribe. He went with his wife, Sarah, to live with the tribe for several years. He learnt their language and culture. One day, when the couple had been fully accepted by the tribe, Brian invited them all to a meeting. The whole tribe gathered around him as he began to tell the story of how God created the world. During regular meetings over the next few days, he told them the whole story of the Bible. The tribal people hung on his every word. Gradually they came to understand that sin was ingrained in their lives. They desperately needed someone to save them. Then they heard that there was an answer to their need. God had sent His Son, Jesus, to save them from their sins. Suddenly every member of the tribe began to jump up and down with joy. They had heard the Good News and their lives had been transformed as they put their trust in the Lord Jesus.

Stephen and Elaine live in the capital city of a north African country. They too are missionaries, but they have a rather different ministry. There are several hundred missionaries working in that country. Stephen and Elaine run a hostel, where missionaries can come and relax away from the pressures of their lives in more rural areas. They are friends, encouragers and counsellors to those who are going through difficult times.

Jean lives in an Asian country. She is a qualified primary school teacher. She is using her professional skills to teach the children of the missionaries working in that area, thus freeing their parents to use their gifts amongst the local people.

God is using all kinds of Christians from many lands. A recent report recounts how God used cross-cultural Iranian missionaries to reach an unreached people group in their own land:

'In the mid-1990s the Y people were considered amongst the hardest people groups to reach: geographically isolated in a remote mountainous area in the south-west of Iran, and most resistant to the Gospel.

Two underground Christians in Tehran were told by God to translate some of the New Testament into the language of the Y people. In obedience, they did as the Lord said, and drove down to the Y region to distribute His Word. As soon as they started to hand out the literature, the Y people ripped it up and said, "Whoever you are, if you don't leave, we will kill you. We belong to Allah." Forced to leave, these two Christian brothers started driving home.

While this was happening, a Friday night mosque service was being held in a Y people village. The imam was reading a story out of the Quaran in which Jesus ("Isa") is mentioned more times than Mohammed. "Isa is mentioned everywhere in the Quaran", he said, "and I don't know a thing about Isa." Neither did any of the other Muslims at the service. "If Isa is in the Quaran so often, then Allah must want us to know about him." So the congregation prayed, "Allah, show us more about Isa."

That evening, Jesus appeared to one of the Muslim worshippers in a dream, and said: "Go to the bridge in the city at 3 a.m. Two men will be there to give you information about Me."

Meanwhile, the two Christian brothers were returning home, wondering why they had obeyed God and nothing had happened. They got to a certain city around 3 a.m. and while crossing a bridge, their Jeep broke down. Getting out to examine the engine, they heard the sound of footsteps and turned to see a Y villager running across the bridge. He ran up to them and said, "I am here for the information about Isa"! They handed over all the literature to the villager, who promptly turned and ran back the way he came.

Never before had the Gospel been introduced to the Y people. They were the hardest to reach, the most resistant. But now the door has been pushed open through the obedience of His servants.

Since that time, overseas Christians have been travelling to the Y region on short term teams to water the seed. There is now a small but growing underground church...' [35]

It is not just individuals who can make a difference. Churches can too. A close colleague and friend shared this thrilling example of how a whole church saw God use them, as the brothers and sisters embraced God's call to reach out to the lost:

'Our local church in Perth, Australia, which had a heart for missions, was challenged by the Lord to adopt an unreached people group. As we had been ministering in Southern India in the Andra Pradesh state, we felt that it made sense to adopt a group in this vicinity. With a little research, and lots of encouragement and assistance from the local Indian Pastors, we decided to adopt the Z people people group. The light-skinned Z people are the gypsy tribe of India, traditionally nomadic, although in recent years circumstances have forced them to settle in villages. They number about 1,300,000 people. They protect their identity by isolating themselves from contact with other peoples, and so are hard to reach. They serve as farmers, construction workers, and wood carriers. Economically, they range from being fairly wealthy to the poorest of India's poor. The people have little education and few are literate. Most Z people groups are animists, offering animal sacrifices to appease the many spirits they worship.

Having seen a few of these Z people tribes-people on our previous travels to village crusades (they were easily identifiable with their distinctive red head coverings) and having also heard about the struggle the Indian pastors experienced in their attempts to reach out to the Z people with the Gospel, we understood that there was a need for much focused prayer to soften their hearts. We decided as a church eldership that unless we were serious about this, it would be perceived by the congregation as just a fad or another programme that would run its course and would not last. We attempted a variety of activities, such as prayer bookmarks for each of the congregation to place in their Bibles, special prayer nights on a regular basis – we even erected a huge banner in the church, so that every time folks came into church they could be reminded to pray for the Z people people. Most of the prayer times were fairly ordinary, but several expressed a growing burden for the lostness of these people.

After some ten months of prayer, a team of around twenty folk went across to Southern India to hold crusades in the villages and also to offer a seminar attended by about one hundred or so village pastors and leaders. On one of the evenings at a remote village, four hours travel by car from Vijawada, we were searching for the bilingual pastor who was going to interpret the meeting. The praise and worship had been going sixty minutes or so with some 100–200 people sitting on the ground, near the tent that had been erected. There were also several hundred folk standing in the shadows some distance from the tent. We eventually discovered the pastor behind one of the huts in tears. He went on to explain. "As I looked out across the meeting, I saw a dozen or so Z people people. We sent no special invitation for them to come. They just felt they should come." His excitement was added to, when, after the salvation message was shared, five or six Z people men and women gave their lives to the Lord.

You can imagine the excitement of the team when they got back to the church in Perth later and reported how God had answered all our prayers for these people in far away India. The prayer focus for the Z people was intensified during the following year, and we could hardly wait to get back to see what God had been doing. As our prayers of faith had increased, we sent a team again to the same villages expecting increased results, and God did not disappoint us. This time there were well over one hundred Z people who simply "turned up" for the meetings with no promotional material or high level marketing programmes ... The Spirit of God had simply drawn them. Forty or fifty of them gave their lives to Christ that year.

Several years later there were reports of great persecution among many of the Z people who had become Christians, but despite this, God was adding to those who were coming to know Him.

What really impacted me from the whole experience was the power of prayer to move the hearts of a hardened people group to respond to the Gospel. What had seemed almost impossible beforehand was now so easy – the way had been prepared for God to move. We discovered that Jesus really meant it when He said, "If I be lifted up from the earth, I will draw all men unto Me."'

There are many such examples of churches and of individual Christians who have experienced God's Hand upon them in thrilling ways. Lives have been changed as God has worked in wonderful ways. It has been my privilege over the years to work with many such folk. I think back to a church on the East Coast of England, where a pastor recently said to me: 'This brother does not seem to be very successful in our local church, but when he gets overseas on short-term teams to the country of God's calling, he becomes a different person.' Mission is the doorway to blessing for him, as it will be for many others.

The second observation I have made in this chapter is manifestly true: it is possible for ordinary people and churches in our generation to make a real difference when they engage in world mission, and to be richly blessed in the process.

Why then do the majority of believers not join in? The current indifference of many Christians to the task of reaching the ends of the world with the good news of Jesus is not easy to understand. God tells us to do it; and He blesses us when we step out. Then why do not more of us do what He says?

It is hard to avoid the conclusion that we have somehow been deceived by the devil. He does not want believers to be blessed, and he does not want unbelievers to be saved. He logically seeks to prevent us from setting out on this path to blessing. As he considers the Church, the devil sees how it is growing. He knows what has happened in South Korea. There was hardly a church there one hundred years ago, and now it is one of the fastest growing churches in the world – all because of missionary work in years gone by. He also sees how these new churches are aggressive in missionary outreach. The Koreans are sending many folk out as missionaries. That cannot be pleasing to the devil. In one hundred years a nation has gone from being almost unreached to being a major missionary sending nation. He knows his time is short. If these models are repeated, then other currently unreached people groups will be invaded by the Gospel and by the Spirit of God. He must act quickly. He must keep in its deep sleep that section of the Church that is slumbering. He must also try to inflict a similar sleep of deception on the churches that are awake and active.

The kingdom of darkness is therefore engaged in implementing an unrelenting and focused strategy. Its major aim is to hinder Christians from obeying the command of the Lord Jesus to reach the ends of the earth with the Gospel. That strategy contains at least four elements, designed to deliver millions of human beings to hell, a place originally reserved for Satan himself.

Satan's first deceptive strategy is to persuade us that mission is the task of a small section of the Church, not the task of the whole Body of Christ

Mission is for the whole Church. The devil wants to fight that. At first, he does not discredit mission, but simply relegates it in our minds to a position of minor importance. He persuades us that mission, though legitimate, is the responsibility of a very limited number of Christians, a specialised task force. Church leaders under this influence begin to believe that mission is not their responsibility before God. They therefore delegate it to mission subcommittees – who are sometimes powerless to get anything much done in the churches. Thus it is easy for the devil to exile mission to obscurity, whilst the prayer, money and energy of the Church is diverted to other less strategic needs.

Churches cannot fully obey God's command to be involved with mission by delegating the responsibility to their mission committees. Instead, mission in a church must begin with the leadership example of its pastors and elders. Church leaders need to go on mission trips themselves, so they can begin to 'live, eat and breathe' mission. The church eldership will then be able to take a leadership role on the mission committee. Ideally, therefore, they will provide the church's mission leadership. Most church members are not slow to test what their leadership really believes. If the leadership does not involve itself specifically in mission trips and mission planning, neither will the members.

Secondly, when the devil has relegated mission to a place of obscurity, he then depicts missionaries as 'odd-balls'

Some modern Christians are easily persuaded that missionaries are out of step with the 'real' Church. Missionaries begin to seem more and more irrelevant. Because they are away for long periods, obeying the Master and going to the ends of the earth, they are seen as less and less in touch with local trends. They are seen as obscure people in pith-helmets and out of date clothing. They do not know the latest worship songs, but rather talk of strange places and peoples which are far from the understanding of mainstream Christianity. Thus, most Christians look upon them as nice, but irrelevant and ill-informed. In modern parlance, they are not 'cool'.

We have to see again that God's only Son was a missionary, and that the apostle Paul, the most significant man in the New Testament apart from Christ, was also a missionary. Missionaries are at the heart of New Testament Christianity. So they should be at the heart of modern church life.

Thirdly, the devil wants to persuade Christians to drift away from submission to the authority of the Bible

The devil hates the Bible. If he cannot get Christians to hate it, he will get them to ignore it or to misunderstand what it says. God's Word is the source of passion for mission, for it shows us the heart of God. As the Holy Spirit opens up God's Word to us with power, we will move out with God's love for a lost world. Thus the enemy must at all costs stop the followers of Jesus from reading, believing – and especially from obeying – the Bible.

For example, a central element of this task of Satan is to convince Christians that Jesus is not the only way of salvation, and that the followers of all religions will be saved as long as they are sincere. Christians who believe that lie will cease to believe that the Gospel of Jesus Christ is the only message of hope for time and for eternity. When that happens, they will also cease to be willing to pay any kind of price for Jesus. They stop going to the ends of the earth with the Gospel.

It is indeed time to stand on God's Word – to live and to die by it. We have to recommit ourselves to the authority of the Bible, the Word of God, on mission and every matter. Christians need to submit again to the truth that Jesus is the only way of salvation, and that we are called to go His costly way to bring that good news to others (John 14:6; Acts 4:12).

Some Christians today have lost confidence in the Gospel. We live in an age when nothing is considered to be black and white, when 'truth' is seen to be whatever is expedient or 'whatever works for you!' It is thus subjective and experiential. It is 'politically incorrect' to talk of ultimate truth. In this climate, any religion is considered acceptable, so long as it is not forced on anyone else. It is very difficult to hold to a view that says that there is only one way to God, only one Name by which we can be saved, one ultimate truth. Many Christians would rather deny or ignore the thought of unbelievers spending eternity in torment in hell. Yet the fact remains that the clearest teaching about the reality of hell came from the lips of Jesus Himself. And He is the One who made the claims – preposterous if they are not true – that He alone is 'the Way, the Truth and the Life' and that 'no one comes to the Father, but by Me.'

It is so much more comfortable to embrace a quasi-New Age view, which states that all religions are good and that we should not presume to meddle with the beliefs of others. Yet the falsehood of this position is easily evident if we are willing to make a visit to other lands and to see the oppression and tangible evidence of the darkness in which they live. These people are not 'better off' if left alone. They often remain in darkness only because no one has yet brought them the Light. That kind of thinking flourishes best when we remain secure in our nice Christian 'Jerusalem' and do not go and see what life's realities are like for most of the world today.

Fourthly, the devil seeks to persuade us that our main concern should be with our own personal needs

Increasingly today we have begun to concentrate on our own hurts and pains – of which the devil may supply an unlimited number. In such a climate we will begin to revel in the subjective experiences of Christianity – those ministries that make us feel good and seem to bless us. We are persuaded to seek after any ministry that brings us physical or emotional comfort, and to avoid any ministry that challenges us to go the way of the cross of Christ.

Sometimes we are offered a model which paints 'me' as the centre of creation, 'my needs' as the focus of all attention, and 'my ministry' as the most important. As Christians thus concentrate on themselves, they forget mission and the missionaries. They do not pray for them, and so jeopardise God's continuing protection upon those who are on the front line of battle. Christians at home no longer care for the families of those involved in mission or for their personal needs. The missionaries are therefore discouraged in the battle, as home churches forget to write to them, and to care for them in practical ways.

Our lives should clearly demonstrate that it is more blessed to give than to receive. Those who spend their Christian lives just waiting to be blessed and healed themselves will have little impact on the lives of others. If our faith today is not strong enough to cause us to send and be sent in the Name of Christ to the ends of the earth, and to give our all to fight Satan's dark strategies, then we do not have a real enough faith.

One modern expression of this self-orientated Christianity is the pressure to succeed in material terms. Many Christians have bought into the myth that life is all about getting an 'upwardly mobile' lifestyle – earning a good salary, owning a nice house, running an expensive car and getting to go on exotic holidays once or even twice a year. Indeed they begin to define the blessing of God in those terms. But the real issue is whether God is in charge of our salaries, our promotions and the disposal of our incomes. One young believer works in the City of London, earning a large salary. But he holds very lightly to all of that, choosing to use his income to finance effective outreach work in both home and overseas missions. He is a committed supporter of many who serve overseas and of their work, while choosing to live in a poor, run-down part of London himself, so as to be involved in cross-cultural outreach there. He is an example of one who uses a successful career to engage in the challenge of reaching both his 'Jerusalem' and also the 'ends of the earth' with the Gospel.

Is mission still required today? Is the Antioch Factor still relevant? God says, 'Yes,' both in His Word and from the evidence of His world today. The devil says 'No,' because he fears what will happen if we hear and obey the Voice of God. God says, 'Yes'; the devil says, 'No.' Whom will you support with your vote – and your life?

Chapter 12

'Walking the Talk'

'The very best proof of your love for God is obedience – nothing more, nothing less, nothing else.'   (Chuck Swindoll) [36]

The challenge of the Antioch Factor needs to be applied to us personally. The heart of the matter is that we should give the right place as churches and as individual Christians to reaching the lost in our world today. My fervent desire is that Christians around the world would embrace the vision of the church at Antioch, and not just sit comfortably in their Jerusalem, basking in the love of God. The Lord would have each church in some way reach out beyond its Jerusalem to its Judea, its Samaria and to the ends of the earth. I long that every Christian might have the joy and the privilege (for that is what it is) of working with the Lord to make a difference for His kingdom.

I trust that, as I have shared with you through this book, you have been encouraged and challenged to play your part in reaching the ends of the earth. We need now to look more specifically at the ways in which this can be done. This is not a calling for a select few, but God's mandate for all of His people. If we do not each play our part, then it is simply a case of being disobedient to our Lord. We risk bearing the responsibility for those people who, because of our disobedience, will enter a Christless eternity without having heard the Gospel.

It is easy to come up with excuses, even legitimate ones, as to why we cannot go overseas. Perhaps because we have a family to support, and argue that we cannot simply 'up sticks' and go abroad. We are not all like William Carey or Hudson Taylor! Others argue that they are not in good health. No missionary society would accept them for service. We need to penetrate through that screen of confusion and avoidance. Mission is God's mandate for every single Christian. It therefore logically follows that He has a role for each of us to play. He may not be calling you to live in a remote African village or high in the mountains of Nepal! But He is calling you to be obedient to your 'heavenly vision' (Acts 26:19). As I suggest some ways in which we can all become involved in reaching the ends of the earth, will you open your heart to the Lord and allow Him to speak to you, to reveal to you His calling on your life in this area?

The first step: Get baptised – into mission!

Before a major sporting event, such as soccer's World Cup, the newspapers and other media are full of articles and reports about the coming matches. The manager or coach is scrutinised. The private lives of the more prominent players are put under a microscope. The different teams are assessed. As play begins, the reporting reaches a crescendo. Many folk may not be in the least bit interested in sport, but one thing is sure – they will know there is a competition in progress. Every newspaper, every broadcasting station will bombard them with information. Even the advertisements often relate to the matches. Indeed the complaint of those who are not interested is that they cannot escape from it, even if they want to!

The church needs to learn from the children of the world in this matter. If Christians in churches are continually taught about mission and given regular information about specific missionary work, they will become more and more involved in it. Many Christians gain their values and priorities from the emphasis of their church. Whatever is clearly a priority for the church will become a priority with the members. Hence my expression above – 'get baptised into mission'. It is not a water baptism but an information baptism; neither should it be a sprinkling, but baptism by full immersion! In other words, people need regular 'soaking' in the work of the Lord overseas, from the Bible and from reports and prayer letters.

There are a number of ways in which this principle can be made to work. Here are three of them:

1. Teach regularly about mission, and have at least one specific missionary weekend per year

Obviously it is important that local pastors and leaders should give regular Sunday and midweek slots to teaching about cross-cultural outreach overseas. Pastors must personally and publicly identify with Antioch values and communicate them to their people. If leaders do not signify their commitment, then the majority will realise that they are not being serious, but are going through the motions. At the same time, it is important for the church to allow mission speakers to share, those who are really involved in this work today. We catch fire from fire in any area of the Lord's work. Where there is vision and burden on the part of those immediately involved, others will experience God's specific calling.

Alongside that, the church should at least once a year arrange a full mission weekend. Clear teaching and challenge from the Word of God should be communicated over this period, as well as specific information about the work overseas that the church supports. The target of this kind of specific weekend is that people in the church should be generally inspired and specifically informed about those areas in which they can be involved.

If believers in a local church are 'baptised' in this way, more missionaries will be raised up.

2. Give prominence in church services to returning missionaries

When missionaries come back on furlough, the church needs to give opportunity to them to share with the whole church. Some missionaries are eloquent and easy to listen to; others are not gifted in that way. The type of opportunity given to them should recognise that reality. Some can preach. Some may only be given a short interview. But whatever method is used, it is important that the missionary should feel that the church knows what they are doing, and has an opportunity to become more involved through that knowledge. It is important to remember that those who have joined the church in the period in which the missionary has been overseas may not even know who he or she is.

The Antioch church's approach towards Paul and Barnabas is exemplary in this matter:

> 'From there they sailed to Antioch, where they had been commended to the grace of God for the work which they had completed. And when they had come and gathered the church together, they reported all that God had done with them, and that He had opened the door of faith to the Gentiles. So they stayed there a long time with the disciples.' (Acts 14:26–28)

The returning missionaries reported, the church gathered, listened, gave praise to God, and was encouraged to support and pray for them. What a wonderful model. By contrast, sometimes those who have laid down their lives for the lost in another nation are given no more than three minutes to share publicly during their time back in their home church. It is even possible that the announcement of the young people's bowling trip may be given equal, or more time. What a travesty.

Of course there are some missionaries who do not communicate well. But, as I have said above, those who are able to communicate can help them present their work effectively.

Imagine your frustration if you were treated in this way. Suppose you worked for a major company and spent three years developing a whole new area of production at an overseas plant. Yet when you returned, the boss announced to you that he could only give you two minutes to listen to your report of all you had done. The message would be crystal clear. He was simply going through the motions and was not interested. That is exactly the situation many returning missionaries face.

3. Encourage the reading of mission materials – individual missionary prayer letters, magazines, books, etc.

Much of this is sufficiently covered in my comments above. It is of course true that normally a smaller group – a prayer group, a cell group or whatever – will have specific responsibility for the missionary. But at the same time every effort should be made to encourage the whole church to read their prayer letters. They can be given out in some form with the church newsletter. They might need to be abbreviated or improved, but they should be read by all. This will be further covered in Chapter 13.

The second step: Pray

> *'The effective, fervent prayer of a righteous man avails much.'*   (James 5:16)

Do we, who have been made righteous through the precious blood of the Lord Jesus Christ, really believe what James said in that verse of Scripture that our prayers make a significant difference – whether on the mission field or elsewhere? Do we really know in our hearts that, as we come before the Lord in prayer, we are releasing the power of God into the lives of others whom we have never met? Why do we spend so much time on idle pursuits when we could be changing the world through our intercession?

Paul, probably the most famous missionary of all time, could not fulfil his ministry without the prayer support of his fellow Christians.

> *'Now I beg you, brethren, through the Lord Jesus Christ, and through the love of the Spirit, that you strive together with me in prayers to God for me ... '*   (Romans 15:30)

> *'Brethren, pray for us.'*   (1 Thessalonians 5:25)

> *'[Praying] ... for me, that utterance may be given to me, that I may open my mouth boldly to make known the mystery of the gospel, for which I am an ambassador in chains; that in it I may speak boldly, as I ought to speak.'*   (Ephesians 6:19–20)

If Paul could not do it alone, how can we expect the missionaries of today to survive and prosper without our committed prayer support?

In my book *The Continuing Heartcry for China* I reported an event in the lives of John and Isobel Kuhn, who worked amongst the Lisu people in Southwest China early in the last century. It is a striking story of the power of prayer and bears repetition. In one village, called 'Three Clans', the Kuhns shared the Word of God and reasoned with the people time and time again, but still they did not see a breakthrough for the Gospel. Then one day, the night before they were due to leave, there was a complete turnaround. As they once again challenged the villagers of Three Clans with the Gospel, one by one they came forward to commit their lives to Christ. It was a wonderful move of God.

Two months later, a letter came from a dear prayer-warrior, Mrs K, who lived in a small town in North America. It read something like this:

'I must write and tell you what happened today. All morning I could not do my housework, because of the burden on me concerning the Three Clan Village, so finally I went to the telephone and called Mrs W. She said that she had been feeling the very same way and suggested that we phone Mrs J and all go to prayer. We did so, each in her own kitchen. This morning we spent in intercession for those clans. We feel God has answered. You will know.'

John and Isobel Kuhn did indeed know. The letter was dated the very day that they had seen that amazing breakthrough in Three Clan Village. God had answered prayer.

A few years ago, a team of believers from overseas were delivering Christian teaching books to China. They arrived at a railway station in southern China, carrying many bags filled with these desperately-needed materials. Their Chinese contact was due to meet them outside the railway station. But as they gathered together in the street outside, they suddenly realised that they were surrounded by Chinese police, who were watching their every move. Any contact with their Chinese friend would put him in danger. What could they do? Then suddenly the way was clear. Their Chinese contact drew up in a taxi. They bundled the bags of books swiftly into the car and off it went. The surrounding police had noticed nothing.

When the team leader returned home to Australia, he was contacted by a lady who had committed herself to support the team in prayer. She told him that at a certain time she had felt a particular burden from the Lord to pray for them, and she had responded in obedience. It was, of course, at exactly the same time that the team was surrounded by police and was wondering what to do. Once again God had answered prayer.

You may not often know of such immediate and obvious answers to your prayers. Only occasionally does the Lord encourage us in such a way. But He has promised that He hears our every prayer, and we can trust that, as we pray, He will make a difference.

How do we begin to pray in this way? The more we know about a subject, the more effectively we can pray about it. As we read or listen to information on the needs of the different areas of the world, the Lord will touch our hearts and burden us to pray for that area. How can we pray for a people of whom we have not heard?

There are many hundreds of missionary organisations that send out prayer information, prayer letters and tapes that will update you on the current situation in particular areas of the world. If you find it difficult to know where to start, get hold of a copy of *Operation World*. This excellent book by Patrick Johnstone gives information and suggestions as to how to pray for every country of the world. It also gives addresses from which you can ask for further information on particular countries. [37] For specific China prayer material, you can obtain information from Appendix C at the end of this book.

Pray for the ends of the earth, not just for your Jerusalem. You can do that without leaving the comforts of 'Jerusalem', though it may be that the Lord will later challenge you to go and see for yourself! There are many folk whose burden for a country has been greatly increased by going to meet the people of that land. Pray individually, in your regular home meetings, in specific missionary prayer meetings – anywhere and everywhere.

J.O. Fraser, the outstanding CIM missionary who was very involved with the Kuhns, used to give two powerful illustrations of the power of prayer. He talked of a boat going down a river and becoming wedged on a rock submerged beneath the surface. The situation is impossible. The rock is too heavy to move; the boat too heavy to lift. And so the boat is stuck – unless the water level rises. If it does, the boat, carried by the water, flows effortlessly over the obstructing rock. The parable is a clear one. Prayer makes the 'water level' rise, and causes us to overcome resistance to the work of the Lord.

Fraser also talked of the work of a missionary as being like that of a man or a woman with a torch (the Olympic variety) in their hand, attempting to set light to the grass and the shrubs. Fraser's point was that if there is prayer, the land is dry and will burn, leaving fires after the worker has gone. If there is no prayer, or insufficient prayer and intercession, the grass is wet, and will not catch fire. The point of this analogy is that the labours of the worker are much the same in either case; they may not be the key to his success or failure. The difference lies in the state of the grass and other materials. Are they dry and will they catch fire? Fraser's point is that this difference is made on the missionary's behalf through prayer.

What a responsibility. What a privilege.[38]

The third step: Give

Those who go overseas need our financial support. Why do we sometimes expect our missionaries to have a far lower standard of living than we do, even sometimes accepting that they should live not too far from the breadline? While some (but by no means all) in the church go on regular holidays overseas and buy the latest model of their favourite car, many missionaries are struggling to survive on a very meagre income. Whilst I am not suggesting we should provide our missionaries with every luxury, we should perhaps consider our priorities. Would a slightly cheaper holiday be so dreadful, when that saving could mean someone in Mongolia coming to know the Lord? Could our waiting another year to buy that new car mean that a missionary in Papua New Guinea can have the means of transport so vital to their work?

The home offices of missions also need financial support. It may not be so romantic as giving directly to a missionary – and we may not see such obvious results – but it is still a vitally important aspect of missionary work, which requires finance. The prayer letters that you receive need to be photocopied or printed. Phone calls and letters to those on the mission field need to be paid for. The staff who give their time to the necessary administration also need to earn a living. Some Christians, who are quick to criticise inefficiency or even a lack of response to a communication, would simply never consider giving to support the administrative side of the work! But how can that work be done without such a team in the background? Reality needs to be recognised here.

Once again we do not need to leave the comfort of our Jerusalems in order to touch the ends of the earth. Even those on very limited incomes can play their part. How about collecting your used postage stamps and passing them on for your favourite missionary society to sell? The members of a church with which I have had contact in Singapore used their Saturday afternoons to collect recyclable materials from the local housing estates. The profits from the sale of these materials are given to mission.

A church in the UK wanted to support a young couple going out from them to serve long-term overseas. They decided that one way they could do this was to provide the couple with items for their kitchen. Each member of the church was given the opportunity to buy one item, such as a wooden spoon, mixing bowl or rolling pin. Everyone in the church could play their part and the young couple were greatly blessed by the provision of so many necessary utensils. At Christmas the church invited everyone to buy a packet soup or sauce mix. These were then packed in one box and posted off to the young missionary couple, living in a third world country where such 'luxuries' were unavailable. These packet mixes helped to liven up their meals for many months to come. With a little imagination we can all play our part in supporting mission financially. Such gifts have a message that is more than just financial. They express personalised care and support for folk on the front line. The message is that the saints back home do really care enough to think about their needs.

The fourth step: Serve

'Serving' in this sense means taking our place to help to reach the ends of the earth with the Gospel by supporting missionaries in practical ways. It is the outworking today of the Barnabas ministry. In the next chapter my wife Christine will share specifically on this topic in a detailed way. It is such a vital and neglected area that it demands a separate chapter.

The fifth step: Go

> *'Go, therefore, and make disciples of all the nations.'*
>   (Matthew 28:19)

In His Word the Lord has told us all to go. It is not optional. It is the Lord's Great Commission to us all. We need to take His Word seriously. We need to come out of our holy huddles to touch the lives of those who are heading for a Christless eternity.

Missionaries and those who go on mission trips are not super-heroes. They are ordinary people with their own different foibles and failings. They are simply people who have been obedient to God's calling and laid down their lives for His purposes.

As international director of Antioch Missions/Chinese Church Support Ministries, I have contact with many folk who join our short-term missionary teams to China. These folk are ordinary people, whom God calls to give a few weeks of their holidays to serve His purposes in China.[39] Different missionary organisations have different kinds of teams. I have listed below some of the ones we organise. They will serve as examples of the kind of opportunities that exist for Christians to serve and to become involved today.

We now send out four different kinds of short-term teams – courier, intercession, mercy and English teaching.

1. Courier teams

Chinese Christians are in desperate need of Christian teaching materials. Very few such books are printed inside China, and this has led to many Christians remaining untaught. Some of them have been led astray into heresies. Our courier teams consist of folk who help to carry Bibles and Christian teaching books to our brothers and sisters in China. They usually travel to several different Chinese cities, each time taking with them several bags full of books. One courier has shared:

> 'The overall perception of the courier trip was that it was exciting, fulfilling and enabled us to gain first-hand knowledge of the need for Christian teaching books to continue to be taken into China. The train trips were also an opportunity to see what the interior of China looked like and also to gain considerable insight into the Chinese culture.'

2. Intercession teams

Intercession teams are organised for those who already have a special burden to pray – or are willing to grow in this area. They travel to a specific area to see the land and the people for themselves. There is no doubt that the Lord can really open our eyes to the needs of an area or a people group as the team meets and prays for them in their own country. One of our team members shared:

> 'To finally arrive in a land that one has wanted to travel to for almost 30 years is in itself a thrilling experience. However, far outweighing that is to finally meet the people of that land that you have been praying for. To cry out more earnestly than ever before that these people would hear the lovely Name of Jesus and be rescued from the kingdom of darkness and brought into His marvellous Kingdom of light. To leave these people and return home was not an easy task. My heart remains in that country.'

On many of our intercession teams, the Lord has brought great encouragement to team members, as they are able to lead local people to trust in Christ.

> 'As we sang and worshipped God on top of a hill, people were drawn to us. Two young men, business partners, had come to burn joss sticks in an attempt to pray for inner peace. As our team responded to their questions, each in his own time met Jesus. They threw the joss sticks on the ground and stomped on them, signifying that they no longer needed these to have peace in their hearts.'

At the end of the team, when we return home, we ourselves can pray more effectively, and we can also share our experiences with others to encourage them to pray as well.

3. Mercy teams

Mercy teams provide a powerful way of presenting God's love in a country where open evangelism is not possible. God's light can shine through acts of mercy, care and a servant heart. These teams often work in orphanages, where many of China's unwanted children end up. One of our mercy team leaders shared concerning a recent team:

'Orphanage work is rarely about looking after children only. God reminded us to look at the spiritual climate in the welfare home, the lives of the officials, the lives of the "aunties" looking after the children, our health worker and finally the children themselves. We saw God actively move hardened hearts, and saw children relaxing as we held them and prayed for them.

Three of our team members gently attended to the needs of all the babies, with special attention given to two new-borns with special needs. One of our team members, an experienced paediatric nurse, cared for the new-borns whilst the staff observed. In this way, she was transferring her skills to them and they expressed gratitude for showing them how to care for such needy cases.

D is a two-and-a-half-year-old little boy, who refused to walk unassisted. He was functioning at an 18-month-old level when we first assessed him at the beginning of the week. Through prayer, therapy, love and play, he was able to function at a two-year-old level by the time we left. He had caught up six months worth of development in one short week. How God answers prayer!'

4. English-teaching teams

Our English-teaching teams help to meet a different need in China. Many Chinese people are learning English, but have virtually no opportunity to practise the language with a native speaker. We therefore send in teams of English speakers who spend time with young people who are learning English at various schools and colleges. As team members make friends with their students, they often have opportunities to share their faith. Thus young Chinese students are exposed to the Gospel, often for the very first time, with those of their own age and educational standing. English-speaking Christians from outside China can play their part in reaching people for the Lord. One such Christian said:

> 'Each one of us on the team was really impressed by the need we saw in China and the potential we had through God to meet that need, and all said how much this time had affected our lives and futures. Coming away from such an awesome time of adventure and learning and seeing God at work in His incredible power, my prayer is that each of us will see Him move us closer to His purposes in our lives, and right into the heart of His service as we give our lives to Him.'

Each of these different teams calls for people who have different giftings and burdens. There is a role for each one of us. Sarah, a sister who joined a team taking Christian literature to Chinese believers, told us:

> 'I thoroughly enjoyed the whole trip, meeting the team and getting to know them, travelling into and through China, and the Chinese and English folk we met. I am grateful to God that we achieved our aim, which was to take the books and Bibles to various people in China.
>
> We did have some opportunities to witness to the Chinese on the train returning from Beijing and that was great. We left people with Bibles and tracts and hopefully some seeds of truth planted in their hearts. It was quite humbling to be able to share with these people. I spent quite a while talking to a young man who is in the army. He was definitely moved and was interested to know more. Being in the position he is, I can understand his reluctance to give his life to the Lord. He has a lot to lose but I hope he will realise that the gain will be greater. I thank God that our prayers are effective and we didn't just have to leave it there. I believe the Lord has His Hand on that young man's life.

I definitely want to go again and will try to encourage others to do the same. In conclusion I have to say it was a precious time and an exciting time. What the Lord taught me in it all (which is something I've been learning for a long while) is that each one of us is a vital part of the body and has a part to play for the successful outcome of whatever it is we're doing, in this case taking precious books to the hungry in China. As I said in the sharing time at the end, I would never have chosen those people to be on that team, but God did and as we got to know one another and worked and fellowshipped and prayed together, one could see the gifts of each person and it was wonderful how the Lord knitted us all together in love.'

'Each one of us is a vital part of the body and has a part to play for the successful outcome of whatever it is we're doing.' How true that is! The vital question is: Are we playing our part? Are we praying, giving, supporting and going in whatever ways the Lord has called us to? The Antioch Factor, this hidden message from the book of Acts, is not something to which we can merely give intellectual assent. It is a challenge from the Lord, a calling on our lives. Will we respond?

Elsewhere in this book I have described a challenge, which goes even further than that. This deeper challenge is for some of those who start with these basic steps to finish on the mission field long-term. [40] Legitimate and vital though the roles described in this chapter are, if they do not result in a steady stream of 'lifers' – of folk going to the field long-term – then they are failing. They will become like a medical inoculation, giving us a little of the virus so that we do not catch the real thing! One of the reasons for running short-term teams in AM/CCSM is that they can be a first step for some whom God is calling into long-term service. Exposure to the needs and realities in other lands can be the fertile soil in which God plants His deeper call and destiny.

God requires ordinary people with an extraordinary vision to pray, give, go; to serve and understand. No more – and no less.

Chapter 13

Caring for Those Who Are Sent

[*This chapter has been written by my wife, Christine, and is therefore unique in the book. The challenge it brings, out of her experience as a missionary daughter, wife and mother on the field, is one of the most important messages of this book.*]

The essence of the Antioch Factor is that it is the job of the **whole** Body of Christ to take the Gospel to the ends of the earth, not just that of a minority of Christians. Obviously, that does not mean everyone will be called to go. If everyone went, who would be left in support? Who would fulfil the equally important task of reaching the home community for Christ? But there should be many standing behind those who do go – in prayer, in giving and indeed in various other ways, giving substance to the sending church's commitment to the task.

The undergirding foundation is one of teamwork. Teamwork means that those who go and those who remain in support are one team, not separate or even competing units. Thus what happens on the field and what goes on at home are both part of the same endeavour, fulfilling the Lord's command to be His witnesses 'in Jerusalem, and in all Judea and Samaria, and to the end of the earth.' Wide personal experience and observation over the years, as well as much discussion with others, has led to the sad conclusion that this kind of support is in reality very rare. It is also extremely contested by the enemy. But where it exists and is sustained, it is exceedingly precious and powerful in winning the unreached. Perhaps that is why the enemy of the souls of men resists it so fiercely.

Ross had been preaching his message of 'Pray, Give, Go and Support' for many years before a book gave us a whole new level of understanding. The book, *Serving as Senders*, by Neal Pirolo,[41] has been described by George Verwer of Operation Mobilisation as 'one of the most significant missionary books of this decade (the 1990s).' Part of its impact is that this missionary book is directed at those who stay behind in support in the home churches, and is not primarily about those who go to the field! I make no apology for referring often to Pirolo's material, as a springboard for my thoughts.

In his preface, Pirolo describes an experience he had one year, sitting in the auditorium at Inter-Varsity's Urbana Student Mission Conference:

> 'I must admit I had begun daydreaming when all of a sudden there was that statement: "In secular war, for every one person on the battle front, there are nine others backing him up in what is called the 'line of communication'."
>
> The concept exploded like a mortar shell! The speaker had been drawing a parallel between secular war and the spiritual warfare that accompanies cross-cultural ministry. He continued, "And how can we expect to win with any less than that ratio? God is not looking for Lone Rangers or superstars; He is commanding an army – soldiers of the cross." '[42]

Pirolo thanked God for confirmation. Without knowing anything about secular warfare, he had already been encouraging students engaged in cross-cultural outreach to build around themselves a team of **nine people** who would pray and support them!

> 'Since that evening at Urbana, with more vigour than ever, I have encouraged, exhorted – even implored – anyone going into cross-cultural outreach ministry not to leave home without a strong, committed support team – a group that accepts the ministry of serving as senders.'[43]

I love the idea of each missionary serving overseas finding nine people at home who are willing to serve in the way Neal

Pirolo describes in the rest of his book. But the reality is that for most missionaries actually on the field today, the picture is far, far different from that. They have the daily challenges of life on the field with which to contend – unremitting cultural issues; difficulty with the language, food and climate; loneliness and homesickness; struggles with indifferent health perhaps; spiritual oppression and stress and so on. Yet, above and beyond that, they also have to wake up to the realisation that the longer they are away overseas, the less connected with those at home they become and the less supported they feel. That double pressure can often be overwhelming. The intent of this chapter is then to encourage local churches to raise up support teams based on Pirolo's nine-to-one ratio.

The term the 'bath-tub syndrome', which represents the level of interest from those back home, has been coined to describe the dynamics involved for many on the field, as Figure 1 shows.

If we take the upper rim of the 'bath' (both sides) as representing the times when interest from back home is at its highest, we will note that this is first the case in the early days when the missionary is sent out and has just arrived on the field. In those early, heady days everything is new and exciting to both worker and sending church. He [44] writes home a great deal, sharing his new life with his church and friends. There then follows a second period when, as the hard grind of language study sets in or the romance dies in the face of every day reality, there is little in the way of exciting 'news' to report. At the same time there is a complementary dynamic back home. Folk get used to him not being around any more,

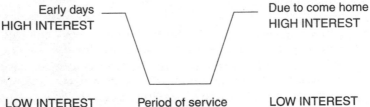

Figure 1

communication wanes and the level of interest begins to die down. Pretty soon he finds himself bumping along the bottom of the 'bath', knowing that very few back home are really remembering him in prayer or standing with him in the work. He feels he is 'out of sight, out of mind', but has no idea how to address the problem without sounding complaining or negative.

Then, after two or three years, the church bulletin announces that the missionary is coming home again and will be available to share in home groups in the church. Suddenly there is a reawakening of interest. It is hard to avoid the perception when this occurs that, as far as the average church member back home is concerned, only what happens in the local church, in the 'here and now' of their Jerusalem, really counts. What the missionary is doing out there in the 'ends of the earth' does not register, after those early days, on the church's care-and-prayer Richter Scale. In reality there is not much of a team concept about it. The missionary's work in faraway places is not perceived as part of the local church's real world. It is part of another alien world.

I agree with Pirolo that this is not how it should be. Romans 10:13–15 shows that clearly:

> 'For "whoever calls on the name of the LORD shall be saved."
> How then shall they call on Him in whom they have not believed? And how shall they believe in Him of whom they have not heard? And how shall they hear without a **preacher**? And how shall they preach unless they are **sent**? As it is written:
>   "How beautiful are the feet of those who preach the gospel
>   of peace,
>   Who bring glad tidings of good things!" '
>   (Romans 10:13–15, emphasis added)

Pirolo shows from this passage that there are **two** dimensions of involvement for those who take seriously the fact that in the world today there are still an estimated 2.5 billion people who have never received a 'culturally relevant presentation of the Gospel'. The first is the involvement of the 'preacher' – the one who is sent (verse 15); the second is the involvement of the 'senders' – those who send the preacher out.

'Those who go and those who serve as senders are like two units on the same cross-cultural outreach team. Both are equally important. Both are vitally involved in the fulfilment of the Great Commission. Both are dynamically integrated and moving toward the same goal. And both are assured of success, for those in God's work are on the winning team!' [45]

Our longing is that local churches and their members would be gripped by this concept in our day – as once used to be the case. Pirolo cites the example of the Student Volunteer Movement, which began with a hundred people in 1886 and went on to send 20,000 missionaries world-wide. This same movement mobilised an army of over 80,000 mission-minded people who pledged themselves to stay at home and support those who went.

Even that does not equate to the nine-to-one ratio mentioned earlier as the ideal, but in terms of passion and commitment it would certainly seem to surpass the average level of support nowadays! In our experience of the modern Church, the task of caring for those who are sent out is frequently relegated to a small group of already hugely over-committed folk, who, on top of other responsibilities, are supposed to pray maybe once a month for all the church's missionaries. How that can be considered as adequate support is a matter of some bemusement, when set against the amount of time that is committed to praying about local concerns! That same imbalance applies to all the required areas of support listed below.

Pirolo has identified at least six distinct kinds of support, which are required. They are, in his words:

1. Moral support – just 'being there'.
2. Logistics support – all the bits and pieces.
3. Financial support – money, money, money.
4. Prayer support – spiritual warfare at its best.
5. Communication support – letters, tapes and more.
6. Re-entry support – more than applauding the safe landing of a jumbo jet. [46]

The particular mix required by the individual, couple or family going to the field will depend very much on their circumstances. The balance will also change from time to time. But whatever the case, one thing is sure: giving adequate support in the long term represents far more work than one or two people, however committed, can do alone. And it is more that one group can seriously do for more than one missionary individual, couple or family. Ideally, each individual or family should have a separate support group, comprised of folk who have expressed a particular interest and commitment specifically to them. The group also needs a committed leader, for the job to be done properly. Moreover, although the different kinds of support overlap to a degree, it is usually the case that folk on the team are drawn and gifted for one aspect or the other, so roles need to be assigned.

The best example we know, where this concept is really working, is actually the couple who introduced us to the whole idea! When they returned to working with Scripture Union in India, after some years of running an international school in that country, they felt a strong need to build up their support systems again. Someone had lent them a copy of *Serving as Senders*, which rang all sorts of bells with them. Based on that and after much earnest prayer, they approached some couples in their local area back home and some family members and friends from further afield, asking them to consider taking on the specific role and responsibilities of being 'senders' for them. The local couples became the core members of the group, taking on responsibility for managing their finances, for prayer cover (including their update letters) and for the short-term missions youth programme they were inaugurating. While most of the 'business' was handled by the core group, the other members were also kept informed, especially of intimate prayer needs, with the aim that they should get together whenever possible.

This has been operating for about five years now, and despite some ups and downs, has been the envy of many, including ourselves. However, the essence of the whole idea is that what works for one family may not fit as a model for another in a different situation. Each couple and each group has to seek for God's leading as to how things are meant to fit together in their own specific circumstances. There is no blueprint that is right for all.

One powerful argument for the need for such support groups comes from the disquieting and sad statistics of those who 'don't make it' on the mission field. [47] The question arises as to whether it is just simply a matter of failure on the part of the missionary, or whether there is more to the picture than that. Most will have gone out with a clear sense of calling, with the promise of strong support and high hopes of being able to make a difference in their adopted culture. It is just when the 'romance' of the early days wears off, where the need for encouragement is at its greatest, that all too often the bottom-of-the-bath-tub experience kicks in. The embattled missionary feels abandoned at the point when he most needs to sense that others are standing with him. This is by no means always the story. But it is nevertheless true that some have returned from the field with the stigma of not being 'suitable material', when, in reality, all they lacked was the tangible support of those who should have stood with them. [48]

Our own particular missionary odyssey serves to illustrate some of these very real issues. At the time that we were married in 1975, Ross had already been a missionary in Taiwan for six years. We then worked together on the field for a further four years, before the Lord redirected us towards serving Christians on the mainland of China, initially from a base in the UK. Up to that point we had been supported totally out of one church in the north. The Lord did not move us out again to the mission field for a further fifteen years, by which time Ross had planted a new church in the UK (where he served as Senior Pastor for a number of years) and also had started from scratch two China ministries from our base in England. When we did finally move overseas again, this time to Singapore in 1994, it was far too easy to make assumptions about support, based on our previous experience in the former church. In the whirl-wind of preparations to move the whole family and the international base of the ministry abroad, we did not realise soon enough that the expectations we had projected had not necessarily been 'owned' or even understood by those back home. Thus, what to us had been a commissioning service when we had been *'commended to the grace of God for the work...*' (Acts 14:26) had been viewed by many in the church as a farewell service, the perception being that we were emigrating and thus leaving the church completely!

In sharing this, I am not attributing blame in any sense. For one thing, we do have a prayer support group in that church, which to this day continues to pray for us and for the work in a committed way. [49] But we are older and wiser now. We now know that certain principles, however clear they may be to us, do not get through to others by some form of 'spiritual osmosis'. These matters need to be clearly discussed and expectations clarified before a couple goes to the field, or certain misunderstanding and pain will follow! If we can do anything through this book, and this chapter in particular, to save others the pain we (and some dear friends because of us) went through, then that will be reward enough.

This matter of support needs thinking through with the greatest of clarity. Those who feel called to give it need to be aware of what it should involve and what it might cost them in the long haul, just as surely as it behoves the one(s) who go to the field 'to count the cost' of going.

One of the specific 'words' the Lord gave us around the time we were seeking Him concerning the timing and location of our return to the field proved very significant and encouraging in the months and years ahead. It came from a dear friend in that church, who felt the Lord say about the base He was taking us to, that He would 'build a fortress right in the lion's den and it shall be secure as a rock – even in the mouth of the Lion.' Little did she know (as we did) that Singapore actually means 'Lion City' and furthermore that we had already been wondering if that might be the place of God's appointing for us! So you can imagine that word proved to be a very solid confirmation of His guiding. However, the prophetic word went on to indicate that it was going to be tough – although we would 'not be destroyed,' yet we would need to experience God's 'rescue'. In all the preparations, we little thought as to what that was likely to entail. Nor did we forearm ourselves for the fierce spiritual onslaught, which began just as soon as we landed. Within a few short weeks, just about everything we thought had been in place before we arrived (house, office and schooling for the children in particular) had systematically 'unravelled' for us; Ross was finding it impossible to find adequate administrative help in the work and we were trying to do everything while 'camping' with a friend in her apartment. All of us were struggling in different ways, probably the children most of all.

The battles that we experienced should not be understood as being related to Singapore as such. Given the 'ends of the earth' agenda in the Lord's call to move there and (specifically) our commitment to serve China and her Church, the attacks against us doubtless would have happened anywhere, in any country where we might have made our base. Singapore indeed in some senses may have made them more (not less) possible to endure because of the quality of its government and environment. It is an unusually safe and 'green' state.

It is also worth observing that both of us are experienced missionaries. Ross had previously been on the field for ten years, and had travelled extensively. I myself was born in Africa of missionary parents, had grown up with mission as my base parameter and had also spent four years on the field. If we faced this kind of battle, and needed help which we did not find in sufficient quantity, what of those who go with no experience into the 'lion's den'? This really is a serious issue.

Satan's strategy against us at that time, it seems to me, was at least threefold:

- **Firstly**, as I said, he brought wave after wave of attack against us, leaving us wondering how the Lord could be with us if things were going so consistently wrong.

- **Secondly**, he sought to undermine our support structures in all quarters back home, so that we would become too worn down from the lack of encouragement on all sides to stay.

- **Thirdly**, on top of everything else, we battled 'offence' against some of our brethren who we perceived to have drawn back from us when we most needed them, so that our spiritual standing was in danger of being compromised, thus rendering us ineffective. [50] I have to admit that there was one point when Ross was in a minority of one in favour of our staying on the field! I have repented of this since, but I became so desperate in the end, that I actually prayed to **die**, not wanting to dishonour my husband by leaving him and the work, but also not seeing how I and the girls could continue to struggle on. At that point communications back home regarding what we were going through dwindled to almost zero, though Ross had to be in regular 'business' contact. Thus one vital lesson for churches to grasp is that there are times when 'no news' definitely is **not** 'good news'!

There were a few people who did stay in close communication with us, however, during that time. They were the ones who we knew were praying fervently for us and encouraging others to do the same. In a very real sense, I believe we owe it to them that we were able to make it through what was for us an 'evil day' (Ephesians 6:13) and still be standing at the end! May the Lord reward them for their faithfulness to us. While their prayer support was vital, and I shall go into that more below, I believe it was just as much the **moral support** these few dear encouragers gave us that sustained us at that time. These Barnabas folk affirmed us by standing with us in our call and vision. They saw the 'reversals' as the enemy's attack, which it was their responsibility to repulse by prayer. What a difference that made. Slowly but surely we turned the corner, seeing with each setback a new answer from the Lord. Little by little we did become established in the 'lion's mouth'!

Our battle involved, as it always does, much more than personal issues. The base that is now established in Singapore has been responsible for considerable blessing to the Church in China. In retrospect we can see that the enemy was seeking to 'kill' this new phase of the work. If we had given up, there would have been serious loss for China. It may seem harsh, but perhaps it is not too much to say that churches who fail to encourage, or who actively discourage, those who are on the field will have to accept a serious measure of responsibility before God for what may be lost as a result.

On the positive side, Pirolo conveys his challenge to the supporter powerfully when he writes:

'God's call on your life to serve as a sender must be just as vibrant as the call on the life of the one you send.

Likewise the commitment you make must be as sure as that of your cross-cultural worker. The responsible action you take is as important as the ministry your field worker undertakes.

And the reward of souls for God's kingdom will be equal to your missionary's faithfulness and your own.'[51]

If it is done to that standard of excellence, this is no soft option!

We need to look in more detail at the list of support categories Neal Pirolo gives.

1. Moral support – 'just being there'

This might involve anything that a good soccer supporter might give to his team – not the hooligan element that is giving English soccer such a bad name abroad, but the best kind of 'fan' who wants to see his team do well and is there to cheer them on. So, in the same way, it means standing with your missionaries through thick and thin, rooting for them, affirming their call, believing in them, encouraging them to hang on till they see a breakthrough, or whatever the need may be. If you do not feel you can have this attitude and maintain it, then do not volunteer! Missionary endeavour has quite enough cold water poured on it and has no need of more, but there is a great need for those who will encourage.

Be a good listener. Do not jump to conclusions. Believe the best, not the worst, if things seem to be unravelling. Let any advice or criticism come after much contact and attempts to understand what is really going on, bearing in mind that otherwise it can be very hard to accept, leading potentially to offence and a breakdown in the relationship.

Front-line warfare often demands extreme measures and in front-line missions the same will be true. It may involve, for example, the necessity of sending children to boarding school to ensure an adequate education for them. In our experience, very few people who have to entertain this option do so easily or willingly, but only after much agonising. Therefore the home-based Christian needs to be very careful not to condemn what may be the **only option** for staying on the field.

Of all the hard issues missionaries face on the field, almost none can be harder than those involving their children. Some couples have even decided not to have children at all in a missions context, in view of such difficulties. Those who do have families will need to resolve the dilemma of how, after a certain age, to educate them. Should they consider home schooling whilst still on the field, with all the time and effort that will entail and the lack of a peer environment for the children? Should they send them to local schools, with the difficulty that will present later when they have to re-insert into the home culture? Should they trust God for the considerable finances involved in sending them to private international schools? Should they 'bite the bullet' over the boarding option? Or should they even leave the field for a season to put their family first?

Another similar 'hot potato' is what to do about elderly parents back home and how to care for them if they become infirm. If education of children is the toughest issue for families, this is often the 'big one' for single folk, women in particular, who often will feel the onus falls on them in this scenario. It is our observation that God seems to guide people differently on a whole range of such issues. We are trying to learn not to criticise or judge if anyone decides differently from us in any of these areas, and I suggest that anyone who is serious about giving moral support to their missionary on the field needs to do the same.

A few years ago Ross and I had to face a certain amount of misunderstanding with some of those who are concerned for us, when we felt God leading us differently from how He led my parents, who were serving in Africa, in similar circumstances thirty years before. In 1964, my parents received news from my sister that things were not going well with one of my brothers and myself back in the UK. They had vowed before the Lord that if ever they heard that any of us children needed them, they would leave the field immediately and return home, which is exactly what they did. My mother was on the next flight home, while my father worked until he could reasonably be released (about six months later) and then he followed. It was not easy for them but they left the field for a total of five years, during which time they saw us come through much of what we had been struggling with and become more established in our lives. Then they returned to a whole new and exciting sphere of service in Scripture Union in Africa, the most fulfilling time of their lives.

In our case, however, while the issues on the surface might have seemed similar, yet the leading we believed we were receiving from the Lord was not the same. Before we ever had children, Ross received a promise from the Lord, which was that if we continued to follow His leading, He would take care of our children's education. This has been extremely contested over the past few years, but the Lord has been true to His promise and provided in some utterly amazing ways for our family. Moreover, with all the 'roller-coaster' experiences they themselves have had, our children have never asked us permanently to return home, nor have they wanted us to – except perhaps during the early days in Singapore.

'Moral support is the very foundation of the support system,' Pirolo states, and it is 'as much an attitude that your cross-cultural worker will **sense** as an action you can **perform**' (emphasis added). [52] Conveying that the missionary is valued, not a nuisance or a burden, and that his concerns are your concerns could make all the difference in distressing or difficult circumstances. It may even make the difference between success and failure on the field. There have been many examples down through the years to show that this is so.

2. Logistics support – 'all the bits and pieces'

In Neal Pirolo's view, logistics support for the missionary is needed on two distinct levels, which we think should probably be the domain for the overall leader of the group. He should at least have a finger on the pulse in both areas. The first is that of pastoral concern for the missionary's personal circumstances on the field; the second is that of giving practical help for any ongoing needs at home.

Firstly, **pastoral awareness and concern for the situation on the field**. This could involve liasing with the sending agency or host churches regarding living conditions, personal needs, utilising of gifts, family issues, policies regarding education and so forth. It requires great finesse and sensitivity on the part of the person concerned, with the ability to ask the right questions, especially if cultural issues need to be clarified. There is also the area of encouraging spiritual growth by sending Bible teaching tapes, books etc.

A note of caution needs to be sounded at this point. It is very important for all concerned that there should be no confusion as to the nature and role of the Support Team here. I am saying in this chapter that every missionary needs to have a solid group of supporters at home who are rooting for him and helping him in manifold different ways. But that is not to imply that the group has any actual 'authority' to override either the sending agency at home or those in charge on the field. That is why 'finesse and sensitivity' are required, lest supporters are perceived to be 'muscling in' inappropriately in areas that are not their proper concern. We are therefore talking only in 'Barnabas' terms here, as discussed in Chapter 8 – that the missionary should feel cared for and affirmed as he seeks to fulfil his vision and call.[53]

The second area is that of **taking care of practical needs at home**. This will involve dealing with house or apartment letting, taxes, letters, bills, pension or requests for items that need to be sent. While one person should probably be in overall charge, there will definitely be a need to spread the load or it can soon seem too much, however willing one may be. The question of the gifting of the support team is important here. Some people love to take on simple practical tasks, like hunting down a vital car part or computer component, whereas to someone else that would be an enormous pressure! Some folk who love systems, find putting out a regular prayer letter and managing an address database to be easy, whereas others would find it extremely burdensome, however vital it may be.

Depending on the circumstances, it might be necessary for someone (probably again the leader) to have legal power of attorney to manage the missionary's financial affairs. It might also involve someone taking on guardianship for younger children or offering support and a free bed to older ones who are at college or working in the home country (patience and persistence required!). Or again, watching over elderly parents, being the first port of call in an emergency.

Knowing that such things are being taken care of will undoubtedly bring real peace of mind to those on the field. Imagine in your life having to deal with all the daily things you carry – from three thousand miles away, and in duplicate (because you must face them on the field as well as at home). If that is not an argument for support groups, nothing else will be!

Giving logistics support is definitely a time-consuming enterprise and can be burdensome and even annoying, unless the right people are doing it. How any given group might determine to cover these areas will differ widely, but whatever conclusions are reached, they should come up for frequent review. Experience shows that otherwise there are all manner of things the enemy would love to exploit in order to undermine this precious support system. For those at home it can be a feeling of being taken for granted. For those on the field it might be a sense of being considered a burden, which could make them reticent to ask for help even when it is sorely needed. Open and honest communication is required on both sides to avoid such misunderstandings and the offences that might arise from them.

3. Financial support

To this section, Pirolo gives as a sub-heading: 'Money, money, money', but this is one of the few areas where I disagree with him! There are too many folk already who feel that is the nub of the issue for us to reinforce that view! To my mind the primary issue is that of the support people taking financial **responsibility** for their missionary and his/her work. That does not mean that they personally have to 'cough up' the necessary finance, but they should help in ascertaining what funds are needed, then stand with them to see that such an amount is raised. At times this solidarity might be quite radical, as with one group, which decided that until funds could be found to buy a car for their missionary on the field, they would go without using their own cars, managing as best they could with walking and public transport. It certainly gave urgency to their prayers!

It is beyond the scope of this chapter to go into all the facets of what is involved in providing financial support for missionaries. Others have already done an excellent job of presenting this need – see Neal Pirolo's chapter on the subject in *Serving as Senders*. [54] I would also highly recommend both missionaries and their supporters to read *Friend Raising*, by Betty Barnett. [55] Its basic tenet, as the title suggests, is the simple fact that **friendship** lies at the root of the support one is seeking, not just money. My purpose, though, in looking at this subject is a little different. I would like to approach this from the missionary's point of view. As a missionary myself, I have some perceptions that may not be immediately obvious to some who have not lived on the field.

Often a missionary has to raise a certain base level of support – financial and prayer – before he can even go to the field. This can result in a certain guardedness among folk on the receiving end of a missionary sermon, as if the perception is that 'all this person is after is my money'. This in turn can give rise to great awkwardness surrounding the whole issue in the missionary's own mind (or perhaps even more in his wife's) There can be a feeling of guilt about spending money that has been given sacrificially or of being in some way a 'second-class citizen', because one is perceived to be living on hand-outs and does not earn a salary in the normal way. Frequently such a perception can even be reinforced by comments that are made, either deliberately or (often) unthinkingly, by others.

I well remember an incident that lodged with me in a very painful way for years. It was 1980. We had been back from Taiwan for a number of months and it was clear by now that we would not be going immediately back to Asia, so we needed a home. We had been housed to date in a place that was awaiting renovation and was damp, having no heating other than an open coal fire, throughout the UK winter! Our second daughter Hannah was imminently due and we simply could not face a second winter in that house with both a toddler and a tiny baby. Then out of the blue we had the offer of using a home while the owner was out of the country; it was in just the right area and seemed to be the perfect answer. However, when we went to look round the house, I made the mistake of asking if we might move a few of the owner's things to make room for some of our own furniture while we were there. Suddenly the dear sister rounded on me with words that cut me to the quick: 'Beggars can't be choosers,' she snapped, dismissing the subject out of hand. A few days later her unbelieving husband rang us and withdrew the offer, much, I have to say, to our relief, since we could not envisage being able to live under the pressure of that kind of attitude. There was a good end to the story – the Lord had a far better solution for us, which only came to light when this fell through!

'Beggars can't be choosers.' Is that really the perception that missionaries are required to embrace and live with – and to raise their children to accept? Jesus certainly did not say that. In Mark 10:29–30 He states categorically that

> 'There is no one who has left house or brothers or sisters or father or mother or wife or children or lands, for My sake and the gospel's, who shall not receive a hundredfold now in this time ... and in the age to come, eternal life.'

What a promise to depend on! This is no niggardly picture of what missionary living is all about. To be sure there are the 'persecutions' that are also mentioned (verse 30) – there is definitely a price-tag here! – but not a hint of penny-pinching or guilt trips.

The Scriptures encourage us to see 'living by faith' as an adventure of experiencing how many and various are the ways our heavenly Father can use to supply our needs. As someone has put it, it can (at times) be a hand-to-mouth existence – His hand to our mouth! But then even those who earn a pay packet in the normal way should also view that as God's provision for their needs – all we have and are is a gift from Him. That is why I prefer to think in terms of responsibility rather than just of raising finance.

Responsibility in Support Team terms means taking a personal interest in the welfare of the one who is sent out, and in his family, and in the work he is engaged in. It means representing his needs to others, so that he does not always have to do so for himself. It means budgeting for quality family time and taking time to find out if there are special needs or concerns. It means being sensitive to the Holy Spirit on the whole issue of giving and cultivating a generous and imaginative heart to consider how you would feel in those circumstances, if you were in his shoes. It might also mean giving practical help in the whole area of managing finance, so that resources can go further. All these issues and more need to be discussed and prayed over and dealt with openly before the Lord.

Our personal testimony is that God is true to His promise quoted above – it is now over thirty years since Ross embarked on his missionary career and, while there have been some tests along the way, we have never lacked for anything. Indeed the abundance of God's provision has often been embarrassing! But that abundance has frequently put us in a position to help others too, which has been a double blessing.

4. Prayer support – spiritual warfare at its best

This is a huge subject to which I cannot hope to do justice here. We have in any case written on it elsewhere in this book. But the bottom line is this: nothing underlines the team aspect between missionary and support group so much as this area of prayer. And it is, as Pirolo's heading here suggests, a case of real spiritual warfare, with your missionary being, as it were, 'on the front-line'. The more strategic the work he is doing, the more 'dangerous' he will be seen to be by the enemy and the more he, his family and his ministry will be targeted for attack. It is our experience that one can almost 'map' the times when bizarre occurrences are likely to occur, because they generally come at moments of attempted spiritual advance in the work.

The enemy's target in spiritual warfare is always to wound and discourage, so that we cannot press home spiritual advances. His methods are as varied as they are vicious. Your prayers could mean the difference between spiritual break-through and continuing discouragement. There really are times, when prayer being offered up on one's behalf can actually be **felt** as the sudden lifting of spiritual heaviness or the sun breaking through the clouds.

On one occasion my sister, a missionary in Rwanda, Central Africa, rang me in England during a time when she and my mother were both feeling under particular attack with all sorts of things going wrong. Mostly these were things of a practical nature – computer problems, electricity failure and other difficulties on top of work and relational pressures. We all know how stressful times like that are even in our own home environment. 'Who is actually praying for us at the moment?' she asked. I quickly rang round their support group, explaining the need.

The next day she sent me the following in a fax:

> 'What a difference it makes to know people are praying! On the way back from Kigali yesterday, I commented that I felt a lightness of the spirit that I had not had for several days. And yesterday was a fantastic day...'

She went on to describe how all the things that we had requested prayer for had been answered. Being interceded for really does make that tangible a difference. It is not that the set-backs or problems necessarily evaporate, but there seems to be a 'bubble' around you, making them not seem so bad!

Of course, the onus in this respect is just as much on the missionary, who must take responsibility for keeping a flow of information going regarding his/her prayer needs – not forgetting to share the encouragement of answers to prayer. We have adopted a catch-phrase, which helps us to keep this focus: 'Information breeds intercession'. If we want folk to pray for us with insight, then it is up to us to keep them informed. That is the almost universal rule, though there are some exceptional intercessors, who do not need that flow of information quite so much.

During that period of blackness mentioned above, when I found it so hard to think of sharing much with anyone back home, one of the intercessors in the UK would telephone us in Singapore from time to time. Because of her intercession, she could actually tell me what I was going through, since she was experiencing it as well – vicariously, as it were, in prayer. But that is the exception rather than the rule. It is more normative for folk to be inspired to pray by the details we furnish in our updates and newsletters. Gradually a picture can be built up in this way of how things are on the field. Thus also the supporters get to know the national and mission co-workers and colleagues by name, so as to pray for them. There is something very heart-warming for a missionary when those who pray ask for the latest on so-and-so, indicating that they really have been following the situation as it has developed on the field. Conversely there is no greater 'give-away' than a revelation of total ignorance about even the most basic details of the missionary's life on the field!

While there are the general intercessors supporting the work, the main role of the support group members should be to take on board the more confidential prayer requests, which cannot really be shared with the wider public. For example, concerns to do with the family, struggles with the work or perhaps with colleagues (being careful not to break confidence), sensitive and personal matters, possible future plans and so on. Along with the moral support mentioned above, it is vitally import-ant to know that these issues will be prayed through with a passion and answers earnestly sought for on one's behalf. How blessed are those missionaries who have folk they can depend on in that way. There is no power on earth that can match what is available to us at the Throne of Grace. Intercessory prayer is the God-ordained channel for bringing that power to bear.

5. Communication support – letters, tapes and more

This whole area is of course closely linked to all the other aspects of support we might care to mention, since without good communication going on, the whole support system breaks down. No one who has not 'been there' can fully understand what getting a letter or a packet from home means to those on the field. Before the onset of email communica-tion, letters were (and in some places still are) the vital link with home, and a visit to the post office to collect mail can be an exciting (or sadly all too often a disappointing) daily ritual. Of course it is a two-way street – even our youngest daughter knows that! She adopted a game-plan early on in her Indian boarding school career that she would write lots of letters, in order to have a good chance of receiving lots! Boarding school as a child and a year abroad in Germany as a student taught me that same lesson too, long before I went to the mission field. Yet busyness and pressure can militate against the practice of good letter-writing, which is why for many of us the potential of email is so wonderful.

We all know that it takes discipline to keep good communication going. Personally, in the press of day-to-day living, I find letters hard to write and even harder to post! One approach that can be helpful in this, is to leave stamped and addressed envelopes on the notice board or stuck to the family fridge, ready for anyone to use who has the time to write a letter and send it off – while in the meantime serving as a reminder to pray. I remember being impressed by the example of one pastor's wife, who would hand out aerogrammes to members of the congregation as they came into church on a Sunday morning. She had already put the name and address of the church's missionaries on the front and put that week's date at the top, to ensure that different folk each week were taking responsibility to communicate with the missionaries abroad.

Equally, if it is your assigned role to pray for your missionary, you should be expecting God to give you words of encouragement or scriptures that might be pertinent to their situation as you pray. If you receive anything like that, do you write and share it? It could be a life-line to them! It would also without doubt deepen the bond between you and those on the field with whom you connect in this way, as they appreciate the care you have taken to share the burdens with them.

Other suggestions might be to send out the weekly church bulletins, tape of the month, wedding cake, photos – anything to help keep him/her up to date with what is happening back home, thus counteracting the 'bath-tub syndrome' and making re-entry easier. You could also do the same in reverse towards the congregation – ask for space to print an extract from a prayer letter in the church bulletin, then advertise that the full letter is available to anyone who is interested. 'Gossip' their news around church to keep their issues alive – especially in the mind of the pastor and leaders. If your church has an email chain, be sure to put out any (non-confidential) emergency items for prayer, being careful also to inform of the answers when they come.

6. Re-entry support

Every missionary knows about and should be, to some extent, prepared to face the culture shock one encounters on going to the field. But how about 'reverse culture shock', which many experience without being prepared for it, on their return to the home country? This is another 'danger point' in the missions experience, parallel to the bottom-of-the-bath-tub one mentioned above. This is when horror stories can occur – contemplated suicides, breakdowns and loss of faith amongst returnee missionaries who feel at odds with life away from the field and with their reception back home. There is, it is true, an increased awareness nowadays of the problems involved in re-entering one's own culture after sometimes years of being away. Whole books are being written and courses are being run on the subject and more and more sending agencies are incorporating a 'debriefing' element into their approach for missionaries both on and off the field. [56]

It is perceived these days that preparation for re-entry is needed and ideally should be started before the returnee leaves the field and should be continued on his return, with feedback being given to the local church for 'debriefing' to continue there. That is the point at which the support group needs to become intimately involved, as the ones who are primarily concerned to walk the returning missionary and his family through any 'matters arising' from the missions experience. They need to anticipate some problems and be on hand with affirmation and understanding, seasoned with a little challenge if need be. They need themselves to have read some of the very helpful books that are now available on the subject of re-entry stress, so as to be armed with insights for the occasion. An example would be *Re-Entry*, by Peter Jordan. [57] Or a chapter in the more erudite *Overcoming Missionary Stress*, by Marjory F. Foyle. [58]

The underlying causes of difficulty for returning missionaries are not hard to find, but it requires time and effort to recognise the signs of impending trouble and take steps to avoid it. Among such causes one could mention the following:

- Everything has changed – the missionary himself by what he has been through; the others he knew, who have adjusted to his absence and moved on.

- Unfamiliarity with what others are so used to and take for granted (for example, hypermarkets, the internet).

- A sense of not belonging any more and maybe even not wanting to belong, because values in the local church no longer sit easily. A constant comparing with life 'over there' is standard. There is also the contrast of feeling useful and appreciated over there, but useless and not understood over here.

- There may be a sense of guilt at leaving the field at all when the needs are so great; anger with the indifference of folk over here; wanting to talk about what one has seen and been through all the time, which can exacerbate the problem of others not receiving what is said.

The support group needs to be alert and watch for signs and 'be there' to listen and encourage. Also to pray for the returnees – and with them. The manner in which they are received back (compare Paul and Barnabas at Antioch in Acts 14:21–28) will determine very much how they cope with the re-entry experience.

If the return is permanent and there is no intention to return abroad, then it will be an issue of helping them reintegrate back into the home environment. There may have been difficult circumstances surrounding the return, so professional help or counselling may also need to be sought. On the other hand, if the missionaries' return is just for a few weeks of furlough, then they need to be refreshed or re-tooled for further service overseas.

In the latter case, the support group will need to monitor the balance between rest, time with family and friends and 'deputation' (going on a preaching tour to represent the ministry) very carefully. The tendency will often be to try and cram in as many speaking opportunities as possible in order to maximise the usefulness of the time at home. It has always been the case that missionaries have been expected to go on deputation during a period of furlough. However, it needs to be borne in mind, that in the old days before the arrival of the jet age, missionaries used to get the rest they needed on leaving the field during the voyage home by sea, which was often weeks if not months in duration. In that time there would be little else to do but eat, rest, read, talk things through and pray about burdens and concerns. That meant that, as soon as they docked in the home country, the missionaries would be quite ready for the challenge of rushing round visiting relatives and/or supporting churches. Nowadays, however, that space for 'R & R' has to be planned for deliberately and ruthlessly, or there may be serious consequences. Getting ready to leave the field, packing up and tying up the details for cover during one's absence can be extremely exhausting. Add to that the disorientation of jet-lag and the confusion of 're-entry' and there is the potential for serious trouble – unless there is care and attention given to the need to 'recharge the batteries' on one's return.

In considering the difficulties potentially faced by adult missionaries at this time, it is imperative not to forget the children, whose 'issues' will not necessarily be the same as those of their parents. If anything they are likely to be even more acute. Remember, the adults have taken part in the cross-cultural experience voluntarily, whereas that is not always the case for the children, depending on their age and spiritual standing. Nor are they as equipped psychologically to handle negative emotions and experiences. Again, there is a generally recognised phenomenon at work here, where kids no longer feel a part of the home culture in consequence of the time they have been away. Yet nor do they feel they 'belong' to the host culture (the people their parents are working with 'on the field') because they look and speak differently, and also for a variety of other reasons. So they tend to feel at odds with both worlds and therefore to gravitate towards others who have had the same 'rootless' existence, forming a kind of 'third culture' amongst themselves. These Third Culture Kids have certain recognisable qualities such as adaptability and love of travel and adventure. But on the negative side, there is a tendency to feel like an oddball or a misfit, especially in the home or sending culture environment.

I well remember returning to England in 1963 just after Beatle Mania hit the scene and being utterly bemused by the screaming and swooning of girls of my age at the sight of the 'fab four'. I remember despising myself for being such a green-horn and not knowing what anything was about and then being angry with my parents and with God for that! In fact my prevailing memory of that period is that of feeling angry and 'out of it' most of the time. You might ask whether that kind of emotion is not shared by most early teen-age kids. It is, but missionary kids have the added burden of feeling utterly different from their peers and of knowing that, however much they try to adapt, that difference may never be erased. Later, when I was soundly converted and reconciled, not only with God and my parents but also with my past, I came to see many of those difficulties in a positive light – as a preparation for my future life, for one thing. But at the time, my anguish was acute!

In order to support young people who are going through re-entry stress, parents and friends need to allow for feelings like this, not denying or minimising them, but helping them to understand why they feel as they do. It may also be necessary to forewarn the school they will be attending, especially if there are likely to be any special needs or gaps in knowledge due to the curriculum they have been studying. Anything that emphasises their difference from others and makes them stand out in any way will be a cause of real pain, especially at the beginning.

All this will, of course, be even worse, if they have had to return to the home culture on their own to continue their education. Sensitive support from family friends will be even more vitally necessary in this situation. And it is no good leaving the ball in their court, to get in touch or 'come round any time you want'. They will never do that, however much they may long to. They need you to take the initiative towards them, to collect them for a meal at your home or include them in a week-end away with the family or for a shopping trip. It may be necessary to persevere through reluctance on their part – teenagers in particular are highly allergic to being considered a 'Billy-No-Mates' who needs befriending! However, if you can provide a genuinely safe environment for them at such a vulnerable stage in their life, you will have performed a major service to your missionary friends, their parents.

In conclusion

If we are convinced that the role of sending and supporting is as vital as that of going to the mission field, then much needs to change! Yet is it really that impossible to achieve? Another way of looking at the nine-to-one ratio of senders to missionaries on the field, is to observe that actually it **only** takes nine in support for one on the field. If churches embraced a specific policy both to release workers and to involve their members, think how many more full-timers could be released, both at home and overseas. If there could just be more senders raised up to be as committed to the task as those whom they are sending, then the challenge that faces us in world missions would become much less daunting.

So often Ross and I, as we travel and share widely about mission today, meet folk who need the help that has been outlined in this chapter. If this book is used by God to help to raise up an army (nine for every one on the field) of Christians in support groups, who then go on to live it out, what a change we would see in the work of mission in our generation.

Lord, let it be so.

Chapter 14

A Message for the Church?

'People need targets, goals, aims – visions. Otherwise they become lackadaisical, lazy, complacent, parochial and ineffective. Christians are no exceptions.'
(Malcolm Widdecombe, in *Ten Sending Churches*, edited by Michael Griffiths) [59]

'How can we, as a church, release more and more resources into the harvest fields of the world?'
(Jim Graham, in the same book)

In the last few chapters we have been dealing with a challenge to the individual Christian. The fulfilment of the ends-of-the-earth mandate is within our grasp if only all who name the Name of Christ, every Christian in every church, would involve themselves in at least one of the ways that have been outlined. Then we really could reach the nations (each individual *ethnos*) with the gospel. Of course, not everyone will 'go' (as we have seen, it takes at least nine to send one), but many more could and should.

The vital key to achieving that mobilisation is the envisioning of the local pastor for the task. He is the one who can inspire his people for the lost world around us. Yet sometimes his leadership can become the bottleneck that hinders the people from becoming involved. As much as any man on the face of the earth, the local pastor needs to embrace the Antioch Factor. The reality is that the dynamics of the Antioch church must be worked out specifically in the local church, not just outside of it. I have personally functioned in both roles – as a local church pastor and as a missionary and mission leader. I am convinced that the Antioch Factor applies to me equally in both roles.

This chapter will draw from the experience and writings of a man who was impacted by the message of Antioch in the book of Acts when he was serving as a local pastor. Kevin Conner is much more than a local pastor. He is an internationally recognised teacher of the Scriptures and a senior elder in the Church of Jesus Christ. He is now in his seventies. But the point at issue is that when God spoke to him in the way outlined in this chapter, his primary role was that of a pastor in a local church.

I first met Kevin Conner around the time that the Lord spoke to him in the manner described below. As we shared spontaneously about Antioch and Jerusalem, it became clear to us that we had both reached the same conclusions in our study of the Word of God. It was a strong encouragement to me, given Kevin's senior standing in the Body of Christ. It may even be that I am included in his comments below, when he speaks of 'various visiting ministries' through whom 'God clearly confirmed the call on the Church to be "as the Church at Antioch"'! Our backgrounds are totally different, but in separate continents and in quite different ministry roles, the Lord had spoken to us both regarding the heart of the Antioch message.

More than a decade ago, the Lord spoke to Conner in the following way:

> 'In 1989, October 14th, San Antonio, Texas, U.S.A., the word of the Lord came expressly by the Spirit, to the heart and mind of the writer, who was, at that time, the Senior Minister of his home church – Waverley Christian Fellowship (Melbourne, Australia). The word of the Lord said:
>
>> "Waverley Christian Fellowship is to maintain the foundation principles laid down in the church at Jerusalem, but not to allow the spirit and attitude that crept into the church at Jerusalem to get into Waverley. Waverley Christian Fellowship is called to be like the church at Antioch."
>
> During a time of prayer, the word of the Lord came specifically and clearly to [my] heart and mind concerning

[my] home church. The Holy Spirit impressed very clearly
the word . . . The word of the Lord to my heart caused me to
do some serious study of the whole matter of Jerusalem and
Antioch, as found in the Book of Acts . . . Through various
visiting ministries, over several following years, God clearly
confirmed the call on the church to be "as the church at
Antioch". Because truth is truth in every generation, what
was truth then is truth now. General truth applicable to the
church at Antioch is truth that may be applied to any
church that is called to be "an Antioch church". Even
though the things written here were quickened by the
Spirit to the writer, and then applied to his home church,
the writer believes that the principles here will be helpful to
any local church . . . in order that there will be many other
"Antioch churches", and they will be strengthened and
encouraged by the same principles set out here. May the
vision of "an Antioch church" grip the hearts of all who
read is the writer's desire and prayer.' [60]

Conner lists in his book the merits of the Jerusalem church.
It is important to bear in mind (as we have observed earlier)
that the Jerusalem church was not a failure. It was a significant,
successful and God-anointed gathering of believers. Its experience of the presence and power of God, its outworking of
Christian community life, and its explosive evangelistic
outreach into its local area probably exceeded that of any
church on earth in our day. Previous chapters have outlined its
exceptional and rapid growth, with literally thousands being
saved and drawn into the Body of Christ. Of the merits of the
church at Jerusalem Conner comments:

'This was the church at Jerusalem. It was the first, the
original church, and here the foundational principles
were laid out for all other churches to follow and maintain (Acts 8:1; 11:22). By these things believers were added
to the Lord, and added to the church, and became
committed members. Such things in God's mind have
never changed.
    Every church that claims to be, or desires to be, a New
Testament church, should have – must have – these

things that were laid down in the original church, the church at Jerusalem, and seek to build thereupon (1 Corinthians 3:9b–15; Ephesians 2:19–22).'

Conner's brief summary is designed to show that the church at Jerusalem was a highly successful model of church life. It was in so many senses experiencing almost everything that the Lord desires to bestow on His Church, and as such should be seen as a model for us today. It is worth recalling the first half of the word that the Lord gave him:

'Waverley Christian Fellowship is to maintain the foundation principles laid down in the church at Jerusalem...'

Jerusalem was and is worth emulating in many ways. For that reason, many today draw from its excellence and seek to experience it again. That is right and godly. Those, like Kevin and myself, who have embraced the Antioch Factor do not deny Jerusalem's excellence. Rather, our observation is that in all its excellence Jerusalem failed to incorporate one major element of the instructions of Jesus, and in so doing, lost the position of prominence (to Antioch) that its quality in many ways rightly merited.

Conner contrasts the positives of Jerusalem with its negatives in the following manner:

'The word of the Lord to the writer continued: "...do not allow the spirit and attitude that crept into the church at Jerusalem to get into Waverley Christian Fellowship..." What was the spirit and attitude that came into the church at Jerusalem and caused its decline from that early glory? Basically, this is seen to be fourfold. It seemed to take place over a period of about ten to twelve years. Such caused the presence and glory of the Lord to decline and thus His purposes moved on to the Church at Antioch.'[61]

Conner then outlines what those 'fourfold' elements were, that crept in and caused Jerusalem to miss a significant part of the purposes of God for their church. They are listed here because of their relevance to our modern local church situations, not the least to those readers who have leadership responsibilities in that sphere. The material below is derived from Conner's book:

1. **A Judaistic spirit.** A spirit of legalism and bondage to external rites of the Mosaic Law crept into the Jerusalem church. Certain of the Pharisees and Judaistic teachers of the Law began to enforce on the Gentile believers that they needed to be circumcised and keep the Sabbath and Jewish food laws in order to be properly initiated ... The Judaizers followed Paul everywhere he went, seeking to bring the Gentile converts into bondage to externals of the Law in order to be saved. They were Paul's greatest enemies ... All Churches have to beware of that spirit of legalism in all of its subtle forms – not adding anything to the simple gospel as the only means of salvation and acceptance before God.

2. **A spirit of centralisation.** Another of the problems of the church at Jerusalem was centralisation. They wanted to stay in Jerusalem instead of spreading the Gospel to Judea, Samaria and the uttermost parts of the earth, as the Lord had commanded (Matthew 28:18–20; Mark 16:15–20; Acts 1:8).

   This is a repeated pattern in Church history and with revival movements. Many movements set up their 'Jerusalem', and have a centralised eldership, centralised leadership and control, or centralised tithing and financial system, and a centralised form of government. God often allows persecution, pressures from without and within and trouble to come, in order to scatter the Gospel seed. It is the principle of Proverbs 11:24 at work: 'There is one who scatters, yet increases more ... ' God scattered the Church to increase it!

   All Churches have to beware of the spirit of centralisation. God wants to multiply the Church and scatter the good seed of the kingdom throughout the earth. He began this at Jerusalem, until they wanted to keep the seed 'in the barn' (Haggai 2:19).

3. **A sectarian spirit.** Acts Chapters 10–11 provide the account of Peter being sent to minister the Gospel to

the Gentiles. It shows how the Lord had to deal with an attitude in the heart of Peter. The Lord granted Peter a vision of the Gentiles coming into the New Covenant. He went in obedience to the vision. Even though Peter preached the Gospel to the Gentiles, it is evident that initially he had no intention of baptising them in water into the Lord's Church.

Sectarian, nationalistic, racist – that was the Jew's attitude to the Gentiles, even in the early Church. They had, as yet, no revelation of 'one body' in Christ (1 Corinthians 12:13); no understanding that the 'middle wall of partition' had been brought down by the cross (Ephesians 2:12–22). All churches must beware of a spirit of sectarianism. It is a work of the flesh.

4. **A spirit of pride.** Over the years, that 'Jerusalem-city' spirit affected also the church at Jerusalem. 'We are the first Church, the original ones to whom the Spirit and the Word came in the first Pentecost'. It is worthy of note that most movements of God eventually decline and set themselves up with the same prideful attitude of the 'Jerusalem-only' spirit. Here (in Conner's words) it manifested in a fourfold manner:

    - *Pride of place* – Jerusalem became a place of pride instead of humility.

    - *Pride of race* – Jewish nationalism was lifted up above the Gentiles.

    - *Pride of face* –The Judaizers sought to 'save face' before the Gentiles.

    - *Pride of grace* – The grace of God was perverted into legalism.

    All local churches must beware of any spirit of pride, or the setting up of their own 'Jerusalem'. Our Jerusalem is above. Pride goes before destruction and a haughty spirit before a fall (Proverbs 16:18). This spirit and attitude must be dealt with at the cross of Christ's humility. [62]

Conner summarises his writings on the church of Jerusalem as follows:

'The Lord showed the writer clearly that the foundation principles laid down in the church at Jerusalem must be maintained, but the spirit and attitude that crept into the church at Jerusalem must not creep into any local church. Otherwise, that church will decline as other churches have over the years, and as the church at Jerusalem declined. These are the lessons one learns from a study of the church at Jerusalem.'[63]

He then also lists the values of the Antioch church, which need not be outlined here, because they have been widely covered in previous chapters. He summarises his general comments on the Antioch church in this way:

'Hence we see the importance of the church at Antioch in the purposes of God. Antioch becomes the great Gentile Missionary church, out of which the Gospel went forth under apostolic teams. Then, from Jerusalem to Rome, Paul went in the purposes of God, as the apostle to the Gentiles and the church planter of that period of time. A church that desires to be "an Antioch church" will have the same evangelistic and missionary burden ... It is the burden of the Lord in the Great Commission. "Make disciples of all nations, and teach them to observe all the things I have commanded you" (Matthew 28:18–20; Mark 16:15–20; Luke 24:47–49; John 21:15–17).

This is "the vision of an Antioch church!" It is a church that maintains the foundational principles laid down in the church at Jerusalem, but does not allow the spirit and attitude that crept into Jerusalem to get into it. It is indeed a church like the church at Antioch!'[64]

The scene we live in now is very different from the one that existed in the first century. When Antioch began to obey the ends-of-the-earth mandate, there were no other churches or movements that we know of doing the same thing. Paul was the pioneer. Everywhere he went was 'virgin territory' for the gospel. Indeed he made it his ambition to keep moving to the 'regions beyond' (2 Corinthians 10:16; Romans 15:20), so as not to build on another man's foundation. In his day that was appropriate and in keeping with his calling as the 'apostle to the Gentiles'.

Now however, two millennia later, the picture is quite different. Most parts of the world have seen centuries of missionary endeavour of one sort or another. There is a proliferation of denominations, groups and splinter-groups, not to mention outright sects, that make the contemporary scene a very difficult one. Surely the very last thing that is needed in this context is more groups going out to 'do their own thing'. We need to think very carefully before applying Paul's church-planting pattern too simplistically in our generation.

Of powerful relevance to our situation today is Paul's teaching in 1 Corinthians 3 concerning the 'carnality' of divisions and the need for all who work in 'God's field' to labour together. One strategic key, then, in our generation is that of unity and co-operation or, in our modern parlance, 'networking'. Networking must focus on two core areas – church working together with church; and church working together with 'para-church'. There must only be one aim – the extension of the kingdom of the Lord Jesus Christ.

But what are we more likely to find, especially it seems amongst local churches or movements that have adopted an 'Antioch vision'? Sadly it is all too common for this to mean that some go out to replicate themselves overseas, without co-operation with or even **reference** to others who may already be working in the same field. The emphasis is on church planting, often in the church's own image and even under its own name. Thus a growing church in the USA, or Australia, or Singapore, or Korea, may go out into different nations to plant churches almost in competition with other churches. The atmosphere can become like that of a multi-national corporation, hastening to extend its own influence in the nations before other rival companies can claim that territory.

I am convinced that that approach is the Jerusalem model, not the Antioch one. In reality, amidst some success, there has been much that brings dishonour to the Name of Christ. I have seen two big churches from the same Asian city both working in another country, yet fighting over territory to plant churches in their own image. Is that really Christianity? I have missionary friends who have been obliged to leave their denomination, because they were not being permitted to co-operate with other groups who are working with the same minority people as they are in a foreign land. Is that really pleasing to God? I am aware of a special and anointed couple, working in a hard but potentially fruitful place, who were in danger of being pulled back 'home'. The reason? They are not planting enough churches each year to fit the church-planting schema of their excellent sending church. I have seen much else in the Jerusalem mould that convinces me that this is not the way. Church must work with church.

Again, if the local church is to engage in world missions, the artificial division that is being created in some quarters between local church and para-church must be removed. There must therefore be a desire to 'network', not to compete with others who are already active in that field. There must be a demonstration of servanthood and co-operation, which to me is the very essence of the 'spirit of Antioch'. Are we as followers of the Lord in our generation willing first of all to take our hands off and release our people to God's deployment in the mission field? Recently someone said of Acts 13: 'It is the responsibility of the church to send its people forth, but it is the prerogative of the Holy Spirit to send them out!' In other words churches, in response to God's prompting and leading, should be willing to release their people for foreign service, but should not demand the right to control or 'own' what they do when they get there. That is the domain of the Holy Spirit and His alone.

Some major churches today refuse to work with para-church organisations – such as missionary societies. They say that such entities are not to be found in the Bible. I would invite such pastors to answer me a simple question. Was Paul 'local church' or 'para-church'. If he was 'local church', which church did he belong to when he went out on his missionary journeys – not just the first two journeys, but all three of them? An honest look at the Bible will show that Paul was para-church (in today's harsh and unbiblical categorisation), not local church. Yet the reality is that none in the Scriptures, apart from the Lord Himself, loved the Church more, or understood it as deeply, as Paul. He would have rejected such an unnatural division, seeing that some were local, some were apostolic (or translocal), but that all were expressions of the same one Church of Jesus Christ. How careful we need to be to go to the bar of Scripture, allowing it to judge us rather than using it to justify our activities.

Practically, then, when people come forward to offer themselves to be sent to a foreign field, the local church leadership has the responsibility to ascertain their gifts and help them, under God's leading, to find a context in which they may be used. They should also ensure that proper support is in place, as outlined in the last chapter. It is not necessary to 'reinvent the wheel' here. There are missionary societies and para-church groups across the globe which are a collective resource that should not be ignored. Most of them have carefully devised procedures for selection, training and placing of candidates, which have been honed out of decades of experience in their fields of service. They have gained a wealth of understanding in cultural and linguistic matters, which simply cannot be instantaneously acquired by new people coming in. Equally, they mostly have good rapport with existing churches and local groups. Working with groups of this kind usually makes the best sense. Even in so-called 'closed' countries, such as China or certain Islamic nations, there are groups which are active in placing people in strategic places as 'tentmakers'. [65] They also have networks in place for giving pastoral oversight that may not always be possible for the church back home to offer.

I am aware that there are horror stories about missionary societies – failure to keep up with the times, to offer real pastoral support, to understand the needs and callings of the individual and so on. But for every one of those there are horror stories about the costly mistakes made by local churches in their sometimes untutored ventures into mission. My plea is that we avoid stereotypes and begin to work together. How often do we as believers 'prove' our way of doing things by using extreme examples to denigrate those we do not want to work with. May God help us to build each other up, not to dismiss and reject the help that we can be to one another.

I am writing the final words of this chapter in Beijing, China. Last night I sat with a local pastor who has responsibility for several hundred churches, and about the same number of workers. He spoke of places in China that pleaded for him to come and help – many churches that have already been planted, but which do not have anyone to help. He welcomed the group that I was with to come and help in any way we could. He himself described how one church, many miles from his home town, had pleaded with him to come, and then had walked miles and miles with him as he left, rather like Paul and the Ephesian elders in Acts 20:37–38, unwilling to let him go.

How wrong it is for us to assume that we need to church plant in such situations. The only thing that his teams of zealous young preachers know how to do is to church plant, and they are doing that to great effect! They ache not for church planters, but for others to come alongside them and to help the young churches that already exist.

Of course there are many areas in China that are not yet reached, and which need church planters. But it is my experience that the Chinese believers are aware of that, and many will lay down their lives for it. Indeed the Chinese brother I am referring to defined his group's aim (in Eastern China) as being that of taking the Gospel back to Jerusalem. That means they would have to work through both the unreached parts of Western China, and then the Muslim lands of the Middle East, before they could reach Jerusalem.

Again, that Chinese model is not relevant to some other lands, where there may be no indigenous churches, or none strong enough to do that work. There church planting from outside – if it is kingdom and networking church planting – is urgently needed. But the cry in my heart, as I listened to this man who even recently has faced arrest, and yet presses on, was a simple one: 'Lord, let every local pastor hear what I am hearing from this Chinese leader, a message I have heard so often – that we might lay down our small empires and give all for Your kingdom, not to rule, but to serve such men and women of God.'

The challenge of this book, of the Antioch Factor, is then applicable to every church, to every local leader. That includes not just the challenge of world missions, but also the way in which we go about that global task. Is it for local church empire or for His kingdom? They are not the same.

If the Antioch Factor is indeed the 'hidden message of the book of Acts', that does not mean it has not yet been revealed by God. It means it is hidden in the sense it has not yet been fully embraced, as it was not embraced by the Jerusalem church. It can be seen, but only by those with a heart to press through to obey all the revealed word of God, including Matthew 28:18–20 and Acts 1:8. May God multiply the Kevin Conners, those who have a heart to be local pastors of churches which not only have the foundations of Jerusalem, but also the 'vision' and the 'spirit' of Antioch.

Chapter 15

The Final Word

Margery Sykes was an Antioch person. I first met her in Taiwan in 1969. I was young, a new missionary worker there. She was an older missionary. She had worked in China, but only briefly – she was amongst the many who were expelled in the late 1940s and early 1950s, after the Communists came into power. Like many fellow missionaries, she had gone to Taiwan, which was one place that offered an open door, under God's leading, to serve the Lord and the Chinese people. But unlike many of them, she did not stay in the big cities. She went to work in the countryside.

Margery settled in a town called Tou-Cheng, which was not a great deal more than a group of houses around a railway on the east coast line in Taiwan. But Tou-Cheng had a poly-technic college. There Margery set to work. Eventually, a church was established as she saw some of the young students from the college and others from the town begin to come to the Lord.

She lived simply. I once fell partially through the wooden floor of her house (it was an old Japanese house and the wood left a little to be desired in places). A friend and I also killed 50 cockroaches in one weekend there, along with some choice spiders – of varied shapes and sizes! But let me not dwell on that.

After a number of years, Margery contracted cancer. There was a battle, a temporary remission, then a further battle. Then she went to be with the Lord.

In some ways, therefore, her life could be seen as a good and godly one, but one that was something of a failure, in part at least. She was after all sadly hindered by the inability to work in China and the work was cut short by her premature death – I think she was in her fifties. But history will not see Margery as a failure, neither do I. I am absolutely convinced that God does not, either.

Those young men and women in whom Margery had invested her life caught her vision. One, David Chen, took over the church in Tou-Cheng. He is still pastoring that church thirty years later. Now, years later at the start of a new century, directly out of Margery's work and that of the successive generations of workers in the church, there are as many as thirty full-time Christian workers serving the Lord. Thirty servants of God have emerged from her labours in a small town in Taiwan.

But there is more. Two of them, Peter and John, visited me in Singapore recently. They have a huge burden for young people's work in China. There is very little material for children there – it is still technically illegal under the Communist regime to preach Jesus to those under eighteen. So they are preparing an eight-volume curriculum of Sunday school materials. The first volume, which they showed me, is already several hundred pages long! When that is completed, they will set up a comprehensive programme which will train believers in China in the use of the materials, to help them lead children to Christ and build those children up in their faith. The material is also being put on to VCD, so that the Chinese believers can see how it should be used, and then use it themselves. Then it will be broadcast into China by radio.

God has been faithful to Margery, because she was faithful to His command to go to the ends of the earth. I have not been back to Tou-Cheng for more than thirty years, and I am sure it has changed greatly. To describe it as 'the ends of the earth' during Margery's lifetime would have been an exaggeration, but not by too much! Yet out of that place not only are there thirty full-time workers, but their labours are spilling back into China, the land from which she was removed. What a magnificent divine irony! She began working with a few young people in a small town. But now millions of young people right across China, the land of her first call, will be reached with the good news about Jesus through the fruit of her work.

Paul expressed it so accurately when writing to the Corinthian church:

> *'Therefore, my beloved brethren, be steadfast, immovable, always abounding in the work of the Lord, knowing that your labour is not in vain in the Lord.'*   (1 Corinthians 15:58)

What an encouragement to increase our labours for Jesus and for the nations. Those labours, according to His immutable promise, will never be in vain in the Lord. What an incentive to lay down our lives for Him, to obey Him in the Tou-Cheng of His calling, and to prove His faithfulness for years to come!

Margery Sykes was an ordinary lady. There was no queue to take her picture or write articles about her. Whatever the people of Tou-Cheng thought about her, the phrase 'Hollywood superstar' would not have come to mind! But she changed lives, caused workers to be raised up for the kingdom, and is still bringing change into many lives through the fruits of her labours – long after her death.

The message of this book is a simple one – that the path that Margery trod is open today to any who will hear the voice of Jesus, just as it was open to the early disciples of Jesus. It is for 'Margery people', ordinary people, who hear God and get up and go.

Many of us hesitate at that gate. So did the disciples of Jesus. There is a powerful illustration of their struggles – and ours – in Matthew 14. To do what Margery did, I believe we need to hear a word from the Lord:

> *'But Jesus said to them, "They do not need to go away. You give them something to eat."'*   (Matthew 14:16)

In that chapter, the disciples, tired after a long day with Jesus as He healed the sick and ministered to a huge crowd, became alarmingly aware of a threatening crisis. There were at least 15,000 people in the crowd – verse 21 says that there were five thousand men, besides the women and children. They were far from home or anywhere where they might eat. The disciples were concerned about the situation as they considered it, because it was quite possible that they would have to do something about it. So they came up with a simple solution:

> '*When it was evening, His disciples came to Him, saying, "This is a deserted place, and the hour is already late. Send the multitudes away, that they may go into the villages and buy themselves food."*'
> (Matthew 14:15)

It was logical. The people should take care of themselves. If they did that, if the responsibility could be pushed back to them, the disciples would not have to face this impossible task of feeding so many people in the wilderness.

But Jesus rebuked them with the direct instruction recorded above: '*They do not need to go away. You give them something to eat.*'

Jesus wanted His disciples to take responsibility for the needs of the multitude. The people did not need to go away and work something out for themselves. That conflict between Jesus and His Church is at the heart of today's battle, as the Church considers – or does not consider – its responsibility to the nations of the world. In effect, though in much more subtle ways, we are often saying that the lost should be sent away, that they should be left to sort out their own problems. It may be hard for us to accept, but the reality is that if we do not go or serve actively as senders, so that others can go, then that is what we are saying.

It may be that the disciples simply wanted to ignore the crowd, because they felt they had nothing to give to them. It was just too much – too many people, too much bread required, too high a mountain to climb. Indeed in verse 17, the text suggests that that was very much in their hearts.

> '*And they said to Him, "We have here only five loaves and two fish."*'
> (Matthew 14:17)

Even if they did respond, what difference would that pitiful supply of bread and fish make? Even if they did begin to feel the compassion of God for the crowd, what was the point? The need so much exceeded their supply. Better perhaps not to begin than to begin and fail to complete the task, offering something and then failing to deliver.

Churches can be like that today. It is not that we do not care for the needs of the world, but that we have so little to offer, as we see it. We consider the vast problems. Sometimes, on the physical level, the television news report of famine and desperate need merely serve to numb us into inactivity by the sheer scope of the problem. The issues they raise are so massive that we would not even know where to begin. We look also at the social needs of the nations, including our own, and the whole problem seems so huge, so intractable. We see the massive spiritual needs of the Muslim world, for example, and we are overwhelmed. Therefore we do nothing.

Jesus answers that attitude specifically in this miracle. He gives four specific instructions to the disciples.

Firstly, in verse 18, He says:

'Bring them here to Me.'

That place is where we begin. It is a place of surrender to the Lord. The opposite of surrender is control. Jerusalem controlled – not all the time, but in some of its key responses. One element of the challenge that this book brings us is to help us reach a simple conclusion: Jesus Christ owns the Church. It is His house, His family, His property, His possession. We therefore dare not control it or its resources. As He spoke to one of His servants a few years ago in respect of the UK church, 'Tell them that I want My Church back.' Will we surrender afresh, and say that it is His Church? Everything we have – our people, our prayers, our finances and resources – all of them belong to Him.

Secondly, Jesus blessed what they had, after they had surrendered it to Him:

'Then He commanded the multitudes to sit down on the grass. And He took the five loaves and the two fish, and looking up to heaven, He blessed ... the loaves ... '   (Matthew 14:19)

How absurd we are! We think that we need to hold on to things, because if we surrender them into His Hands, we will have too little. How ridiculous to think that we can do better than He can! If Jesus blesses our efforts for the nations, there comes into them a whole new dynamic. Ordinary people suddenly connect with the dynamite of God, as they did when they walked into Antioch and preached to the Greeks. God literally multiplies in a way that goes beyond anything we might imagine. The Scriptures say that the blessing of God makes us rich. They also make it clear that those who obey Him are in the best place to receive His blessing. When we understand that, and we energise that through waiting on God, in prayer and in worship, we come to a whole new place of experience in God.

I have seen that in my own life. God stepped into my life when I was a Cambridge University student in the early 60s and instructed me to give my life to mission in general and to the Church in China in particular. I was not aware of ever having talked to anyone Chinese, or of knowing anything about China, or even of caring whether it existed or not. As I set out to obey that call of God, God began to release His blessing. God has given me the privilege of seeing phenomenal growth in our service of the Church in China. We have seen about four million books printed and given into the hands of believers in China. We have seen seventeen years of Bible teaching radio programmes broadcast throughout China, in Mandarin and other dialects. We have seen hundreds of people go into China on short-term teams and some also go in long-term. We have seen many folk raised up to pray regularly for the Church in China. We have seen key workers raised up, both in our organisation and in other ministries, to serve the Church in China. As I look at all of that, I remain puzzled. How could that possibly happen? How could God possibly use me to impact literally millions of lives through His Word? The answer is simple. It is totally to do with His blessing and absolutely nothing to do with me – except in the matter of obeying Him.

This principal holds true for any individual or for any church, if we will obey the Great Commission, and go to the ends of the earth to serve Him. If He can do that with me, think what He could do with you!

Thirdly, Jesus broke the loaves (verse 19):

'*And He took the five loaves and the two fish, and looking up to heaven, He ... broke ...*'

All of this involves a place of brokenness. Recently God spoke to me through the writings and the experience of Johannes Facius. [66] After a period of significant and fruitful service for the Lord, Johannes went into a deep tunnel of depression and struggle. After three years of failure to find any place of relief, God suddenly set Him free. This happened specifically at the point when he had been willing to lay down everything before the Lord – to give up in brokenness as to his ability to serve the Lord at all. At that point, the Lord spoke to him:

'The first thing the Lord said to me was this: "Johannes, all along this way you have been walking I have been longing to extend to you My healing touch, but I could not do it until you had been utterly broken before me. For in the days to come I cannot use you in a way I have planned and give you my anointing in an increasing measure unless I know that your spirit is broken and your heart is contrite. I will not entrust My power and a heavy anointing of My Spirit to anyone who has not been broken."' [67]

The impact of those words in my life recently was profound. The awesome truth struck me that I might know a measure of blessing and anointing, such as I have described above, and then settle back into it. If I do that, I may not allow God to continue His work of brokenness in my life. It was a frightening moment. I saw that it may not be 'no blessing' that is the stumbling block in my life. It may be a measure of blessing and anointing – enough to keep me satisfied, and therefore to miss the 'much more' that God wants to give. Those words impacted me deeply:

'For in the days to come I cannot ... give you my anointing in an increasing measure unless I know that your spirit is broken and your heart is contrite. I will not entrust My power and a heavy anointing of My Spirit to anyone who has not been broken.'

Many churches and Christians do not struggle with the fact that they are empty failures, simply because they are not! God has blessed, and there are definite results of which they can boast. It is not the fact that we have nothing that holds us from a deeper anointing from God. It is the fact that we will not allow Him to break us, because we think we have 'something'. We will not allow Him to have His way.

Isaiah sums it up powerfully, as he describes the person upon whom God will look, in whom He delights:

> *'But on this one will I look: On him who is poor and of a*
> *contrite spirit,*
> *And who trembles at My Word.'*   (Isaiah 66:2b)

Fourthly, we need to distribute the blessing that we receive. We need to share:

> *'And He took the five loaves and the two fish, and looking up to*
> *heaven, He ... gave the loaves to the disciples; and the disciples*
> *gave to the multitudes.'*   (Matthew 14:19)

There is a powerful truth here. Jesus gave the loaves to the disciples and they handed them on to others. That is the correct procedure. Today, many believers are flocking to spiritual meetings, where they encounter God in new and exciting ways. Many sit under anointed Bible teaching and they grow in the Lord. But it can be self-orientated Christianity. The danger is that Jesus gives to them, but they do not give to others. No wonder that so many find after a while that the experiences become stale, and their edge for the Word of God is dulled. That is because their failure to reach out to others has rendered them increasingly a 'Dead Sea'. It is only when we aim to give to others that God can continue pouring fresh water into our lives.

It is all so worthwhile, this surrendering to God that He might make us Antioch people – people whose lives impact and change the world around us.

> *'So they all ate and were filled, and they took up twelve baskets*
> *full of the fragments that remained.'*   (Matthew 14:20)

The disciples saw the power and the glory of God manifested into lives. They saw the Son of God work miracles and were impressed and built up in that encounter. Something amazing happened in their lives, which they would never forget. Surely it is worth pressing out to the nations to see the hungry fed, to see lives changed, to see men and women come to Christ. How much they would have lost if they had refused to respond, if they had demanded that the crowd be ignored and sent away.

That core phrase of Jesus in verse 16 is the key to all of this. It is the heart of the Antioch factor.

> *'But Jesus said to them, "They do not need to go away. You give them something to eat." '*   (Matthew 14:16)

Jesus' command to His disciples is as direct as it is brief – 'You give them something to eat'! I believe it is a word of God to our generation of Christian believers. Let us tease out its meaning by closer examination:

The first word in this statement is **'you'**. Who is 'you'? You is plural; it is everyone who reads this book. It is not 'them'.

John Angell James was a man burdened for China more than a hundred years ago. He saw the opportunity and the challenge for Christians outside of China to take spiritual advantage of the open door and to help China's Church. He had a long-standing friendship with Robert Morrison, the great early missionary pioneer to China mentioned elsewhere in this book. James organised an appeal to send a million New Testaments to China through the British and Foreign Bible Society. The appeal was so successful that twice that number – two million New Testaments – were sent to China. So James was not given merely to theory in the matter of serving China's Church. In 1858, the year before he died, James penned these words:

> 'The conversion of China is, one way or another, the business of every Christian upon earth – and every Christian upon earth can do something for it and ought to do what he can. The man who says, "What have I to do with this matter?" is either ignorant, indolent or covetous, and is altogether heartless towards the cause of Christ. He that says, "What concern have I in China's conversion?" just

asks the question, "What fellowship have I with Christ?" We are all too apt to think of what the Church can do and ought to do, and not what we individually can do and ought to do, and either through modesty, timidity or avarice, we lose ourselves and our individual obligations in the crowd. Do you then ask whose business the conversion of China is? I answer, "Yours, whosoever you are who may read this page. Yours, I say, as truly as that of any other man on the face of the earth." Here it is, I offer it to you, and in the Name of Christ bid you take it. Take it into your hand, your heart, your purse, your closet – you dare not refuse it!'

Perhaps we find that kind of language and challenge a trifle strong, with its powerful emphasis on 'you' – or 'me'! Should it today not be even stronger, given the massive population growth in China and India and in so many nations of the world – and the corresponding growth in spiritual need? Dare we say the words are any less relevant today?

The second word in Jesus' short command to His disciples is '**give**'. That surely is the heart of Christianity. So many just want to receive, not to give. But God gave His only Son for us. Surely we then need to give to a dying world.

The third word is '**them**'. Who is 'them'? It covers anyone, any person upon the face of the earth, whatever their background, creed or colour, or social status. 'Them' is anyone whom God leads us to meet in our generation. 'Them' is not just our people, but **everyone**. Is that not what Jesus was saying, when he told the story of the Good Samaritan? 'Them' is anyone who needs what we can give them.

The book of Revelation describes it this way:

> *'And they sang a new song, saying:*
> *"You are worthy to take the scroll,*
> *And to open its seals;*
> *For You were slain,*
> *And have redeemed us to God by Your blood*
> *Out of every tribe and tongue and people and nation,*
> *And have made us kings and priests to our God;*
> *And we shall reign on the earth."'*   (Revelation 5:9–10)

'Them' is to be drawn from out of 'every tribe and tongue and people and nation'.

The fourth word that we need to study in the command of Jesus is '**something**'. The best definition I can give of 'something' is that it is basically the opposite of 'nothing'! May God have mercy on us, if when we go to meet Jesus, having enjoyed Him in our churches and in our lives, yet there is nothing in the hands of others.

I listened to a great man of God once as he expanded the story of the Syro-Phoenician woman. In the middle of the story, his voice broke and he looked up and said 'I have a continuing vision of peoples of every colour, background, nation, and tribe. Like the woman they stretch out their hands and they say: "Do not give me a loaf of bread, nor even a slice of bread, but just crumbs that fall from the Master's table."' That is all they ask of us – 'something'. Not the sophisticated healthy loaves of the churches that many of us enjoy, nor our conferences, nor our resources. They ask for anything – something that falls from the Master's table as we feast there ourselves. What 'something' will be left over from your life, when you depart to be with the Lord?

That is the challenge of the Antioch Factor. That is the question that we must face. That is the Word of the Lord to us in our generation: *'You give them something to eat.'*

This final chapter began with the testimony of one sister, Margery Sykes, whose life, given over to Jesus and to mission, made a difference. It is therefore appropriate to let another such sister in Christ have the final word.

'Amy Carmichael grew up in Belfast, enjoying a carefree life until her father died and left the family debt-ridden. The ensuing pressure helped direct her attention to spiritual things, and in 1886 she gave her life to Christ. She struggled vocationally till the words "Go Ye" so impressed her that on January 13th, 1892, she yielded to overseas service. She sailed to Japan. But she did not seem to fit there, and Amy struggled to find her place. She left for Shanghai, then, to the dismay of family and friends, abruptly sailed for Ceylon. Returning to England, she decided on India. But for several years, she could not find her niche there, and she was often criticised by fellow missionaries.

But she gradually noticed that children were drawn to her, so much so that Indian parents feared Amy was "bewitching" their youngsters. One day, she met a girl who had escaped from a Hindu temple with stories of horror. The Hindus were secretly using children as temple prostitutes. Evidently, parents sold baby girls to the temple, and when the children were eight or nine, they "married" the idol and were pressed into harlotry.

Most people disbelieved such stories, and for several years Amy worked as a detective, assembling evidence to prove the atrocities real. She rescued several more children, and by 1904, was responsible for seventeen youngsters. Amy was occasionally hauled into court for kidnapping, and death threats were common.

But children multiplied on her doorstep, and by 1945, thousands had been placed in Amy's Dohnavur Fellowship, a series of homes for outcast children. Many youngsters grew up becoming Christian husbands, wives, and leaders.

During these years, Amy Carmichael also made time for another ministry – writing. By the time of her death at Dohnavur in 1951 at age 83, she had written thirty-five books on her work in India and on the victorious Christian life. She had found her place and filled it well.' [68]

Amy is in many ways a great example with which to finish this book on the Antioch Factor. She was one who seemed to be going nowhere, attracting it seems much criticism in the process, before she hit her destiny in Christ – on the mission field of India. There she made a difference to many lives. She is indeed classic Antioch Factor material – a 'nobody' who went, and by the grace of God, became a 'somebody' to countless hopeless lives.

But she was more than that. She was one who heard from God. We need to hear, in our generation, what the Lord showed her: [69]

'The tom-toms thumped straight on all night, and the darkness shuddered round me like a living, feeling thing. I could not go to sleep, so I lay awake and looked; and I saw, as it seemed, this:

That I stood on a grassy sward, and at my feet a precipice broke sheer down into infinite space. I looked, but saw no bottom; only cloud shapes, black and furiously coiled, and great shadow-shrouded hollows, and unfathomable depths. Back I drew, dizzy at the depth.

Then I saw forms of people moving single file along the grass. They were making for the edge. There was a woman with a baby in her arms and another little child holding on to her dress. She was on the very verge. Then I saw that she was blind. She lifted her foot for the next step ... it trod air. She was over, and the children over with her. Oh, the cry as they went over!

Then I saw more streams of people flowing from all quarters. All were blind, stone blind; all made straight for the precipice edge. There were shrieks as they suddenly knew themselves falling, and a tossing up of helpless arms, catching, clutching at empty air. But some went over quietly, and fell without a sound.

Then I wondered, with a wonder that was simply agony, why no one stopped them at the edge. I could not. I was glued to the ground, and I could not call; though I strained and tried, only a whisper would come.

Then I saw that along the edge there were sentries set at intervals. But the intervals were too great; there were wide, unguarded gaps between. And over these gaps the people fell in their blindness, quite unwarned; and the green grass seemed blood-red to me, and the gulf yawned like the mouth of hell.

Then I saw, like a little picture of peace, a group of people under some trees with their backs turned towards the gulf. They were making daisy chains. Sometimes when a piercing shriek cut the quiet air and reached them, it disturbed them and they thought it a rather vulgar noise. And if one of their number started up and wanted to go and do something to help, then all the others would pull that one down. "Why should you get so excited about it? You must wait for a definite call to go! You haven't finished your daisy chain yet. It would be really selfish," they said, "to leave us to finish the work alone."

There was another group. It was made up of people whose great desire was to get more sentries out; but they found that very few wanted to go, and sometimes there were no sentries set for miles and miles of the edge.

Once a girl stood alone in her place, waving the people back; but her mother and other relations called, and reminded her that her furlough was due; she must not break the rules. And being tired and needing a change, she had to go and rest for awhile; but no one was sent to guard her gap, and over and over the people fell, like a waterfall of souls.

Once a child caught at a tuft of grass that grew at the very brink of the gulf; it clung convulsively, and it called – but nobody seemed to hear. Then the roots of the grass gave way, and with a cry the child went over, its two little hands still holding tight to the torn-off bunch of grass. And the girl who longed to be back in her gap thought she heard the little one cry, and she sprang up and wanted to go; at which they reproved her, reminding her that no one is necessary anywhere; the gap would be well taken care of, they knew. And then they sang a hymn.

Then through the hymn came another sound like the pain of a million broken hearts wrung out in one full drop, one sob. And a horror of great darkness was upon me, for I knew what it was – the Cry of the Blood.

Then thundered a voice, the voice of the Lord. And He said, "**What hast thou done? The voice of thy brother's blood crieth to Me from the ground.**"

The tom-toms still beat heavily, the darkness still shuddered and shivered about me; I heard the yells of the devil-dancers and the weird wild shrieks of the devil-possessed just outside the gate.

What does it matter, after all? It has gone on for years, it will go on for years. Why make such a fuss about it?

God forgive us! God arouse us! Shame us out of our callousness! Shame us out of our sin!'

'What does it matter, after all? It has gone on for years, it will go on for years. Why make such a fuss about it?' The Antioch

Factor is not just biblical truth, though it is that. It is also eternal responsibility for the lost. May God help us to hear their cry in our generation. May He also help us to see that if we will only rise and go, these needy people can be reached. And if we will but support those who go, many 'nobodies' can be used of God, even as Amy Carmichael was. May that be so of many readers of this book – even to the ends of the earth.

'What does it matter, after all?' The purpose of this book is that we might be the generation who says that it does matter. Then we will be Antioch people, who pray and give and support – and go – so the dead might live.

Notes

1. From *Ripening Harvest, Gathering Storm*, by Maurice Sinclair (STL Books, 1988), pp. 74–77.

2. *Eternity In Their Hearts*, by Don Richardson (Regal Books, 1981), p. 197.

3. William Carey has been given this title in the English-speaking world, but many from Europe would dispute that and with good reason. Long before Carey went to India, the Moravians had already moved out from Count Zinzendorf's community in N. Germany, taking the Gospel to various foreign lands. It is documented that Carey was himself greatly affected by the example of the Moravians. See *Ripening Harvest, Gathering Storm*, by Maurice Sinclair (STL Books, 1988), pp. 74–77.

4. *On This Day*, by Robert J. Morgan (Thomas Nelson, Inc., 1997). Entry for May 12th.

5. Ibid, also May 12th.

6. AM/CCSM sends teams of believers into China. See Appendix C for more details.

7. This and other material above is taken from the Preface to *Life Of William Carey, Shoemaker & Missionary*, by George Smith C.I.E., LL.D., 1909. Reprinted 1913, 1922.

8. *Eternity In Their Hearts*, p. 197.

9. Please see Appendix A for a brief explanation that no references to 'Jerusalem' in this book should be taken to imply that God does not have a 'special place' in His heart for the Jewish people and for the land of Israel! That is a quite separate issue. These chapters refer to the Christian church in Jerusalem in the First Century only.

10. The unreached people group amongst whom she is working.

11. Quoted in *New Frontiers* magazine.

12. Comment by C.T. Studd. Studd was captain of the English cricket team. He then forsook all, including personal wealth, to be a missionary first in China, then in India and finally in Africa. He was the founder of the Worldwide Evangelisation Crusade.

13. *On This Day*, January 14th.

14. Scripture Union notes: *Encounter with God*, 1999.

15. Taken from *Let Your Glory Fall*, by David Ruis (Copyright © Mercy Publishing, 1993).

16. *Every Day With Jesus*, by Selwyn Hughes.

17. The Coptic Church in Ethiopia still has an oral tradition that goes back to these events.

18. Material taken from *Every Day With Jesus* and *On This Day*, October 24th.

19. *On This Day* – February 28th.

20. Quoted from Bob Gass. Details of source unknown.

21. This material is taken from Tony Lambert's book *China's Christian Millions* (Monarch Books, 1999), (pp. 15–20). I strongly recommend the reading of this book and also Tony's book: *The Resurrection Of The Chinese Church*.

22. Taken from *The Continuing Heartcry for China*, Ross Paterson (Sovereign World, 1999).

23. The use of this word here will become clearer in Chapters 8 and 9!

24. Taken from *Every Day With Jesus*.

25. *On This Day*, June 17th (with slight alterations).

26. These headings are taken from a verbal conversation with James Hudson Taylor III in the Garden Hotel, Singapore c1990.

27. *On This Day*, July 21st (slightly modified).

28. See my book *China: The Hidden Miracle* (Sovereign World, 1993) for an account of these events in China.

29. Taken from British Airways In-flight magazine, Summer 2000.

30. *On This Day*, February 29th.

31. *Unveiled At Last*, Bob Sjogren (YWAM Publishing, 1992), pp. 28ff.

32. Quoted in Scripture Union notes, *Encounter with God*, July 2000.

33. *Unveiled At Last*, pp. 28ff.

34. *Unveiled At Last*, pp. 35ff.

35. Transcribed from comments by Fred Markert of YWAM speaking at a Perspectives class.

36. Quoted in Scripture Union notes, *Encounter with God*, 21st July 2000.

37. *Operation World*, by Patrick Johnstone (Zondervan Publishing House).

38. Those who feel challenged to take up the ministry of intercession but do not know how to begin, would find the book *Don't Just Stand There, Pray Something*, by Ronald Dunn (Scripture Press, 1992) particularly helpful.

39. See Appendix C for addresses from which you can obtain further information on these teams.

40. Opportunities for serving overseas in a full-time capacity are many and varied. Sending organisations are also manifold, ranging from the traditional missionary societies to those that aim to place people in strategic 'tent-making' situations in countries that are closed to the Gospel. It has been beyond the scope of this book to cover all these issues, but please see the Appendices for a few 'pointers', which might be helpful.

41. *Serving As Senders. How to Care For Your Missionaries*, Neal Pirolo (Emmaus Road International, Inc., 7150 Tanner Court, San Diego, CA 92111. Tel: 858 292-7020; email: emmaus_road@eri.org; website: www.eri.org).

42. Ibid: first page of the Preface.

43. Ibid: first page of the Preface.

44. Or 'she'. The use of the male pronoun should be not be taken to exclude the female missionary, who is, after all, the more common of the species.

45. Ibid: p. 5.

46. Ibid: p. 11.

47. One shocking report we have heard is that one in four missionaries or missionary couples fails to last even to the end of a second term on the field.

48. See Appendix D for a very helpful diagram from Pirolo (ibid p. 6) showing the 'roller-coaster' experience of many on the field. It indicates the danger periods, when 'failure' is most likely to occur and support is most needed.

49. Amongst them are those who prayed a significant part of our China ministry into existence. We certainly would not wish anything shared in this chapter, much as it needs to be said, to reflect badly on that church!

50. We received great help at that time from a book by Barney Coombes called *Snakes and Ladders*, especially chapters 8–10 dealing with the whole issue of 'skandalon' or 'offence' – and how to get out of it.

51. *Serving as Senders*, p. 10.

52. Ibid: p. 29.

53. See Appendix A for further brief comments regarding sending agencies and service on the field.

54. *Serving As Senders*, Chapter 5, pp. 90–116.

55. YWAM Publishing, 1991.

56. In the UK, courses are being run regularly on the subject of 're-entry stress' and how to deal with it at Bawtry Hall near Doncaster, as well as by an increasing number of missions agencies. Global Connections of the EMA-UK has a useful summary of what ought to be included in 'debriefing' in their *Code of Best Practice in Short-term Missions* booklet.

57. YWAM Publishing, 1992.

58. Published by Evangelical Missions Information Service (EMIS), 1987.

59. Published jointly by Marc Europe, STL Books and Evangelical Missionary Alliance, ISBN 0-9508396-7-1. (Although this is an older book, published in 1985, it contains much relevant and helpful material on the subject covered by this chapter.)

60. Material taken from *The Vision Of An Antioch Church*, Kevin J. Conner (KJC Publications). Conner's small book is well worth studying alongside this one, as it includes some very useful details of the nature of Jerusalem and Antioch churches drawn from the book of Acts.

61. Ibid: p. 14.

62. Ibid: pp. 14–17.

63. Ibid: p. 17.

64. Ibid: p. 27.

65. Refer to Appendix A.

66. Johannes Facius heads up the ministry of Intercessors International, which has established prayer movements in some 45 nations around the world.

67. *God Can Do It Without Me*, by Johannes Facius.

68. Taken from *On This Day*, January 13th.

69. Excerpt taken from *Thy Brothers Blood Crieth* from *Things As They Are*, by Amy Carmichael of Dohnavur Fellowship.

Appendix A

There are a number of issues that have not been covered in this book, though they are nonetheless important and related to the Antioch theme.

1. The biblical revelation regarding the status of the land and people of Israel. The discussion of Jerusalem in this book relates only to the church there in New Testament times. The whole issue of the Jewish people and their 'specialness' is a totally separate issue, and nothing that is said in the pages of this book should be taken to relate to that issue. My position is that there is a special place in covenant history for the Jewish people, a truth that is revealed both in the Old Testament and in the New Testament (Romans Chapters 9–11, etc.). Of course, the Scriptures clearly state that the only way of salvation for the Jewish people is through the death of Jesus on the cross and His subsequent resurrection. For further study of this issue see *Destiny of Israel and the Church*, by Derek Prince (DPM Publications).

2. The issue of the poor, the disadvantaged (orphans, widows, etc.) and the oppressed has only been covered in passing in the chapters of this book. It is nonetheless, according to the Scriptures, a major responsibility for Christians, not the least in the field of mission, as revealed in both the Old and the New Testament. Derek Prince's recently published book, *Who Cares For Orphans, Widows, the Poor and Oppressed?*, subtitled *God does . . . do we?*, is a masterly statement on this subject from the pages of the Bible. I would urge the reading of that little book.

3. Tent-making, or the opportunity for missionaries to take up secular employment in foreign lands (for financial reasons, or because it is the only way into certain countries), has not been touched on in any detail. It is important. You can contact AM/CCSM (see addresses in Appendix C) for details of tent-making opportunities in China.

4. The indigenous church. The whole aim of missionary work is to serve and release a local indigenous church, and then to back off! Some of the books on the book list will cover that theme.

A related theme is that of the internationalisation of the mission force. Again, more information on this can be found in the book list in Appendix B. I happen to believe that we may see the loosing of a mission force from the Church in China that will astonish us in our generation! We are already seeing amazing mission activities from certain South American lands, from India and Africa, as well as some of the Asian nations.

Appendix B

Other books by Ross Paterson

The Continuing Heartcry for China (Sovereign World, 1999).

Explaining Mission (Sovereign World, 1994).

China: The Hidden Miracle, by Ross Paterson and Elisabeth Farrell (Sovereign World, 1993).

Other recommended reading

The Vision of an Antioch Church, Kevin J. Connor (KJC Publications, 1999).

Snakes and Ladders, Barney Coombes (Sovereign World, 1993).

Don't Just Stand There, Pray Something! Ronald Dunn (Here's Life Publishers, 1992).

God Can Do It Without Me, Johannes Facius (Sovereign World, 1990).

Nests Above the Abyss, Isobel Kuhn (Overseas Missionary Fellowship, 1947).

China's Christian Millions, Tony Lambert (Monarch Books, 1999).

Resurrection of the Chinese Church, Tony Lambert (Hodder & Stoughton, 1991).

On This Day, Robert J. Morgan (Nelson, 1997).

Ripening Harvest, Gathering Storm, Maurice Sinclair (STL Books, 1988).

Life of William Carey, Shoemaker and Missionary, George Smith (1909, reprinted 1913, 1922).

Top 25 recommended books on missions

(Taken from http://www.calebproject.org)

This list was compiled by Nate Wilson through the **Brigada-orgs-missionmobilizers@XC.org** conference.

1. *Let The Nations Be Glad! The Supremacy of God in Missions*, by John Piper (Baker Books). This book will give you a great biblical understanding of the real purpose of missions to glorify God. Written in a fast-paced, exciting style, with a good challenge to missions involvement.

2. *Operation World*, by Patrick Johnstone (Zondervan Publishing House). This is a classic for missions, an invaluable resource. It lists all countries of the world (about 200) in alphabetical order, and gives information about and prayer requests for each. Read and pray through this book and your life will never be the same.

3. *The Great Omission*, by Robertson McQuilkin (Baker Book House). A relatively short book (100 pages), *The Great Omission* is easy to read and an excellent introduction to the urgent need for missions in our day. This book is a great starting place for those interested in learning about the biblical priority of missions.

4. *Shadow of the Almighty*, by Elisabeth Elliot (Harper & Row, Publishers). Of all the missionary biographies I've read (and I've read quite a few), this is the best one. It is well-written and shows a passion for God and for taking the Gospel to those who have never heard. You can learn a lot about God, life, missions, and your own life through this biography of Jim Elliot. Also *Through Gates of Splendour*, Elizabeth Elliott, The account of the martyrdom of Jim Elliot and four other missionaries by the Auca Indians.

5. *Unveiled at Last*, by Bob Sjogren (YWAM Publishing, 1992). This book will show you God's unchanging purpose – to redeem some from every tribe, tongue, and people. Filled with exciting stories, this book also gives a great biblical understanding of missions from God's perspective.

6. *Touch The World Through Prayer*, by Wesley L. Duewel (Francis Asbury Press). This book has short chapters, which will teach you about the power of intercessory prayer and encourage you to really pray! You can touch the world, without ever leaving your home, through prayer.

7. *Serving As Senders*, by Neal Pirolo. A great book, showing how a church or missions committee can care for missionaries as they prepare to go, while they are on the field, and when they return home. Full of clear, practical, helpful ideas and information. Available from Emmaus Road International Inc., 7150 Tanner Court, San Diego, CA 92111, USA. Website: http://www.eri.org

8. *I Dared to Call Him Father*, by Bilquis Sheikh (Baker Book House). The true and riveting story of a Muslim woman in Pakistan, married to a high government official, to whom Jesus appears in a dream. She became a Christian, she says, 'When I dared to call the awesome God my Father!'

9. *The World at Your Doorstep*, by Lawson Lau (InterVarsity Press). It's so important for us to realise that even as God is sending us out into all the world, He is also sovereignly bringing people from all over the world to us! This is a helpful and encouraging guide to befriending and reaching out to Internationals as a way to reach all nations.

10. *Death of a Guru*, by Rabi R. Maharaj (Harvest House Publishers). Autobiography of a man, born to a high caste Hindu family, destined to become a Guru, but instead became a follower of Jesus. It will help you understand the tenets of Hinduism and make you really glad you are a Christian!

11. *From Jerusalem to Irian Jaya*, by Ruth Tucker – History of Missions.

12. *Eternity in Their Hearts*, by Don Richardson (Regal Books) – Case studies of how God puts cultural keys in every culture to help them understand the Gospel. Also *Peace Child*, Don Richardson, The account of how the Peace Child brought peace to the Sawi People of New Guinea.

13. *Until the Day Breaks*, by Patricia St John (OM Publishing). The life story of Lilias Trotter, a young, passionate, talented artist who worked with the prostitutes and homeless girls of London, and at the age of 25, went to North Africa.

14. *Run With the Vision*, by Bill & Amy Stearns, Bob Sjogren. This book gives an overview of what the Bible says, what God is doing around the world, and helps the reader begin to find their 'niche' in God's global agenda … I haven't seen anything this 'user friendly' for people who are wanting something clear and helpful.

15. *Bruchko*, Bruce Olson. Hair-raising adventures among South American Indians.

16. *Evidence Not Seen*, Darlene Deibler Rose. A missionary's miraculous faith in the jungles during World War II.

17. *A Chance to Die*, Elizabeth Elliott. The life of Amy Carmichael, an Irish missionary who spent 53 years in S. India without a furlough.

18. *Giving Wings to The Gospel*, Dietrich Buss. The ministry of Missionary Aviation Fellowship, Baker Book House.

19. *By Their Blood*, James & Marti Helfey. Christian martyrs of the 20th Century, Baker Book House.

20. *The Liberating Gospel in China*, Ralph Covell. Information and stories never published before, Baker Book House.

21. *The Short Term Missions Boom*, Michael Anthony. A church's comprehensive guide, Baker Book House.

22. *Marching to a Different Drummer*, Jim Raymo. Rediscovering missions in an age of affluence and self-interest, Christian Literature Crusade.

23. *St. Luke's Missiology*, Harold Dollar, William Carey Library.

24. *Crisis and Hope in Latin America*, Nunez & Taylor. An evangelical perspective, William Carey Library.

25. *God's Power, Jesus' Faith, and World Missions*, Steve Mosher. A study in Romans, Herald Press.

See also:

Costly Missions, Michael Ducan. Following Christ into the slums, MARC.

Ministry and Theology in Global Perspective, Don Pittman. Contemporary missionary challenges for the Church, Erdmans Publishing Co.

Evangelical Missions Quarterly (Vol. 33, No. 1, January 1997) contains an article featuring 30 books that could be of help to missionaries. The list was compiled by Kelly O'Donnell and Gerald Reddix and includes features in Member Care, Self-Help, Team Life and Conflict Management, Psychology, and Children, Marriage, and Family issues.

Appendix C

Ministry Addresses

For further information on the situation of the Church in China and what you can do to help, please write to your local AM/CCSM office or the DPM-China office:

Singapore
Antioch Missions Singapore
(Chinese Church Support Ministries International HQ)
PO Box 2046
Robinson Road Post Office
Singapore 904046
email: amspore@singnet.com.sg

Derek Prince Ministries China Outreach
PO Box 2046
Robinson Road Post Office
Singapore 904046
email: dpmchina@singnet.com.sg

Derek Prince Ministries International
PO Box 19824
Charlotte
North Carolina 28219-9824

Australia
Chinese Church Support Ministries
PO Box 2187
Warwick
WA 6024

Germany
Chinese Church Support Ministries e.V.
Gueterstr. 37
D-46499 Hemminkeln

Malaysia
Chinese Church Support Ministries
c/o Roland Kok
41 Jalan Bakawali 54
Taman Johor Jaya
81100 Johor Bahru

New Zealand
Chinese Church Support Ministries
PO Box 7156
Taradale
Napier

South Africa
Chinese Church Support Ministries
c/o 998 Kraanvoel Ave.
Silverton 0184
Pretoria

Taiwan
Antioch Missions
PO Box 117–432
Taipei

UK
Chinese Church Support Ministries
PO Box 73
Bury
Lancs BL9 7FW

USA
Chinese Church Support Ministries
1230 Bardstown Road
Louisville
KY 40204

Or visit the ministry websites:

www.am-ccsm.org or www.derekprince.com

Appendix D

A Diagram from Serving As Senders by Neal Pirolo, p. 6/7
(used with permission; slightly amended)

The 'Cross-cultural worker's life time-line', represents the physical/
emotional/mental/ spiritual experiences of a cross-cultural worker
before, during and after his or her missionary experience:

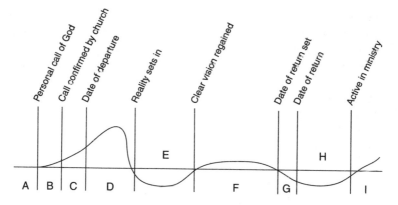

Figure 2: A cross-cultural worker's life time-line.

Explanation

1. The horizontal line represents the 'normal living' base line of life
    before going to the field (not that it was flat, except by comparison
    with life in a foreign culture!)

2. The line resembling the dips and curves of a roller-coaster ride
    represents 'the changing pulse of your missionary's being in
    passing through a missionary experience.' One veteran said about
    the ups and downs of missionary life:

    'Missionary living takes me on a trip that is totally outside the
    realm of every comfort zone I have come to enjoy!'

3. The vertical lines indicate periods of time, milestones along the missionary venture. Relative spaces may vary. But these are the expected phases of which you, his support person, should be aware. As you are giving your support, anticipate the next milestone of your cross-cultural worker's life time-line. And be available to offer your assistance.

4. The capital letters represent phases or time periods along the way:

   A. Life before even considering the mission field.

   B. Period while waiting for approval from church and/or mission board.

   C. Anticipation of Departure; hectic preparations.

   D. 'Honeymoon period' on first arriving on the field, when everything is still fun and 'interesting'!

   E. Culture Shock! A normal stage, but one of the 'danger times'.

   F. Ministry of Love – the 'great door for effective work' Paul speaks of in 1 Corinthians 16:9.

   G. Anticipation of Return – mixed feelings.

   H. Culture Stress in Reverse – another danger period.

   I. Full Reintegration – or preparation for returning to the field.